Spirituality
Without
Religions

LOVE: Nurturing The Essence Of Spiritual Birth

Meek as a lamb.......

.......Confident as a lion

ASHER
Poetic Feelings Analyst
Author of The Human Soul

ISBN 978-0-9636109-6-6

Printed in the USA

Edited by Lori B. Johnson

Formatted and Cover Design
By William Alderman
Oltermann@hotmail.com

WHY A BOOK ABOUT SPIRITUALITY WITHOUT RELIGIONS?

Religions do a good job in helping the poor and needy. Religions do a better job in giving spiritual fulfillment to individual devotees. But what religions do best is divide people and separate communities.

Spirituality *without* religions reaches creations' **'Inner Light' of Innocence and Grace at the core of our Being.** When this Light shines in all its Holiness its Spiritual Brightness paralyzes the Ego-centered Power and Glory we put in *man-made institutions*.

Asher

CONTENTS

INTRODUCTION

Peace on earth goodwill to all men. If our destination is peace on earth, the journey to our destination is inner peace, and goodwill to all men is rooted in inner peace. That's what this book is about—inner peace and love.

Love builds a world in which every child feels loved, and every adult answers the call to love. We all came into this world with high spiritual self-affirmation, inner peace, and goodwill to men of all religions, as well as goodwill to men of *no* religion. My hope and aspiration is that the book will transport you, the reader, to a spiritual journey of inner peace, where love flows generously into your heart.

This book is about a journey towards a brighter consciousness of the spiritual love that's the source of all creation. It's about spiritual love, the source of life at the core of every human soul. It's not about religion, but it's not anti-religious either because I believe all religions seek to cultivate spiritual love and spiritual fulfillment.

History shows plenty of evidence that mankind's deepest hunger and most fundamental need is for spiritual significance and spiritual fulfillment. On every page of this book, I've tried to write words that will inspire you and move you into the path of fewer Material desires and more spiritual fulfillment. My words are intended to compliment and spiritualize religious ideals, rather than destroy them.

I believe we were all filled with the grace of God when we were born. Long before we were able to embrace any religion, we were in God's spirit-filled embrace. But our journey into adulthood empties our spirit and separates us from God. This book is intended to light the way back into the kingdom of the soul where we can be reunited with the peace, goodwill and spiritual grace of our birth.

At the dawn of creation, the gift of life appears and every living soul is filled with the seeds of inner peace and goodwill. Like the sun and the rain, loving parenting makes these seeds bloom and grow in the celebration of life. If parenting is anything less than unconditional love, however, the ego's weeds of self-doubt and fear will choke out the inner peace and goodwill of creation.

This book will show you how to walk by faith and goodwill for the rest of your life's journey. It will show you how to be reunited with the inner light of divine love and root yourself in a brighter spiritual consciousness of human kindness.

Some people believe spirituality has everything to do with religion, while some say spirituality has nothing to do with religion. I say the gift of life came out of creation in a spiritual birth, not religion. Babies are the most spiritual people, but by the time they learn to walk, talk and read a book, they move into spiritual separation and need a religion to light the path back to a spiritual second birth. Spiritual separation is the fate of mankind, and since the beginning of time, religion has always been mankind's hope to reunite himself with his creator.

Were it not for the fact that religion divides people and therefore, is unable to offer goodwill to all men, religion would be the best place to start towards world peace. It would be the place where saints and sinners sit down together like the lion and the lamb and show Brotherly Love, every man to his fellowman.

This book endorses one religion, not many religions. I call it the

Religion of the Holy Spirit, promoting first the tender loving care of children. It also promotes the essence of spiritual birth, along with the divine love of creation, Brotherly Love and human kindness. If a man is a loving father, loving husband, loving brother and a loving person, he's rooted in faith and hope. He's rooted in the source of his creation. He's his brother's keeper, and every time he loves his brother, he feels loved. When his religion is stronger and deeper in the core of his being than any manmade institution, he's rooted in the institution of love and the institution of God. He's everything God created him to BE.

My hope is every reader of this book will move deeper into the consciousness of spiritual love. I hope you will diminish your material desires and seek happiness in the cultivation of satisfaction, not in the satisfaction of desires. I hope you'll feed the little child of innocence and grace inside of you. I also hope you'll set free the inner yearnings of your soul—feed your soul and starve your ego. Free yourself to express the love that created you. Then you'll be free to feel the love, and you'll be free to love and be loved.

I define love as the ability to surrender without the fear of being conquered. We came into this world waving a white flag in total surrender to love. Egoless, innocent and helpless, we surrendered to a world with a heart that is as cold as ice. Very soon we discovered that selfishness and materialism were the weapons this world of sin and shame used for survival. The fear of being conquered rooted itself into our sub-consciousness and our personality. Then, the ego appeared to diminish our fear, but love was gone. Our life became a struggle on the spiritual battlefield with everyone calls for love and fights against the fear of being conquered.

I hope this book inspires you to hold on to love. Don't give up your religion if you have one, but give up the struggle. With or without religion, you can follow the path to love. Self-examination and self-discovery will renew your faith and free you to surrender to love once again.

If we want a world of peace and goodwill, we need a revolution of faith, hope and love. We need a revolution of human kindness and tender loving care for all the children of the world. Science, religion and every social institution in every culture must teach, preach and practice the idea that from the source of divine love grows Brotherly Love, parental love and every other kind of love, even romantic love. Love is the only weapon against the ego's fear, selfishness and materialism that threatens to destroy the whole human race.

Finally, let me say that I use the word "he" throughout the book to refer to everyone and I include all of mankind in that term. Not just men but women as well as little children. Also there's a lot of repeating on these pages, because like a poet or a songwriter, I repeat my lines for emphasis. I hope you enjoy them.

FOREWORD

If "God is Love" then Asher's latest book is one of the most "God Filled" volumes ever written. Every page reaches out and hugs the reader's heart. Asher's words flow from the page and into the reader's mind in a stream of consciousness, sometimes like a gentile stream and sometimes like a torrent. At a time when self inflicted Armageddon is a very real possibility, Asher offers a way to prevent this tragic World Suicide.

Unlike many books written today Asher's book doesn't just raise questions but offers realistic, workable solutions to problems caused by the world's major organized religions (and even the disorganized ones). Asher's book gives the reader the choice to determine what the truth is for him or herself.

Asher breathes new life into the ordinary meanings of "Spiritual Humanism" and "Spiritual Materialism" as he leads the reader on a journey into inner peace.

He explains how work can become a labor of love when body, mind, and soul are unified by the spiritual harmony of motion. Hopefully, Asher's latest book will burn away the impurities of Spiritual Materialism that pervade many Religions, leaving only a Spiritual Humanism, a blend of the best qualities many Religious Traditions have to offer.

Asher and I still serve as Volunteer Chaplains in a State Prison located in Central Florida where we met in 2002. We became "Spiritual Brothers" and I consider Asher to be my closest friend despite my many glaring and obvious character defects.

Asher, the epitome of Unconditional Brotherly Love, practices what he preaches. Asher believes Mahatma Gandhi was the most "Christ Like" human to ever walk the face of the earth.

Born in Jamaica, raised Quaker and without benefit, or perhaps bias of a college education, Asher rejects the Christian Dogma of Original Sin. Asher's book makes clear his beliefs that all people are born good and that "man built" institutions called "Religions" can actually separate people from God. Perhaps this is why Asher believes that Sunday is the most segregated day of the week.

This book distills the very essence at the heart of all religions – Love! But it is a Love that can and must begin for the Baby in the Crib.

Rev. Mr. Michael V. Shortell

HUSH...HUSH...LISTEN...LISTEN

Hush...Hush...Listen...Listen.
Love...Love.
In the silence of my meditation,
I can hear my brother calling for love.
I can hear him slip and fall.

Give thanks and praise to the
Holy Spirit above.
My calls for love have been
Answered all,
Every time I answer my brother's call.

Be still my soul, in love, silence and tranquility...
I am my brother's keeper.
When I love my brother, I feel loved.

1

A Prayer for Inner Peace
and Human Kindness

Lord, make me a vessel of your divine love.
Grant me inner peace, like still water drawn
From your source of infinite love.
Let me be a fountain of human kindness.

Where there is hate, let me bestow love.
Where there is darkness, let me glow light.
Where there is injury, let me show forgiveness.
Where there is fear, let me sow faith.
Where there is despair, let me grow hope.
Where there is arrogance, let me flow humility.

Wherever religious or racial prejudice,
Or any social rejection afflicts the human soul,
Let me be there.
Not to curse the darkness more,
but to be the light of a thousand candles,
glowing to make humanity whole.

Lord, grant that I may seek first not
to be loved but to show love.
Grant that I may pour contempt on my own
selfish-obsessive material desire, so forever
higher and higher may flow a spiritual river of
Human Kindness.

2

WHAT IS MAN?

If he must feel whole and not fall to pieces
If he must be for himself but not for himself alone
If he must walk and not feel abandoned
If he must talk and not feel unfilled by his words
If he must work and not blame and complain

If he must give and not feel misused
If he must have a lover and not feel unloved
If he must eat to a belly full and not feel half
empty
If he must have this world's riches and not feel
like a pauper"

THEN: he must labor tirelessly fueled with his
Passion in the vineyard of all the Virtues of
Spiritual Wholeness.

ONE

SPIRIT:

THE SOURCE OF LIFE

Creation

The story of Adam and Eve is the story of every man, created in innocence and living in a spiritual paradise. He's a spiritual giant but a physical and mental midget. By the time he learns to walk and talk, his innocence is lost. His journey from soul-centeredness to egocenteredness causes him to cover himself with a fig leaf and live in sin and shame. He must be born again to save himself from the torment of evil.

The source of divine love creates every human soul. At the dawn of each man's creation, his body, mind and soul appear in perfect wholeness, oneness and holiness. We call this paradise—no sin and no shame are found there. In the realm of creation after his birth, man is given the awesome task of cultivating his own inner life—the wellspring of divine love—and his own outer life—the source of human love.

The interplay of divine love and human love is the essence and bliss of human living. The infant is the source of divine love and the mother with the baby on her breast is the source of human love. The mother cultivates human life with her tender loving care of the infant.

For about the first eighteen months of any infant's life, the child is whole and holy. He or she sees no evil and does no evil. This is a place of peace on earth, goodwill to all men. It's a place of oneness with God, oneness with self, and oneness with the universe.

But this state of spiritual bliss lasts only as long as tender loving care is given the child from loving adults. Any kind of neglect or any kind of abuse from the outside world causes the child to suffer an inner conflict of spiritual separation and also conflict with the outside world.

Caring for the infant requires twenty-four hours a day, seven days a week of uninterrupted love, food and attention. These can be days of paradise in the Garden of Eden, with the child in the arms of the creator and at the same time in the arms of the mother, family and community, cultivating the growth of human life. It can be days of paradise, days when mind, body, and soul are in harmony, days before the ego comes to divide man against himself and isolate him from the spiritual connectedness of his fellowman.

In those innocent days with plenty of tender loving care, the infant lives in celebration of life. However, too little tender loving care or abuse makes the child live in fear of life, which can last a whole lifetime for some people.

For about the first three years of life, the child is filled with the grace of God, filled with the inner peace of divine love when nurtured by the source of human love. The child has no consciousness of God or gods, nor does he or she hunger for any religion. But he hungers deeply for love. The most spiritual action for anyone is to let his or her love flow into nurturing the spiritual grace of little children.

This situation clearly illustrates that the most Godly and most spirit-filled people on earth (children) have no religion. Furthermore, there will be no peace on earth and no goodwill to all men until religions stop promoting their self-righteousness. Instead, every one of them should preach and practice tender loving care of children and also accept the holiness and righteousness of little children.

Evolution and creation

There are hundred of stories about creation—all religions have them. All religions also believe in some kind of supernatural higher power, some kind of God or god-like entity. The scientist who says there's no God was born filled with the grace of God and so lives in self-denial. And the preacher who says there's no evolution is blind to the mountain of evidence that shows the common thread of DNA that runs through all living things. It's obvious that both creation and evolution are the works of the creator.

Tender loving care

Love—tender loving care—is the key to a happy, meaningful life. Love and only love nurtures and shelters the spiritual holiness of the infant child. Tender loving care saves all of mankind.

The most important period for spiritual growth and maturity is the first three years of a human life. With loving care of the soul, the child is filled with God's grace. He has inner harmony and unity of body, mind and soul. Deep easy breathing is at its peak, and he has inner peace and peace with the outside world. In the arms of love little children are the happiest and most spiritual people on earth up to about three years old.

Between the years of three and six, the ego—mental and psychological development—along with walking and talking, running, and jumping for joy come into play. Loving any little child brings the adult, who is the source of human love, closer to the source of divine love—the source of all creation, the source of life.

Filled with spiritual grace, the infant has no consciousness, no image of God or gods, and no religion. It's only after man's fall into spiritual disgrace that he is put in the fear of life. It's only then that he must find a **religion**—any religion—to **save** his tormented soul from pain and evil.

7

All the great religions are the result of man's search for the inner peace of *Spiritualism*. The baby's passionate and holy kicking and crying to the mother for love and life becomes the religious man's passionate cry, praise and worship to the Holy Spirit, "Save Me."

Spiritual wholeness

Man is born whole and holy. In this state of righteousness he's one within himself, in harmony with body, mind and soul. He feels a oneness with his creator and at one with his universe. This is a place of spiritual wholeness and spiritual bliss in the garden of paradise.

In this place of spiritual wholeness, we breathe deep. We breathe strong. We breathe easy. The baby is on its mother's breast. Hope and joy abound. The whole universe is our playground.

Studies have shown that a baby's breathing quality is stronger than any adult's. This is because by the time we grow up we've lost our spiritual wholeness and lost the spiritual quality of breathing in and out in celebration of life. We become spiritually alienated, and our breathing becomes shallow and weak. Our journey from infancy into adulthood is a journey from spiritual righteousness into sin and shame.

Man is born ***spiritually whole***, so a little baby is incapable of sin. In the state of spiritual wholeness, a baby has the utmost capacity to experience love, more than most adults. We see love as the only reality in life, and we have no illusions about body and mind significance. Our soul is filled with spirit, and our total being is filled with the passion of life. Body, mind and soul harmonize in the key of life and bubble to the rhythm of life.

Born Again

Man is born spiritually whole but also spiritually immature. He's born fragile, innocent, and meek but with little or no mental capacity. Emotionally he's like a rollercoaster. He's more animal than human.

But the human side of his nature commands him to escape the place of innocence and spiritual bliss and move quickly to find his full human potential where every adult human must fight spiritual battles with sin and shame.

What seems to be the fate of mankind puts him in a dilemma. He must escape himself, or more accurately, escape part of himself to become himself. The Bible says: "Man cannot live by bread alone." He must have spiritual significance or lose his will to live, but at the same time, he must have bread or die.

This is man's dilemma. He struggles for bread for his survival and more bread to feed his greed. Yet he finds himself dying of spiritual emptiness.

The solution: man should struggle for bread in the daytime and at night, journey back into the kingdom of his soul, back to find that little child inside. He should go back to the man or woman crying for God and crying for love.

Spiritual Separation
The story of Adam and Eve tells of man's loss of paradise, plus his loss of innocence and grace and his fall into spiritual disgrace. As the story goes, "By the sweat of your brow you must eat bread."

Maybe man was lucky just to fish and hunt in primitive or tribal cultures. Fathers didn't have to work, mothers had time to raise kids, and kids had time to grow without suffering much spiritual separation.

But no modern man wants to be primitive. As mankind's culture grew to include weapons, machines and agriculture, children paid the price in spiritual separation.

Let me say, I don't believe spiritual separation in itself is a curse, because man must *evolve* or die. With love as the foundation, mankind must seek work and knowledge to reach the peak of his human potential.

9

In the days of spiritual affirmation, ways of love are the only reality. But in days of spiritual separation, the call for love becomes mankind's constant possibility. Either way, love is man's only reality. Either we experience love or we call for love.

What is the result of spiritual separation? It's fear, anger and self-doubt, which are caused by spiritual emptiness. Babies are very good at spiritual self-affirmation, but once they suffer spiritual separation, love is diminished, and they're open to fear, anger and self-doubt.

Spiritual reaffirmation with the creator, spiritual reaffirmation with self, and spiritual reaffirmation with fellowman are the keys to peace of earth and goodwill to all men. Interpersonal relationships—people loving people—are the most spiritual relationships.

The Breath Of Life
The breath of life is manifested in our spiritual condition, which includes love, anger and fear.

Love. With love we breath easy. We breath deep, totally free to experience the inner and outer limits of life in all its glory. Love is faith and hope. Love is the breath of life.

Anger. When we are angry we breathe strong, tense and uneasy. Anger comes to fight for love and against all enemies of love. Anger is a fight for affirmation, a fight for the breath of life.

Fear. Fear is a flight from life. Breathing is cut short and shallow. The body trembles and the soul weeps. Life suffers a spiritual breakdown.

Characteristics Of Love, Anger And Fear
Love, anger and fear are our three primary emotions. They're our instincts for survival given by the creator. Anger and fear are instincts for our survival, but love is for our survival *and our salvation*.

When we define someone as a loving person, he usually is peaceful and kind, hopeful, humble, full of self-affirmation. He sees the world as a good place. We define an angry person as someone who hurts inside, is quick to condemn. He blames and complains, and he looks at the world with contempt. A person in fear has plenty of self-doubt, is quick to attack, and also quick to give up the fight. He hungers for success, but fear is a harbinger of failure.

The infant child is more spiritually free and more equipped than adults to experience the full range of these emotions. Paradise is when the infant is in a constant state of love, and negative emotions last for just a moment. But paradise is lost when the infant is separated from love by too much neglect or abuse. Joy and all the positive emotions last for just a moment, and negative emotions become a state of constant existence.

In paradise lost, mankind finds himself in a no man's land, wandering in the darkness of despair, alienated from his inner self and his creator, and isolated from his outside world. Greed, envy, selfishness, fear, and materialism contaminate his soul, and his spiritual affirmation is lost. All the great religions offer man a second chance to find spiritual affirmation.

A spiritual energy of divine virtue is the essence of all creation. It has no name, no image, no forms, no shape, no beginning, and no end. It's eternal. Man must see God in every living thing in creation and feel God in the innermost core of himself. It's a mistake to think that God only belongs to those who believe in him. Little children are the Godliest people on earth. The soul of a child is filled with the grace of God but has no ego-consciousness of God.

GOD
God is in the innermost core of our being,
in the heart and soul of every innocent little child.
Within the human mind and in his imagination,
Images and thoughts of God take many different shapes,
names and forms.

11

But all will agree there's a spiritual higher power seated
within the soul of man and that this spiritual

higher power is one and only in the universe.
Since I am a Christian I believe this higher power is my creator
and my spiritual power is *God*.

**Throughout this book, I will use the name God to represent
my belief, but the reader is free to use any names or images
to represent his or her personal spiritual inclination.**

How does one feel the presence of God?

It's an inner peaceful feeling, a feeling that I'm loved. I want to
love the world, and I want to love all of God's little children. Faith
and hope abound. All of God's creations are in my playground.

Even when sorrow comes to capture my soul, it lasts only for a
little while. Soon a river of joy will wash away my tears. When I
feel God, hate, envy and fear may knock on my door but my
spirit says, "Go away. You're not going to break my day. I've
found the truth and the way."

When my granddaughter was about ten months old, I watched
her go from smiling to anger, to fear, and finally, to crying in just
a few minutes. She could run through the full range of all her
emotions in just a few minutes. But most of the time, she was in
a happy peaceful mood, laughing and jumping for joy.

How does on feel the inner presence of God? I wish my
granddaughter could have talked and had the wisdom of a high
priest at ten months old. She could have told me.

Religions And Spirituality
Man is born centered in the light of spiritual consciousness. He's
filled with spiritual grace, and he's holy and righteous. He's filled
with the grace of his creator but has no concept or
consciousness of God or gods. His righteousness is a gift from
his creator and not an offering from any religion.

12

The most righteous people on earth have no religion and all the saints on earth cannot surpass the righteousness of a little child. All the books that man have written about God, gods and about righteousness cannot surpass the righteousness of other creatures of creation that have never read a book.

Religions are not the source of man's righteousness. Only the creator sows the seeds of righteousness. Man and his religion are only the cultivators that water the seeds to make righteousness bloom and grow.

Love is the foundation of man's spiritualism, tender loving care to little children, and brotherly love in the world of adult. Any experience of love is a spiritually fulfilling experience, and any spiritually fulfilling experience is an experience of love.

All religions aim to light man's pathway to spiritual fulfillment. All religions aim to seek the path of righteousness. But there is only one way, one truth and one light to righteousness, and it is *LOVE*—divine love and brotherly love.

Love and spiritualisms are the same, with or without a religion. But every religion embraces ways that conflict with brotherly love. They embrace too many ways that divide people. If any man seeks a total spiritual affirmation, he must step outside the ideals of his religion. If he does that, like a little child with innocence and love, he'll be able to find total oneness with his creator and total oneness with all of humanity.

Images Of God

An adult human, separated from his soulful spiritual consciousness, lives in an ego-centered physical consciousness. In our state of physical consciousness, we pay all our attention to the material side of life. We're in a material state of mind, a state of mind that leaves the soul feeling empty. Feeling empty and lost, man must look for salvation and the salvation he finds is the image of God in his consciousness.

When mankind brings God into his material consciousness, it's easy for him to take God out of his spiritual consciousness and have images of God. But God is a spirit and no image of God is worthy of divine grace and spiritualism. Some men say God made us in his own image, while some men make God in their own image. Let's do away with all the images of God or gods so we can experience God as little babies do, in spirit, truth and light.

The most significant parts of human history involve man's relationship with some kind of God-like entity. Empires were built with images and myths about God. People of God have killed people they said served the wrong Gods. Religions imbued with the spirit of Gods have built some of the greatest human cultures and at the same time, religions imbued with the spirit of Gods have been the destruction of many people of many cultures.

The evidence is very clear. Man has a permanent presence of God in his psyche—he cannot rid himself of some essence of God. Even the man who claims to be an atheist has some kind of godlike image on his consciousness.

The trouble with man's experience with God is that man makes many material images that take God out of the purely one universal spirit—no shape, and no form—and put God into a material concept. Every material concept or image of God is an illusion that creates deep conflicts in human relations. These images cause racial conflicts, gender conflicts, conflicts between man and animals, conflicts with brotherly love, conflicts of hate, and war between man and his fellowman.

Concept Of God
When man loses his spiritual gracefulness, he wanders in a world of spiritual darkness. Alienated from his inner self and isolated from his fellowman, he suffers a loss of faith and evil thoughts corrupt his soul. This is the condition for most if not all human suffering.

There's hope of salvation and redemption, but it takes profound mindfulness, images, myths and praise, along with worship and devotion. In many ways, thoughts and dreams, man can develop his own knowledge and his own concept of God in his never ending search to find God and end his suffering.

Denial Of God

Christian, Islamic and Jewish religions all believe in the same God as the one supreme ruler and creator of all the earth. Some other religions define their god as a superhuman spirit or being. Still, there are many who say there's no God or gods. But I've never met a man who didn't believe in some kind of superhuman spirit on earth, in heaven or in hell.

In trying to understand God, we can look into the mind of man to see what he believes. There are so many different ideals, many images, myths, and conflicting theories that it's almost impossible to find a concept of God that doesn't conflict with others. But if we put aside all the beliefs and mindfulness of God, we find one spirit that runs through every man and indeed, all of humanity.

We call that one spirit love. It's the spiritual grace of God, the fountain of life that flows in the innermost being of every person. There's no conflict in this oneness of spiritual grace in every man.

That such grace exists is as sure as there's a liver and a heart in every man. Ask the Godliest people—the little children. Ask a little girl or boy if they have a liver or a heart or a God inside of them, and they most likely to deny the existence of all three.

For those who believe in one God, those who believe in many gods, and for those who say there is no God? Tell the little children, tell the communist and the atheist, and give them the positive reality:

There is spirit in you and your denial can do nothing to change that reality.

The adult denial of God is only for those who refuse to love. If a person is a loving mother, a loving father, or a loving person of faith, hope and charity, they surely are filled with spiritual grace.

15

Words may speak in denial of spirit but for sure, his soul is filled with the gracefulness of the Holy Spirit.

The Need For Love And God
If a child is raised with plenty of tender loving care and he feels loved, he will love the world. He'll have only joy, and no sorrow. He'll never have an enemy. That child may go from cradle to grave and never have to say, "**I need God**."

God is love and the need for love is the need for God.

In this world of sin and shame, everyone suffers from some kind of spiritual dis-grace, so everyone needs God to get back to amazing grace.

In the history of humanity, the need for God has been mankind's deepest need. Religions have taken up the task of saving mankind from the pain and terror of materialism and evil by centering him in the mindfulness of his need for God. History shows plenty of evidence that religion is the only reality in many cultures. People live for religion, die for religion and kill for religion. Take away all their material possessions and they'll forgive you, but mess with their religion and they will kill you.

Wherever a baby cries, there's a need for God. Wherever people are oppressed, there's a need for God. Wherever spiritual emptiness starves the human soul, there's a need for God. Wherever there's too much famine, too much rain, too much war, too much sorrow, or too much pain, God is man's only salvation.

God, My Mother And Me
I was born in Jamaica, West Indies on May 3, 1941, the last of six children. Till this very day, I believe my mother and father were two of the most honest, most humble and the hardest working people I know. I say I'm lucky to have been the son of two very Godly people.

However, my mother used to beat me. Whenever my disobedience made her angry, she beat me saying, "You need Jesus, you need Jesus." My mother was a very angry person

16

and she had to work too hard to give me loving care. So I suffered those beatings and worse, neglect, in my crib.

I felt like I was all alone in the world. It was little me, alone against the world. Throughout my young life, I was full of sorrow and terror of emotional pain, horror of loneliness, and fear caused by spiritual emptiness.

My family were Quakers. Christians and we call ourselves Friends Church. Quakers came to Jamaica during times of slavery. They built churches and schools, they fed people and best of all, they were very much anti-slavery. My wife, who was born in the same place I was, always sings the praises of the Quakers.

My Mother. To this very day, I don't know of a person who is a better Christian than my mother was. Her Christian life of following Jesus was a twenty-four/seven experience. She beat me to get me to read the Bible. She made me read the Psalms and pray every morning, go to Church, go to Sunday school, sing and praise God, and Jesus, Jesus, Jesus.

In defense of my mother, she did not know **love** when she was a child. Her parents emotionally and even physically abandoned her. I do believe it was her belief and following Jesus that saved her to live a good life for eighty-two years.

My Father. On the other hand, my father just worked, worked and sang. He was a man of high integrity—a kind, honest and loving man to his family and to the people in our little village of Hectors River, Portland. He was also a good provider for his family, so we were never hungry.

But I never saw my father in any religious activity. Emotionally speaking, I always felt as if my father was a total stranger, and I had no close contact with him.

My mother was the most religiously active person I know. My father had no religion but was most honest, humble and kind.

But who of the two was more spiritually filled? I believe my mother was full of religion, while my father was full of the Holy Spirit.

I want the reader to understand where I'm coming from when I speak and write about spirituality without religion. I lived most of my life trying to serve God, reading my Bible, going to Church, singing in the Choir, and praying, always singing and praying.

But at the same time I was spiritual rebel. Every spiritual rebel is rebelling against the core of his innermost self. Man is a spiritual being living in a material consciousness. I'm alive and doing very well today only because after fifty years of rebellion, I have learned to *separate* my religion from my inner most spiritual self. My religion is manmade, but my inner most spiritual self is God created.

I have learned to put my religion aside and I'm taking a journey back to God—back to visit the holy and innocent little boy crying in his crib. I'm traveling a dark and dismal distant journey back into the kingdom of my soul.

God is love, and spiritualism is love. *I* must learn to love again. Love is the only thing that can save me from the pain and torment of living a loveless life.

Born Free
Mankind is born free—free from fear, free from anger and free from sin. But most of all, he is born free to love. Love, anger and fear are his three primary emotions, but love is the foundation of all our emotions. When we experience the emotion of love, we experience the spiritual fulfillment of life.

The child is born free to love, love, and love. But if love cannot be found the child quickly swings into the emotions of anger and fear. We must seek to love little children at any cost. Love keeps them free as the day they were born, free from the spiritual bondage of anger and fear that can last a lifetime.

Infants are closer to God than adults. Parents who neglect little children or punish and push them to get closer to God cannot be more wrong. As a matter of fact, loving a baby will bring the parent closer to God's little creature and closer to God. Any kind of neglect, such as leaving the child alone for too long, separates the infant from inner peace and separates the infant from God. Mothers must be tender and soft, and there must be rays of love shining from their eyes into the eyes of the baby.

Sad to say, this world we live in today is obsessed with material consumption in which everybody works too much and shops too much. There's not one child born in this modern world who is given adequate tender loving care. So every child suffers the sin of a short supply of spiritual love and a short supply of spiritual love. They are born spiritually free but soon suffer the fate of all humanity born in the age of information and technology.

Born Again
"Ye must be born again," the holy Bible says. What does this mean? I believe it simply means the place of one's birth is certainly a place of salvation. It simple means the place of one's birth is a place of holiness and not a place of sin.

My mother was born free, free to love and be loved. But her parents abandoned her, physically and emotionally, and that experience of rejection conquered her freedom to love and put her in spiritual bondage. The reason this world is such a sinful place is because every day millions of little children suffer the same rejection as my mother did over a hundred years ago.

I believe the Christian religion has the widest road to salvation, because of Jesus Christ. Jesus showed man the open road to salvation and the road to freedom from the torment of living in anger, fear and self-doubt. Freedom to go back to the place of his birth, to go back into the kingdom of his soul to be embraced in the arms of love. Freedom to go back to the place where love is the only reality.

Man can find a place where he is given a second chance at salvation because the second time around, the adult is the mother of the little child crying inside of her, "Save me, save me," and then the mother can be born again.

TWO

SPIRITUALITY WITHOUT RELIGION

I Believe

I believe God is a spirit, God is love, and God is light and truth. I also believe every man has a soul, and the spirit of God is in every man. Love is the manifestation of God in every man, and this love will manifest itself in the seven spiritual virtues of love. God is an inner feeling of spiritual love, rather than what we believe.

I believe in the God of creation, the same God found in little children. Little children, who have no consciousness of God and no religion, are closer to God than adults.

The essence of God is spiritual grace seated in the soul of every man. If we truly see love in everything, we can see a trace of God in the sinner but more of God in the saint. However, it's the same God in both.

I believe the person who worships idols or many gods simply suffers from a case of mistaken identity. And I believe the grace of God is still in the person who says there's no God, as long as that person is able to love—meaning he's a loving father or she's a loving mother or any other loving person.

21

If a man wants to truly experience the word of God, it's written on the wind. It's written on the first breath of life a baby takes, and it's written on the baby's deepest breathing. It's even present in the baby's cries to its mother for love and as it cries out for life and cries out to God.

God's word is written on the seed that's planted and grows into a tree a hundred feet high and on every flower that blossoms. The grace and the word of God also are seen every time an animal suckles its young.

On the other hand, every book that's written is written on manmade paper. Whether or not the words of God are in the book, one thing is certain—the book is manmade. And everything man does is subject to mistakes and errors. Some things are left out, subject to the unrighteous thinking every man is capable of.

We see God in everything that's created in nature, not in a book made by man. Sure, there are many holy books written by many holy men. But no man is perfect, only creation is perfect. Every book that's written has some imperfections and some prejudices. We find perfection only in creation.

Many inspiring books have been written and have inspired mankind about righteousness. Books may be written about God, but the only true book of God is written on the wind. Only nature provides mankind evidence of God.

If every man looked to nature in his search for God or gods, then and only then, every person in this world will be devoted to the one and the same Holy Spirit Religion. The whole world would be united in peace and harmony with only one religion, with one denomination and one love, one peace on earth, goodwill to all men, one sect, one name. We would be devoted to the religion of every child. Every child would feel loved and all of mankind would be free to love. The Holy Spirit Religion.

Religions

The source of our spiritualism is a higher infinite spiritual power. It's the source of all creation, not religion. This source of spiritual power is what we call love. This one and only source of spirit, I call God, with a capital G.

Spiritualism is God-made while religions are manmade. Spiritual significance is the heart of mankind's living. It's the inner core of our self without which life is not worth living. Many men have taken their own lives when they were in perfect physical shape, simply because their lives were spiritually empty.

Religions are manmade, the strongest thing made by man. The dictionary defines religion as a belief, the belief in and worship of God or gods, a particular system of faith and worship. So belief, faith and worship are the foundation of all religions. These same three—belief, faith and worship—seem to define the very core of our human nature. Worship transcends our animal nature, so it's safe to say the need to have a religion is at the very core of our human nature.

If man doesn't have a religion or more accurately, doesn't have the belief, faith and worship that are at the heart of all religions, he can face feelings of nothingness. He may feel lower than an animal or feel like a thing. Throughout human history we've seen how greed, selfishness, power, and materialism have captured the passion of many cultures. And we've seen mankind spend his passions in search of material significance.

But if there is no spiritual significance throughout the culture and within the inner life of each citizen, there's a danger that every culture and every man with material significance will self-destruct. A man with spiritual significance and no material significance will struggle very hard to live. But the rich and powerful man who has lost all his spiritual significance will seek to destroy his fellowman and destroy himself in the process as well. Only with spiritual significance can man find the freedom from living with the terror of the fear of death.

Human nature can be characterized as a search for material

significance for his survival and at the same time an inner need for spiritual significance for his salvation.

Religion is the strongest manmade entity on earth. In a battle between the will to survive and the fear of death, fear will win every time. Fear can terrify a man's soul so much that he will take his own life, rather than keep fighting the fear. Religion is man's search for God or gods, his search for spiritual significance. Sometimes it's the only way he can have and hold his spiritualism, so he may live for his religion. He also will die for it, and he will kill for it.

It's best for man to build his cultures on God (or with God) and religion, because human history shows that cultures that refuse to do so spend much of their power fighting against religion and fighting against man's most fundamental need, the need for spiritual significance. Man's religion helps him fight all enemies, whether it's the inner enemies of self-destruction, fear and self-doubt, or the outer enemies, such as oppression and destruction coming from his fellowman. The boldest force on earth is the man with the Ten Commandments in one hand and the sword of God in the other.

All the great religions teach against materialism and for spiritualism. The million-dollar question is—is there a way or ways for man to promote his spiritual needs without a religion? Or an even more important question—can man find a better way to nurture spiritual love while a baby is in the crib? So adults don't have to live in deep spiritual emptiness, don't have to live so obsessed with religions. So adults would be free from all the prejudices and wars of religions.

Flesh And Spirit
At the inner core, man is a spiritual being, but his outer layer is flesh. Which is more important, spirit or flesh?

The history of man's behavior suggests we're first, last and always a creature of spiritual significance. Give a baby all the food in the world but no love, and the baby will die. Take away

24

any man's food for his flesh, and he will struggle to get more. But let him be faced with a total rejection, betrayal or denial of love, and he will kill or be killed—or even kill himself.

We're born rooted in a spirit-emotional expression of life. Spirit and emotions express our lives. The flesh is just a byproduct of that expression.

Human life is a transformation from the eternal, mortal essence of the soul, which is changed by the power of spiritual love into a living, breathing being of body, mind and soul. Life is a myth. It's a miracle, it's magic. Spirit takes the breath of life we call love and love become flesh. At birth man's flesh in rooted in the embryonic state of spiritual love only for the time it takes to become enlightened into the consciousness and shame that the flesh is naked. The human infant, like every other creature on earth, has no shame of the naked flesh. The consciousness of the nakedness of the flesh takes mankind away from the inner spiritual self of love and soul and puts him into a material outer self of flesh, sin and shame.

All the great religions teach man to seek first to live in the consciousness of the inner spiritual self, through prayer, worship, praise and meditation, and to live in the denial of the consciousness of the outer flesh.

Life is a struggle for survival and salvation. Mankind's greatest struggle is between his secular living and his religious living, as well as conflicts between those who put secular living first and those who   put religious living first. **Secular** living provides material food, water and comfort for the consumption of the flesh, while **religious** living provides spiritual food and water for the fulfillment of man's soul.

This struggle cannot be won by social means. It can only be won by psychological and spiritual means, because it's a struggle to fill man's most important needs. Man struggles for survival and at the same time, he struggles for salvation. Both are struggles to find freedom from pain and suffering. Some of the great prophets believed that life itself is a struggle—to find freedom from human

SPIRITURALITY WITHOUT RELIGIONS

suffering and pain, to find consumption for the flesh, and at the same time fulfillment for the soul.

Is man to live first for the material survival of his belly, or live first for the spiritual salvation of his soul? This is a question about human nature that we've yet to answer. That's why so many people turn to God or gods. But scientists and philosophers also must have input in finding the answers to the miracles of human nature. Man's historical struggles, between secular and religious, between flesh and spirit, have been the cause of many wars, oppressions and many other conflicts in human societies. Is there any end to war and oppression in the lives of mankind?

Yes, there is a solution.   It's **Brotherly Love**. Only brotherly love has the power to break down all walls of conflicts and bring harmony between religious, secular, social and ideological factions. Only brotherly love has the power to bring peace on earth, goodwill to all men.

God, Spirit And Love
God is the spiritual essence of life that's at the core of every human life. It blooms and grows onto the substance we call the flesh. Life is spirit and substance. God is likened to the spirit in alcohol or the scent of a flower. The soul is the essence of God in the body of every man.

If man hears the words of God, he'll hear it on the wind for as the wind blows, so we breathe in and out the breath of life. We can hear the voice of God in the ocean's roar and in the river rushing to the sea.   We hear God in the baby's cry and in a bird singing its songs of glory. Most of all, we hear God in our inner intuition, our inner voice.

We hear God in our feelings—feelings that tell us to love, forgive, and be kind. Feelings that tell us to be still and tranquil. We can hear the voice of God connecting us to an infinite flow of divine love. This divine love comes as a n inner fulfillment of joyful emotions that flow from our soul into our hearts where they flood our entire being with love. We feel loved and we love the world.

26

We hear God in the good feeling that moves in our conscience to tell us when something is going right in our words, thoughts or deeds. We also hear God in our conscience in feeling bad when something is wrong in our words, thoughts or deeds. Our conscience is the book of God written with moral and ethical codes. It's open inside us for every man to read, but man doesn't write it. There's no language for God because God is not a person, place or thing. God is the spiritual essence of life.

Brotherly Love

Brotherly love is the only thing that can remove, resolve or even bury all conflicts in every human-to-human relationship. In all inter-human dealings, there are conflicts. Disagreements are unavoidable, and a difference of opinion is often necessary. Wisdom will conflict with folly, love will conflict with hate, selfishness will conflict with kindness, and knowledge will conflict with reason.

But in all these things, man should seek first the redemption of brotherly love, because it's only in the face of brotherly love that the wise man will pour kindness, not contempt for the folly of his brother. Only brotherly love will pour kindness and not contempt on his brother's selfishness. Only brotherly love will pour goodness, mercy and forgiveness on his brother's character defects.

God is the light of kindness and love. Any man who picks up the sword of contempt in words, thoughts or deeds against his fellowman moves against his own inner spiritual self and also moves against the God who lives and breathes within him.

Brotherly love is the foundation—the essence—of spiritualism. Religious men have paved the roads of history with the blood of their fellowmen, as they held the Holy Book in one hand and the sword of contempt in the other. Simply because they were Without brotherly love. But with brotherly love, man will hold the Holy Book in one hand and the light of forgiveness and redemption in the other.

Brotherly love is peace on earth, goodwill to all men.

27

Pleasure is an emotional sensation. It's the movement of feelings that diminish pain and move towards a desired satisfaction. But it's just a superficial sensation, whether neurotic or emotional.

The "real deal" is not pleasure—it's feelings of joy. Feelings of joy start with an inner spiritual liveliness of emotions that flow from the soul into the heart and radiate throughout man's blood into his veins and indeed, into his whole body. The experience we call love is to feel spiritually alive, and any experience of love makes us feel spiritually alive.

Little children are the most spiritually alive humans, more than most adults. Most adults don't remember when they were super-spiritually alive, when they were in a state of spiritual bliss. They don't remember smiling while at their mother's breast, filled with inner peace and the grace of God.

Children are at one with God, at one with self and at one with all of humanity. They are the essence of spiritual aliveness. But there's a downside to all this baby and baby-like spiritual aliveness. You see, a baby is a spiritual giant but it's emotionally fragile. It's also a mental and physical midget. The baby's very life depends on tender loving care from adults. The baby's inner spiritual life needs food for the soul, along with love and food for the body. These two kinds of food must be nurtured and supplied by adults.

If the baby is hungry and left alone for long periods—kicking, screaming and crying—he suffers the pain of a hungry stomach. And because of his fear of being alone, he suffers an even deeper pain and t error, which is the death of his inner spiritual being.

This helpless infant, once spiritually alive with joy and happiness, is put on an emotional rollercoaster. His ego is too weak to Handle too much joy, too much fear, or too much crying. Emotional suppression is spiritual separation. To stop the Pain of crying and the fear of spiritual death, babies soon Learn to suppress their inner aliveness. They learn to suppress the unity and harmony of self and we become adults of disunity and anxiety.

Man becomes alienated from God, disunity within self —

body, mind and soul—and is isolated from his fellowman.

God-Filled
Human life is meant to be a God-filled journey from cradle to grave. We call these God-filling, life-filling experiences love. I believe the holiest of these is the one between mother and child. The mother nurtures life while the child experiences God, drinking from the life-saving spring of mother's milk.

Later in this book, I write about the Seven Virtues of Love. Each one is an experience of the spiritual essence of God. Each fills the soul with the spiritual essence of God.

The Seven Virtues of Love: Faith, Hope, Charity, Humility, Gratitude, Forgiveness, and Spiritual Self-affirmation

Spirit God
God is a spirit, a divine higher power that's the source of all creation. This spiritual energy dwells in the soul of every man, rather than in the ego-consciousness of the mind. I will tell the true believer, the agnostic and the atheist that every man is born with the Holy Spirit in his soul. God is in man before he can have any belief in God. If the sprit is the source of all creation and there's only one creation, then there must be only one spirit. There's only one spirit with no name, no shape, no form, no begging, and no end. All the great religions believe in the Holy Spirit. Some call him God and some say gods, but all believe in spirit.

In the book of Genesis it's said, "God made man in his own image." Since God is a spirit—nothing more and nothing less—any image of God must be something we cannot see. Can we see the wind? No! But we're sure it's there. And we know we would die without it. We cannot see God or any image of God with the naked eye. In fact, any image of God we can see with

29

the naked eye is an illusion. Man can only see God through the eyes of faith.

Any man who believes he can see God or any image of God is in trouble. Any man who believes he can make an image of God With his hands or naked eyes also is in trouble. Because when the sun goes down, in the midnight hour, when the lamp that man has made runs out of oil, he's left in darkness. Wherever there's darkness, there's fear. Fear that makes the soul weep and the body tremble. Wherever there's darkness, there's doubt and plenty of anxiety. And there in the darkness, man has always picked up his sword to fight.

Any man who believes he can see God or any image of God with his naked eye suffers with the illusion of spiritual materialism. That makes it easier for him to fight holy wars, with the Holy Book in one hand and his sword of God in the other.

Faith
In faith, there's no darkness. Faith is the spiritual light of God, And it's the key to God. Faith lets us believe in something we cannot see, God.

In all the great religions there's a foundation of faith in their teachings. They all have faith in a spiritual higher power. They teach and preach faith but they cannot truly follow faith. The ego must have images to go by.

Because man has lost his soul and is alienated from God, he wanders off into no man's land. But faith is the foundation of happiness and inner peace. Without faith we worry about every little thing, and we make a mountain out of a molehill. Anxiety, fear and insecurity are the constant companions of a faithless man.

Modern man is gripped in the arms of machines, making bigger and bigger machines with his computers. He has lost faith in himself. Today's little children are given machines—cold, hard machines—to comfort their souls. In this world with all the glory given only to machines the soul of very child weeps and when the soul weeps, the body trembles. This brings the ego in to the rescue. Man becomes an empty soul with an overflowing ego.

The super ego comes to rescue each individual from the sorrow and loneliness of a world of selfishness, greed and materialism. We live in a world where man has lost faith, not only in himself but also in his fellowman. Faith in God is his only hope of finding meaning in his meaningless world.

This faithless world is run not by those who embrace love. Instead, its run by those who think love is only for the meek and the weak. Those who've lost faith in brotherly love run it. They bring the message of the love of God to the world with power and glory, but this message is wrapped up in ego-centeredness and spiritual materialism.

The ego said, let's go back to God, but the ego is in the darkness, and not knowing that it is not God that is lost, but faith. Faith in God, faith in himself and faith in his fellowman is lost.

The history of the human race is filled with faithless man looking for God and gods in his ego-centered world. He looks for his God, not only in spirit but also with his spiritualism contaminated by materialism.

The history of the human race shows plenty of evidence that man is a very highly spiritual being. But on his journey into adulthood in this material world, he loses some of his spiritualism. So much so that he's bound to live an active life of searching to rebuild his spiritualism or else live an empty life that's not worth living. In his never-ending search to recoup his spiritual self-affirmation, man has the need to promote a bright spiritual consciousness in his mind. His mind must become active with spiritual matters.

In the ego consciousness of the mind, however, man searches for spiritual significance. Without it, he has no significance at all. Without it, his life becomes an empty soul that's lifeless inside and meaningless on the outside.

It seems the fate of mankind is to live with plenty of suffering and sorrow, to be victims and victimizers, to live with wars, fear, and oppression. But all these sins only happen because man has lost his way to a life of salvation. He has lost his spiritualism.

Love is man's only salvation to regain his spiritualism. "Save me, save me, " he cries. "Give me something to live for because this empty soul is killing me. I need someone to trust and obey, someone to give my praise and worship, someone to renew my faith. Someone to give me a reason to love and to live. Give me a place where I can find enough spiritual meaning to make me want to live and love. If that someone is God, then I will serve him. I'll serve the moon and the stars, I'll build my own gods with spiritual powers, and t hen I'll serve him or them. I'll serve and worship my God or gods and him, her or even it."

Spiritually Graceful
Spiritual gracefulness is the key to happiness. If a man is filled with spiritual grace, he has inner peace, which is the foundation of self-love and love for the world. Each human is created full of spiritual grace. This amazing grace is the core at the center of our being. It's the living wellspring of waters flowing, giving life to the flesh. There's no human life that goes on living totally void of spiritual grace, because such a life would feel empty, meaningless and worthless. It would seek ways to destroy itself.

Next time you talk with an atheist, especially one who is able to show love, assure him or her they have this spiritual grace inside. Most people who kill themselves are materially full and healthy but are spiritually empty. Before we could walk and talk when we crawled on our bellies, our soul was filled with spiritual grace, but no spiritual mindfulness. By fate we developed into a person running on two feet, with strong ego mindfulness. We have knowledge of good and evil but are separated from our spiritual grace.

The key to a happy life of salvation is to seek a soulful, spiritual, gracefulness with a *mindful* spiritual awareness.

Spiritualism

The essence of human life is love, spiritual love. The scientists with their bag of DNA and Big Bang Theory will disagree with me only because they're unable or unwilling to differentiate between essence and substance on the issue of human life. Essence is the flavor we can't see, while substance is the salt we pour in a spoon. We cannot pour flavor in a spoon.

The substance of human life *is* DNA, chemical matter we can see or measure. Furthermore, scientists have done plenty of good to the human quality of life with their DNA theories. But they cannot create life. With his theory of evolution, Darwin contributed much virtue to human living. And consider the accomplishment of the scientist who invented the vaccine to prevent polio. He had the same DNA makeup as millions of people, but by inventing the polio vaccine, he did something that was one in tens of millions. He must have something in him greater than his material self, something extra in his soul, faith, hope and inspiration. Otherwise, he could never have succeeded.

Faith and hope are two of the main ingredients in man's spiritualism. They're part of the infinite source of the spiritual love that creates man. And so we say, leave it to scientists to glorify and magnify the substance of life. But the spiritualists will give worship and praise to spiritualism, the essence of life.

In the history of the human race, religions have played a far more significant role in life than anything science can do. Superficially, there are sharp differences and conflicts between religions and even sharp and deep conflicts within each religion but at the inner core, all religions deal with mankind's most fundamental meaning and fulfillment in life. All the great religions seek to promote spiritualism, the essence of life. But the essence of life is love, not religion. All great religions seek what is most important in human living—faith, hope and love—not the DNA in life but the essence of life.

33

Spiritual Significance

Evolution deals with life in regard to instincts, and chemical and biological changes in mind and body for survival of the species. Creation, on the other hand, is not just about survival. It deals with mortality and salvation, and there are hundreds of different stories about it. Salvation is found in the immortal soul of every man, the wellspring of eternal spiritual enlightenment, and the love that transcends all humans from the grips of evolution and into the tender embrace of the creator.

Spiritual Beings

Human spiritualism is what separates us from animals. It's not good enough to say we're spiritual beings because at the core of our being is the spiritual wellspring of life. In substance, we're flesh, bones, big brains and blood, but we live in the consciousness of spiritual love. When ego-centeredness puts human living in the consciousness of only the material self, the spiritual light of eternal love within us glows dim and dimmer, until finally, we're plunged into the darkness of sin and shame.

Sad to say, at the peak of his spirit-fullness man cannot walk, talk or stand on his own two feet. He has little or no intellectual reasoning. This being that seems to be more animal than human is an infant child. The animal-like infant is dependent on this sinful world shaped in inequity for his survival and for his salvation. The child needs food for his belly for survival and tender loving care from adults for his salvation.

Love Or Fear?

Our spiritualism is at the heart and soul of our humanism. It's wrapped up in our capacity for love. How we show love and can be loved is the indication of our spiritualism. At the core of life, we are spirit. Spirit is love and love is spirit, the essence of life. Whenever we choose to love, we choose the celebration of life. On the other hand, when we refuse to love we choose the fear of life.

In the spiritual realm of life, we must choose to love or fear will choose us. The fear of life, that is.

The history of the human race is characterized by expressions of fear more than love because we've been caught in the grips of selfish materialism. Today very little is said about love and even the little that is said gives lip service to love more than real expressions of love. Even though religious organizations still talk about the glory of love, they're more about power, egoism, and materialism, rather than brotherly love.

Children today have been given such a loveless world to live in that they live in the sub-consciousness of fear. This means their words, thoughts and deeds are motivated by fear rather than love. All our faith and glory is given to technology and information. We give the glory to relationships with things rather than to relationships with people.

The happiness we find today is void of simple joys because it's not the freedom to love that makes us feel good but the freedom from fear.

Spirit In Children
To be happy, children of today need the same things as children did a thousand years ago. They need to live in a world of love and be given an abundance of tender loving care. The biggest mistake we make is not to accept fully and wholeheartedly the holiness and righteousness of little children. Little children are the most spiritualized people on earth.

Not understanding the Godly gracefulness in children, self-righteous parents say they have to bring the child to God. They don't understand that the kicking, crying and screaming the child does is because of the spiritual aliveness in the little ones. What the parent sees as unrighteous behavior by the child is nothing more than a fear-bound child demanding the spiritual and material necessities to live, love and eat.

Loving a little child is the most spiritual way to nurture life, and it is also the holiest way to bring the parent closer to the love of God.

35

Inner Light: Union With The Spirit

All the great religions accept that there's one universal spiritual infinite source in all of nature. But in human life, we also must accept that there's the same *one* spiritual source of love that's at the core of every one of us. It's this source of inner spiritual light that unites our souls with the infinite source of life. It also unites our consciousness with the universal light and with life itself.

Universal unity: The spirit soul, united with physical body, united with mind consciousness

In this state of universal unity, man is totally in the embrace with his or her universe. Free from sorrow and fear, spiritual self-affirmation is high, which gives rise to self-esteem. Self-awareness is high, also giving rise to self-esteem. Finally, self-position and self-control are high and that also gives rise to self-esteem. This tranquil state of universal unity and harmony leads to love, and love is the only thing for someone in love with self, in love with divine love and in love with the universe.

This place of universal unity is a place of spiritual bliss. There man will find peace with God, a peace that's beyond all concepts and all understanding. It's the peace of a sleeping child who has no concept of God, no evil thoughts, words or deeds, and a child who has no religion but is filled with the grace of God.

Spiritualized

Mankind is born embraced in the grace of God, fully spiritualized. A baby's soul bubbles with spiritual energy, a wellspring of spiritual love flowing from the soul into a heart that beats in harmony with the rhythmic waves of life.

Since the human spirit is the heart of human life, the man with a broken spirit is a man with a broken life. His flesh becomes tense, and his mind grows weak and wanders into nowhere. His whole being feels lifeless, and he's ready to give up his struggle for life. Finally, he gets depressed.

You'll never see a little baby who's depressed unless he's not getting enough love. Without love, the baby's spirit is broken. Otherwise, the innocent child with plenty of tender loving care is the most spiritualized person on earth. No saint, no prophet, no high priest, no imam, and no rabbi is more spiritualized than an innocent little child.

De-Spiritualized

The most complex thing on earth is human nature, because there are many contradictions within our nature. A man's character often seems to be one thing at first sight, but a deeper analysis may show it to be just the opposite. Man's actions can be the exact opposite of his innermost feelings.

The confusion arises because of mankind's dual nature. He's born with an animal nature but has to seek a productive and active life of love, work and knowledge to reach his full human potential. Born fully spiritualized in the bright light of spiritual consciousness, it seems man must seek to de-spiritualize himself in order to reach his full human potential with his mind, body and soul. But the "Catch 22" is that too much de-spiritualization means de-humanization.

Man must transcend his *spiritual* world in order to fully understand and prosper in his material world. It's a tale of two towers, where spiritual fulfillment conflicts with material consumption. The challenge is to nurture the spiritual aliveness in little children and at the same time, teach them the wisdom and necessary skills to prosper in the material world.

It seems human nature is one of transcending from inner self of soulful spiritualism into an ego-centered, de-spiritualized development of body and mind. The fate of mankind is to transcend from a vessel of spiritual love into an instrument of work and knowledge.

De-spiritualization is an inner-outer split, a spiritual transformation of soul separated from body and ego. It is the ego abandoning the soul that seeks to gain the world so the body may wallow in material consumption.

Man is created fully spiritualized, filled with the grace of God, whole and holy. But most adults block out these days of holiness and grace, especially those who have a loveless first three years in life.

But these spiritual days of grace are also the days of physical bondage and an empty mental slate. Even though this spiritual holiness is at its peek at birth, those are the days of spirit-emotional immaturity, physical immobility and mental pity. Those are the days of de-spiritualization and days of spiritual separation.

Love is the key for body and mind development. But in today's world of selfish materialism, very few children are given enough love to enjoy freedom from de-spiritualization.

Holiness And Fear
If you could look back at the place of your birth, there sometimes would be nothing to see but fear. You would see scorn and sometimes even punishment for your spiritual aliveness, the same spiritual aliveness that makes you kick, scream and holler for loving care food and attention.

The same loving care that keeps you alive causes you to be punished for boldly expressing it. Neglect and punishment put fear into your soul, your soul weeps and your body trembles. Fear becomes a constant companion and stifles your ability to experience love. It dims the inner lights of faith and hope, and it puts you in the darkness of de-spiritualization. Sin and shame become you.

Re-Spiritualization
Mankind is born fully spiritualized, but he's also born more animal than human. However, his fate is to transcend his animal-like self and live in the glory of spiritual love and a full human potential—no matter what it takes. If it takes sin, shame, greed, selfish-centeredness and dreams of heaven, we must follow the yellow brick road to find the wizard of human nature. The wizard is the material monster, but the

essence of human nature is spiritual love. If we must de-spiritualize to become fully humanized, then we must do it because we must evolve or die.

The best part of human nature is that when we become adults, we're given a second chance to be born again. Every man is given the freedom to be re-spiritualized. Every man is given the chance to go back to his place of innocence and gracefulness to reunite and reacquaint himself with the Holy Spirit of love. He's allowed to go back into the kingdom of his soul, back to redeeming grace.

All the great religions have a basic foundation to show the light and give the enlightenment to mankind's re-spiritualization. All the great religions believe that spiritual essence is mankind's only salvation. Everyday spiritual activity is the aim of the great religions.

Man's journey from spiritual expression to spiritual separation is a journey from soul-centeredness to ego-centeredness. The ego or ego-centeredness stands in the way of man's journey back to reunite himself with the spiritual grace of his creator.

The ego is really not in a child at creation. Ego develops in the first few years after birth. It's our bright mindful consciousness and power of intellectual and rational reasoning that comes into full development at about three years old. It's a material consciousness that's anti-spirit and anti-love, and it seeks to find a world where there's freedom from fear, not where there's freedom to love.

In order for an adult man to fully re-spiritualize himself, he must first **de-ego** himself. A friend told me once, "Get rid of the ego and God will show up."

Every ego trip that promises man freedom from fear puts excitement and sometimes pleasure in his heart. Imbued with this excitement and pleasure, man seeks more and more to affirm his egotism. We see mighty religious men, centered in egotism, fight holy wars, and we see men in the secular world, military dictators, fight brutal and bloody wars. The light of brotherly love is the only weapon against the ego's ways of fear and darkness.

Love, Work And Knowledge

Wilhelm Reich, one of the Twentieth Century's foremost authors and psychoanalysts, said, "Love, work and knowledge are the wellspring of our lives. They should also govern it."

LOVE is the essence of life, the passion of life, and the wellspring of the spiritual passionate emotion that flows from the soul and fills the heart. It sweetens the body and sends peaceful tranquil waters flowing into the mind. For people who know love, it's the only thing in life.

All great religions teach about love. Sad to say, they glorify divine love but fail, miserably and shamefully, to practice brotherly love. The true experience of love permeates the whole being with an expression of spirit and emotional joy. It's an inner peace and at the same time, peace with the whole world.

The wellspring of life flows at the innermost core of our being, and when we let it flow into our words, thoughts and deeds, love governs our life. We feel loved and spiritually alive and we celebrate life, because the passion of love fills our life with meaning. The only time we truly celebrate life is when we love. We may celebrate life with divine love, parental love, brotherly love or the most compulsive love of all, romantic love.

Work

As mankind transcends his animal nature and moves into the glory of his human nature, he must have a productive, creative and inspirational life to feel complete and find significance in his living. He must work, not only for his daily bread but also for his daily dose of self-esteem. In the Garden of Eden, so the story goes, God told Adam, "By the sweat of your brow, you shall eat bread." Man must decide for himself whether work is a curse or a blessing.

Even in the subject of work, we come back to the issue of love. The labor of love adds passion and joy to any experience of work. In days of old before techonology unfolded, man used to work with passion, with a wellspring of joy in his soul. Every man once again must seek to find his passion in every work that he does. Passionate work is a blessing, while passionless work is a curse.

Knowledge

Once again it's all about love. The foundation of human nature is to love, but as we transcend our animal-like nature into the courage and glory of our human nature, we must increase in wisdom and knowledge to fulfill the full potential of all our humanism.

To increase in wisdom and knowledge, mankind must use his most unique virtues, the power of intellect and reason. Through these, he gains knowledge of his creator, knowledge of himself and knowledge of creation. Man makes love to feel the completeness of himself, because love is the only experience that makes him feel complete. But he makes work to survive and to feel the vibration of himself. Throughout history men of knowledge have ruled and changed the world.

Love is necessary to fulfill the soul, while work is needed to build the body and knowledge feeds and stimulates the mind. But love is the root of the tree of life, while work is the trunk of the tree and knowledge represents the branches. **Without love, there is no life**.

Having a proper balance of love, work and knowledge puts man in the glory of all his humanness. His life is filled with spiritual significance at the core of himself, and he has the necessary amount of spiritual, mental and material significance to make him feel perfectly whole and holy. This is true with or without a consciousness of God and with or without a religion.

Passionless Days

These are the most passionless days for people in the world.

41

Parents tell their children, "You must work hard, you must get a college education, or you will suffer the shame of poor people."

Are these the right words to way to every child, "Get rich, gain the world and lose your soul?" Remember, the soul is the well of man's passion and love. Only the labor of love will make that well of passion flow into a wellspring of inner spiritual life and give meaning to life. Without the passion of love that flows from the soul, knowledge is uninspiring and work becomes boring and unfulfilling.

People used to say, "Follow your passion." Today it's "Passion be dammed." Technology is king and information is queen.

But these passionless days leave the king and queen feeling lonely and empty, sitting on the throne in the darkness of a haunted palace.

Music, poetry and art are some of the most passionate ways to express life. Today computers are taking over, while the passion and inspiration of the soul is quickly diminishing.

Today, a computer makes soul music.

What good is work without passion or knowledge without wisdom and reason? This situation stifles our spiritual fulfillment in life and leaves us with an inner life of emotional and spiritual emptiness. If we pursue work and knowledge void of love, we will lose the innermost core of the self. We lose the soul. We lose God, we lose self and we lose our human-to-human connectedness.

One Universal Religion Of The Holy Spirit
Although there are sharp differences in superficial ideals and practices between religions, there's a common core of humanistic need and a search for the meaning and fulfillment of spiritual significance that unites all religions at the core.

So the question is why religions will not, or cannot, promote the things that unite mankind, rather than promote the very differences that often bring war and destruction on the human race? Why do religious people have the most conflicts and disagreement with other religions? I believe it's because religion is manmade, and anything that one man makes for himself will be envied and despised by other men. We need spiritualism, which is about the human soul that God created.

If we want to unite the world I suggest one religion or no religion.

"THE UNIVERSAL RELIGION OF THE HOLY SPIRIT"
(one world, one spirit, one creation, one love, and one soul)
Let the divine holiness and gracefulness that unite the soul
of every child be the essence of this religion.

Knowledge And Grace
Look at the inner peacefulness and grace of a little child. It has no sin and no shame, just gracefulness and love. In this inner place of spiritual bliss within little children, there's no knowledge of God and no consciousness of God. This shows that man doesn't need to have knowledge or consciousness of God to be holy and intimate with God.

Knowledge and consciousness are ego-centered, while gracefulness is soul-centered. Every adult has lost some of the gracefulness he had with God when he was born. So any adult who wants to be holy and righteous needs to seek God in the light of knowledge and spiritual consciousness, where he is open to the temptation of self-righteousness.

In human history we see the inner grace of God decrease as knowledge of God increases. Just watch a crocodile on TV pick up its young and put them under its tongue to safely protect them. The crocodile is motivated by the grace of God. It doesn't need a religion, nor does it need to read holy books to do the will of God. The crocodile doesn't have to believe in God to do the will of God.

I believe that tender loving care of little children is the Godliest experience anyone can have. Once again mothers don't need a religion to be perfect in motherly love. In man's darkest nights when he has gone astray like sheep, he needs God. But the ego says, "Let's seek a religion to **fight** the path back to God, the holy book of knowledge in one hand and the sword in the other hand." The soul says, "Let's not deny the power of knowledge. Let's have the holy book of knowledge in one hand but let's have a candle in the other hand to **light** the path back to God."

The salvation of this world is one universal soul-centered religion to unite all of mankind, not many ego-centered religions that will forever conquer and divide mankind.

The creator gives mankind choices. Mankind has the ego's power and the knowledge that can bring the darkness to destroy him and all of creation. But we also have the gracefulness and love of the soul that can bring the light to glorify ourselves and all of creation.

Human Nature
Mankind's biggest challenge in living is to understand himself. Simply to **BE** himself. But man has no time for that because there's an outer world he must conquer. Or he trembles with fear that the outer world of sin and shame will conquer him. In as much as man lives in fear of being conquered by his outer world, he keeps running away from a deeper fear. He fears the demons of his past, the demons of sin that invade his soul.

The trouble that man has in understanding his true nature is that demons stand in his way going back into the innermost core of himself where his true nature abides. Today's man has lost his courage and he's unwilling to go back into the kingdom of the soul to be reunited with his true inner self. So he runs, runs and runs, ego-tripping in his effort to gain the world but with a lost soul.

From the industrial to the technological ages, man has found a seemingly prefect way to deny his need for love and plunge himself through work and knowledge into machines—bigger, better and faster machines.

Love is the passion uniting mind, body and soul.

The nature of man as God created him is no more man's glory. Today we let machines be our glory. We express our nature in machines and let machines express our nature. As technology advances more and more, man tries to make machines more and more human-like.

This Frankenstein Syndrome is a big mistake, because it's a soul bubbling with passion that is the essence of human nature and the source of human life. Until man learns to put the passion of love in his machines, technology will never be his salvation. Until man is able to put the passion of hate in his machines, he will fail miserably to make truly human-like machines.

The passions of love and the passions of hate are the two positive and negative extremes in human nature. No manmade machine and no manmade institutions in this world will ever be able to put these two extreme emotions in a blender and spin them into one big ice cream and soda milkshake we call human nature.

Man is born to love, in as much as we experience love as the measure of our fulfillment in life. Even today, I believe most people live for love, but how safe is love? What good is love when wars and destruction reign throughout human history?

More and more, **evolution** has provided man with the ability to suppress his nature and to suppress his feelings and emotions. When sorrow, anger and love come, they interrupt our daily activities of making money and building war machines to keep us safe from the wrath of our fellowman. When we have stress, anxiety, boredom or any kind of mental dysfunction, we take pills. We let technology remove the symptoms of an empty soul and a broken heart.

Spiritual Nature
Man is a spiritual being who lives in a spiritual and physical consciousness. The essence of our spiritual nature is love—to love and feel loved. But love cannot bring money, so we suppress the spiritual consciousness and live in a material world. We give all the glory to scientists who study the mental and

45

biological sides of our nature. We also give glory and power to religious men who study the nature of God, the creator and the keeper of our souls.

But still today the innermost part of man—his spiritual nature—lurks in the darkness of his soul unknown. We know shamefully little about our innermost self, about our spiritual nature. We know shamefully little about our need for love, why the rich man in perfect health kills himself, or why people who are sick and starving struggle for every drop of the breath of life.

We don't understand why a man slaves all his life to get rich, while the rich man who worships his money only wants to use it to get love and attention. We don't understand why men make slaves of other men.

Man is born to love, and love is life, but hate and human destruction seems to be more in our nature. But the best things in life—love and attention—are free. So there's plenty of hope for humanity and human nature. Every time a mother loves a child as most mothers do, it shines the light on the glory of love and on the glory of man's spiritual nature.

Dual Nature
Man is born fully with an animal nature, more animal than human. It takes about ten years for him to fully develop and cook his first food. But make no mistake about it, from the day of his birth he fights to transcend the bondage of his animal nature and to reach his full human potential. He works hard for his daily bread and seeks knowledge. This dualism of nature does nothing but cause confusion. He becomes so confused he brings self-hate and scorn on humanity.

Most adult pour scorn on the wild animal-like ways of babies. The biggest scorn on man's created nature is by some religious people who say that man is born a sinner with a sinful nature. They maintain that man's purpose in life should be "Every man for himself." They believe man must save himself from sin and make himself righteous.

Because of dualism and confusion in human nature, self-righteousness is the biggest cause of human-to-human destruction.

At the innermost part of our being, our animal nature is driven by an instinct for survival. But also at the innermost part of our human nature lies a weeping soul that longs for love, redemption and salvation.

Looking at human nature, we see not only confusion of dualism but we see also many self-defeating ways. For example, man's greed for money stifles his need for love, the breath of life. And suppressing his emotions stifles his need for the self-expression that lifts his self-esteem.

 What is human nature? Is it to lie and deceive or is it to be truthful and honest? It sometimes seems as if every man is two people in one. Does that mean that every man is a victim of a split personality? Is every man's personality split between ego-centeredness and soul-centeredness?

Human nature is the only place in creation where we find sin and all kinds of evil. If we want to be sinless and do no evil, we have to go back into our animal nature, back to the place where we were born. However, the ego-centered part of our nature pours contempt on the part that is animal nature.

So what is man that God makes him a little higher than the animals? Is man an animal-like human or a human-like animal? Whatever mankind is, we know he's split within himself and split against himself.

There will be no peace on earth until mankind unites himself within himself and that unity is a unity between body/flesh (the material part) and mind/ego (the mental part) on one side and spirit/soul (the Godly part) on the other side. Peace on earth, goodwill to all men will come only when we solve the problem of dualism, a split, with soul on one side and body and mind on the other side. Peace on earth will come only when inner unity and harmony enables the spiritual side to take the sword out of the hand of the ego and replace it with a light so bright that it will take all of human nature out of the darkness of spiritual separation and make every human whole.

The Kingdom Of God

"The kingdom of God is within you," Jesus said. That means God is deep within the soul of man. The expression of God in man is his expression of love, spiritual love, the divine love that exposes him to brotherly love. The essence of this spiritual love is man's only reality in life. So every man who has lost total connectedness with the grace of God lives in the illusion of darkness and is like a living dead.

The soul is the kingdom of God in man. Many books have been written saying the kingdom of God is only for those who **believe**.

Every human soul represents the kingdom of God in man. The man who has lost his soul has lost intimacy with God and has lost intimacy with the innermost part of himself. Only babies have this complete intimacy with God and at the same time, babies have complete unity and total integration within self and with the universe.

The kingdom of God is in every baby in the crib.

The "Monkey Syndrome"

Man looks at the monkey and is totally perplexed. The monkey's nature is very close to the human infant. When Charles Darwin came out with his theory of evolution, all hell broke loose. Religious leaders got angry. They asked, "How could it be that man is descended from monkeys? Only man is created in the image of God. Man is created to worship, serve and obey God. Man is created by the hand of God." They poured scorn on monkeys, saying a monkey has a dumb animal nature while human nature is close to God.

If you think about it, the theory of evolution and the theory of creation are not mutually exclusive. God created every monkey as well as every man. We didn't need Darwin to tell us that we're

48

close relatives to animals. It's foolish to think that mankind is more Godly than the monkey.

God is love righteous and divine. All the evil and destruction in history has been done by man, not by monkeys.

If mankind would cease to be ashamed, cease to pour scorn on his monkey nature and instead start to embrace it, some of the monkeys' kind and loving ways might rub off on him and he'd cease doing so much evil and do more good. Then there would be peace on earth, goodwill to all men—and to all monkeys as well.

One religion or another has started most of the wars in human history. People who believe in God or gods. If monkeys cannot believe in God and cannot start wars, then let us pray that we can be more like monkeys and also be more like little babies who are filled with the grace of God but cannot believe in God and cannot start wars.

That mankind pours scorn on animal nature gives us the obvious reason why man is afraid to look at himself when he was lying helpless in his crib. Lying in his crib, he was more animal than human. He crawled on his belly before he could walk. He couldn't talk more than to say "wa-wa-wa" as animals do, and he couldn't pray or worship God. Still, he was filled with the grace of God long before he could read a Bible.

The man who rejects his animal nature rejects the grace God in him. It does not matter how much he claims to worship and serve God, he has alienated himself from God.

The Ego
Animals live within the spiritual laws of nature, and they do it without having any religion. Why can't man be the same? The answer is easy. Animals have no egos. All men do. From the weak to the strong to the super-ego, mankind is blessed with egotism in the morning and cursed with it in the night. And as long as the ego remains dominant in man's psyche, ego-

centeredness will motivate mankind to praise and worship God in the morning and kill off his fellowman at night.

The choice for man is either ego-ism or God-ism.

Creation Without Evolution
Every human is created. None was made by him or made by another human. The evidence of the animal nature in humans and of human nature in animals is so overwhelming it's very difficult for any person with sound reasoning to deny it.

World-renown scientist Carl Sagan wrote about the roots for the human species. In his book, "Shadows of Forgotten Ancestors," he gathered plenty of evidence of the astonishing similarity between animal and human nature. According to Sagan, there's nothing unique about human nature. There's nothing we do that some other species doesn't do in some minute way.

Here's something very important about Sagan—he didn't believe in God. So it's safe to say, he did not believe in creation either. But with every bit of evidence he had, not one drop of it proved there is in no creator.

When someone once asked him if he believed in love, he did not say no. I say, God is love and the love in every man is the God in him. Mankind needs only faith to believe in God. And he needs only to look at the scientific evidence to believe in creation. Mankind's best hope to save this world from total destruction is for all religions to unite with science within the essence of the spiritual gracefulness of God in little children.

The aim is a religion of Spiritual Humanism.

THREE

SPIRITUALISM

The essence of human life is love, spiritual love. The scientists with their bag of DNA and Big Bang Theory will disagree with me only because they're unable or unwilling to differentiate between essence and substance on the issue of human life. Essence is the flavor we can't see, while substance is the salt we pour in a spoon. We cannot pour flavor in a spoon.

The substance of human life *is* DNA, chemical matter we can see or measure. Furthermore, scientists have done plenty of good to the human quality of life with their DNA theories. But they cannot create life. With his theory of evolution, Darwin contributed much virtue to human living. And consider the accomplishment of the scientist who invented the vaccine to prevent polio. He had the same DNA makeup as millions of people, but by inventing the polio vaccine, he did something that was one in tens of millions. He must have something in him greater than his material self, something extra in his soul, faith, hope and inspiration. Otherwise, he could never have succeeded.

Faith and hope are two of the main ingredients in man's spiritualism. They're part of the infinite source of the spiritual love that creates man. And so we say, leave it to scientists to glorify

51

and magnify the substance of life. But the spiritualists will give worship and praise to spiritualism, the essence of life.

In the history of the human race, religions have played a far more significant role in life than anything science can do. Superficially, there are sharp differences and conflicts between religions and even sharp and deep conflicts within each religion but at the inner core, all religions deal with mankind's most fundamental meaning and fulfillment in life. All the great religions seek to promote spiritualism, the essence of life. But the essence of life is love, not religion. All great religions seek what is most important in human living—faith, hope and love—not the DNA in life but the essence of life.

Spiritual Significance
Evolution deals with life in regard to instincts, and chemical and biological changes in mind and body for survival of the species. Creation, on the other hand, is not just about survival. It deals with mortality and salvation, and there are hundreds of different stories about it. Salvation is found in the immortal soul of every man, the wellspring of eternal spiritual enlightenment, and the love that transcends all humans from the grips of evolution and into the tender embrace of the creator.

Spiritual Beings
Human spiritualism is what separates us from animals. It's not good enough to say we're spiritual beings because at the core of our being is the spiritual wellspring of life. In substance, we're flesh, bones, big brains and blood, but we live in the consciousness of spiritual love. When ego-centeredness puts human living in the consciousness of only the material self, the spiritual light of eternal love within us glows dim and dimmer, until finally, we're plunged into the darkness of sin and shame.

Sad to say, at the peak of his spirit-fullness man cannot walk, talk or stand on his own two feet. He has little or no intellectual reasoning. This being that seems to be more animal than human is an infant child. The animal-like infant is dependent on this sinful world shaped in inequity for his survival and for his salvation. The child needs food for his belly for survival and tender loving care from adults for his salvation.

Love Or Fear?
Our spiritualism is at the heart and soul of our humanism. It's wrapped up in our capacity for love. How we show love and can be loved is the indication of our spiritualism. At the core of life, we are spirit. Spirit is love and love is spirit, the essence of life. Whenever we choose to love, we choose the celebration of life. On the other hand, when we refuse to love we choose the fear of life.

In the spiritual realm of life, we must choose to love or fear will choose us. The fear of life, that is.

The history of the human race is characterized by expressions of fear more than love because we've been caught in the grips of selfish materialism. Today very little is said about love and even the little that is said gives lip service to love more than real expressions of love. Even though religious organizations still talk about the glory of love, they're more about power, egoism, and materialism, rather than brotherly love.

Children today have been given such a loveless world to live in that they live in the sub-consciousness of fear. This means their words, thoughts and deeds are motivated by fear rather than love. All our faith and glory is given to technology and information. We give the glory to relationships with things rather than to relationships with people.

The happiness we find today is void of simple joys because it's not the freedom to love that makes us feel good but the freedom from fear.

Spirit In Children
To be happy, children of today need the same things as children did a thousand years ago. They need to live in a world of love and be given an abundance of tender loving care. The biggest mistake we make is not to accept fully and wholeheartedly the

holiness and righteousness of little children. Little children are the most spiritualized people on earth.

Not understanding the Godly gracefulness in children, self-righteous parents say they have to bring the child to God. They don't understand that the kicking, crying and screaming the child does is because of the spiritual aliveness in the little ones. What the parent sees as unrighteous behavior by the child is nothing more than a fear-bound child demanding the spiritual and material necessities to live, love and eat.

Loving a little child is the most spiritual way to nurture life, and it is also the
holiest way to bring the parent closer to the love of God.

Inner Light: Union With The Spirit
 All the great religions accept that there's one universal spiritual infinite source in all of nature. But in human life, we also must accept that there's the same *one* spiritual source of love that's at the core of every one of us. It's this source of inner spiritual light that unites our souls with the infinite source of life. It also unites our consciousness with the universal light and with life itself.

Universal unity: The spirit soul, united with physical body, united with mind consciousness

In this state of universal unity, man is totally in the embrace with his or her universe. Free from sorrow and fear, spiritual self-affirmation is high, which gives rise to self-esteem. Self-awareness is high, also giving rise to self-esteem. Finally, self-position and self-control are high and that also gives rise to self-esteem. This tranquil state of universal unity and harmony leads to love, and love is the only thing for someone in love with self, in love with divine love and in love with the universe.

This place of universal unity is a place of spiritual bliss. There man will find peace with God, a peace that's beyond all concepts and all understanding. It's the peace of a sleeping child who has no concept of God, no evil thoughts, words or deeds, and a child who has no religion but is filled with the grace of God.

Spiritualized

Mankind is born embraced in the grace of God, fully spiritualized. A baby's soul bubbles with spiritual energy, a wellspring of spiritual love flowing from the soul into a heart that beats in harmony with the rhythmic waves of life.

Since the human spirit is the heart of human life, the man with a broken spirit is a man with a broken life. His flesh becomes tense, and his mind grows weak and wanders into nowhere. His whole being feels lifeless, and he's ready to give up his struggle for life. Finally, he gets depressed.

You'll never see a little baby who's depressed unless he's not getting enough love. Without love, the baby's spirit is broken. Otherwise, the innocent child with plenty of tender loving care is the most spiritualized person on earth. No saint, no prophet, no high priest, no imam, and no rabbi is more spiritualized than an innocent little child.

De-Spiritualized

The most complex thing on earth is human nature, because there are many contradictions within our nature. A man's character often seems to be one thing at first sight, but a deeper analysis may show it to be just the opposite. Man's actions can be the exact opposite of his innermost feelings.

The confusion arises because of mankind's dual nature. He's born with an animal nature but has to seek a productive and active life of love, work and knowledge to reach his full human potential. Born fully spiritualized in the bright light of spiritual consciousness, it seems man must seek to de-spiritualize himself in order to reach his full human potential with his mind, body and soul. But the "Catch 22" is that too much de-spiritualization means de-humanization.

Man must transcend his *spiritual* world in order to fully understand and prosper in his material world. It's a tale of two towers, where spiritual fulfillment conflicts with material consumption. The challenge is to nurture the spiritual aliveness in little children and at the same time, teach them the wisdom and necessary skills to prosper in the material world.

It seems human nature is one of transcending from inner self of soulful spiritualism into an ego-centered, de-spiritualized development of body and mind. The fate of mankind is to transcend from a vessel of spiritual love into an instrument of work and knowledge.

De-spiritualization is an inner-outer split, a spiritual transformation of soul separated from body and ego. It is the ego abandoning the soul that seeks to gain the world so the body may wallow in material consumption.

Man is created fully spiritualized, filled with the grace of God, whole and holy. But most adults block out these days of holiness and grace, especially those who have a loveless first three years in life.

But these spiritual days of grace are also the days of physical bondage and an empty mental slate. Even though this spiritual holiness is at its peek at birth, those are the days of spirit-emotional immaturity, physical immobility and mental pity. Those are the days of de-spiritualization and days of spiritual separation.

Love is the key for body and mind development. But in today's world of selfish materialism, very few children are given enough love to enjoy freedom from de-spiritualization.

Holiness And Fear
If you could look back at the place of your birth, there sometimes would be nothing to see but fear. You would see scorn and sometimes even punishment for your spiritual aliveness, the same spiritual aliveness that makes you kick, scream and holler for loving care food and attention.

The same loving care that keeps you alive causes you to be punished for boldly expressing it. Neglect and punishment put fear into your soul, your soul weeps and your body trembles.

Fear becomes a constant companion and stifles your ability to experience love. It dims the inner lights of faith and hope, and it puts you in the darkness of de-spiritualization. Sin and shame become you.

Re-Spiritualization
Mankind is born fully spiritualized, but he's also born more animal than human. However, his fate is to transcend his animal-like self and live in the glory of spiritual love and a full human potential—no matter what it takes. If it takes sin, shame, greed, selfish-centeredness and dreams of heaven, we must follow the yellow brick road to find the wizard of human nature. The wizard is the material monster, but the essence of human nature is spiritual love. If we must de-spiritualize to become fully humanized, then we must do it because we must evolve or die.

The best part of human nature is that when we become adults, we're given a second chance to be born again. Every man is given the freedom to be re-spiritualized. Every man is given the chance to go back to his place of innocence and gracefulness to reunite and reacquaint himself with the Holy Spirit of love. He's allowed to go back into the kingdom of his soul, back to redeeming grace.

All the great religions have a basic foundation to show the light and give the enlightenment to mankind's re-spiritualization. All the great religions believe that spiritual essence is mankind's only salvation. Everyday spiritual activity is the aim of the great religions.

Man's journey from spiritual expression to spiritual separation is a journey from soul-centeredness to ego-centeredness. The ego or ego-centeredness stands in the way of man's journey back to reunite himself with the spiritual grace of his creator.

The ego is really not in a child at creation. Ego develops in the first few years after birth. It's our bright mindful consciousness and power of intellectual and rational reasoning that comes into full development at about three years old. It's a material consciousness that's anti-spirit and anti-love, and it seeks to find a world where there's freedom from fear, not where there's freedom to love.

In order for an adult man to fully re-spiritualize himself, he must first **de-ego** himself. A friend told me once, "Get rid of the ego and God will show up."

Every ego trip that promises man freedom from fear puts excitement and sometimes pleasure in his heart. Imbued with this excitement and pleasure, man seeks more and more to affirm his egotism. We see mighty religious men, centered in egotism, fight holy wars, and we see men in the secular world, military dictators, fight brutal and bloody wars. The light of brotherly love is the only weapon against the ego's ways of fear and darkness.

Love, Work And Knowledge

Wilhelm Reich, one of the Twentieth Century's foremost authors and psychoanalysts, said, "Love, work and knowledge are the wellspring of our lives. They should also govern it."

LOVE is the essence of life, the passion of life, and the wellspring of the spiritual passionate emotion that flows from the soul and fills the heart. It sweetens the body and sends peaceful tranquil waters flowing into the mind. For people who know love, it's the only thing in life.

All great religions teach about love. Sad to say, they glorify divine love but fail, miserably and shamefully, to practice brotherly love. The true experience of love permeates the whole being with an expression of spirit and emotional joy. It's an inner peace and at the same time, peace with the whole world.

The wellspring of life flows at the innermost core of our being, and when we let it flow into our words, thoughts and deeds, love governs our life. We feel loved and spiritually alive and we celebrate life, because the passion of love fills our life with meaning. The only time we truly celebrate life is when we love.

We may celebrate life with divine love, parental love, brotherly love or the most compulsive love of all, romantic love.

Work

As mankind transcends his animal nature and moves into the glory of his human nature, he must have a productive, creative and inspirational life to feel complete and find significance in his living. He must work, not only for his daily bread but also for his daily dose of self-esteem. In the Garden of Eden, so the story goes, God told Adam, "By the sweat of your brow, you shall eat bread." Man must decide for himself whether work is a curse or a blessing.

Even in the subject of work, we come back to the issue of love. The labor of love adds passion and joy to any experience of work. In days of old before techonology unfolded, man used to work with passion, with a wellspring of joy in his soul. Every man once again must seek to find his passion in every work that he does. Passionate work is a blessing, while passionless work is a curse.

Knowledge

Once again it's all about love. The foundation of human nature is to love, but as we transcend our animal-like nature into the courage and glory of our human nature, we must increase in wisdom and knowledge to fulfill the full potential of all our humanism.

To increase in wisdom and knowledge, mankind must use his most unique virtues, the power of intellect and reason. Through these, he gains knowledge of his creator, knowledge of himself and knowledge of creation. Man makes love to feel the completeness of himself, because love is the only experience that makes him feel complete. But he makes work to survive and to feel the vibration of himself. Throughout history men of knowledge have ruled and changed the world.

Love is necessary to fulfill the soul, while work is needed to build the body and knowledge feeds and stimulates the mind. But love is the root of the tree of life, while work is the trunk of the tree and knowledge represents the branches. **Without love, there is no life**.

Having a proper balance of love, work and knowledge puts man in the glory of all his humanness. His life is filled with spiritual significance at the core of himself, and he has the necessary amount of spiritual, mental and material significance to make him feel perfectly whole and holy. This is true with or without a consciousness of God and with or without a religion.

Passionless Days
These are the most passionless days for people in the world. Parents tell their children, "You must work hard, you must get a college education, or you will suffer the shame of poor people."

Are these the right words to way to every child, "Get rich, gain the world and lose your soul?" Remember, the soul is the well of man's passion and love. Only the labor of love will make that well of passion flow into a wellspring of inner spiritual life and give meaning to life. Without the passion of love that flows from the soul, knowledge is uninspiring and work becomes boring and unfulfilling.

People used to say, "Follow your passion." Today it's "Passion be dammed." Technology is king and information is queen.

But these passionless days leave the king and queen feeling lonely and empty, sitting on the throne in the darkness of a haunted palace.

Music, poetry and art are some of the most passionate ways to express life. Today computers are taking over, while the passion and inspiration of the soul is quickly diminishing.

Today, A Computer Makes Soul Music
What good is work without passion or knowledge without wisdom and reason? This situation stifles our spiritual fulfillment in life and leaves us with an inner life of emotional and spiritual emptiness. If we pursue work and knowledge void of love, we will lose the innermost core of the self. We lose the soul. We lose

God, we lose self and we lose our human-to-human connectedness.

One Universal Religion Of The Holy Spirit
Although there are sharp differences in superficial ideals and practices between religions, there's a common core of humanistic need and a search for the meaning and fulfillment of spiritual significance that unites all religions at the core.

So the question is why religions will not, or cannot, promote the things that unite mankind, rather than promote the very differences that often bring war and destruction on the human race? Why do religious people have the most conflicts and disagreement with other religions? I believe it's because religion is manmade, and anything that one man makes for himself will be envied and despised by other men. We need spiritualism, which is about the human soul that God created.

If we want to unite the world I suggest one religion or no religion.

"THE UNIVERSAL RELIGION OF THE HOLY SPIRIT"
(one world, one spirit, one creation, one love, and one soul)
Let the divine holiness and gracefulness that unite the soul of every child be the essence of this religion.

Knowledge And Grace
Look at the inner peacefulness and grace of a little child. It has no sin and no shame, just gracefulness and love. In this inner place of spiritual bliss within little children, there's no knowledge of God and no consciousness of God. This shows that man doesn't need to have knowledge or consciousness of God to be holy and intimate with God.

Knowledge and consciousness are ego-centered, while gracefulness is soul-centered. Every adult has lost some of the gracefulness he had with God when he was born. So any adult who wants to be holy and righteous needs to seek God in the light of knowledge and spiritual consciousness, where he is open to the temptation of self-righteousness.

In human history we see the inner grace of God decrease as knowledge of God increases. Just watch a crocodile on TV pick up its young and put them under its tongue to safely protect them. The crocodile is motivated by the grace of God. It doesn't need a religion, nor does it need to read holy books to do the will of God. The crocodile doesn't have to believe in God to do the will of God.

I believe that tender loving care of little children is the Godliest experience anyone can have. Once again mothers don't need a religion to be perfect in motherly love. In man's darkest nights when he has gone astray like sheep, he needs God. But the ego says, "Let's seek a religion to **fight** the path back to God, the holy book of knowledge in one hand and the sword in the other hand." The soul says, "Let's not deny the power of knowledge. Let's have the holy book of knowledge in one hand but let's have a candle in the other hand to **light** the path back to God."

The salvation of this world is one universal soul-centered religion to unite all of mankind, not many ego-centered religions that will forever conquer and divide mankind.

The creator gives mankind choices. Mankind has the ego's power and the knowledge that can bring the darkness to destroy him and all of creation. But we also have the gracefulness and love of the soul that can bring the light to glorify ourselves and all of creation.

Human Nature
Mankind's biggest challenge in living is to understand himself. Simply to **BE** himself. But man has no time for that because there's an outer world he must conquer. Or he trembles with fear that the outer world of sin and shame will conquer him. In as much as man lives in fear of being conquered by his outer world, he keeps running away from a deeper fear. He fears the demons of his past, the demons of sin that invade his soul.

The trouble that man has in understanding his true nature is that demons stand in his way going back into the innermost core of himself where his true nature abides. Today's man has lost his courage and he's unwilling to go back into the kingdom of the soul to be reunited with his true inner self. So he runs, runs and runs, ego-tripping in his effort to gain the world but with a lost soul.

From the industrial to the technological ages, man has found a seemingly prefect way to deny his need for love and plunge himself through work and knowledge into machines—bigger, better and faster machines.

Love Is The Passion Uniting Mind, Body And Soul
The nature of man as God created him is no more man's glory. Today we let machines be our glory. We express our nature in machines and let machines express our nature. As technology advances more and more, man tries to make machines more and more human-like.

This Frankenstein Syndrome is a big mistake, because it's a soul bubbling with passion that is the essence of human nature and the source of human life. Until man learns to put the passion of love in his machines, technology will never be his salvation. Until man is able to put the passion of hate in his machines, he will fail miserably to make truly human-like machines.

The passions of love and the passions of hate are the two positive and negative extremes in human nature. No manmade machine and no manmade institutions in this world will ever be able to put these two extreme emotions in a blender and spin them into one big ice cream and soda milkshake we call human nature.

Man is born to love, in as much as we experience love as the measure of our fulfillment in life. Even today, I believe most people live for love, but how safe is love? What good is love when wars and destruction reign throughout human history?

More and more, **evolution** has provided man with the ability to suppress his nature and to suppress his feelings and emotions. When sorrow, anger and love come, they interrupt our daily activities of making money and building war machines to keep us safe from the wrath of our fellowman. When we have stress, anxiety, boredom or any kind of mental dysfunction, we take pills. We let technology remove the symptoms of an empty soul and a broken heart.

Spiritual Nature

Man is a spiritual being who lives in a spiritual and physical consciousness. The essence of our spiritual nature is love—to love and feel loved. But love cannot bring money, so we suppress the spiritual consciousness and live in a material world. We give all the glory to scientists who study the mental and biological sides of our nature. We also give glory and power to religious men who study the nature of God, the creator and the keeper of our souls. But still today the innermost part of man— his spiritual nature—lurks in the darkness of his soul unknown. We know shamefully little about our innermost self, about our spiritual nature. We know shamefully little about our need for love, why the rich man in perfect health kills himself, or why people who are sick and starving struggle for every drop of the breath of life.

We don't understand why a man slaves all his life to get rich, while the rich man who worships his money only wants to use it to get love and attention. We don't understand why men make slaves of other men.

Man is born to love, and love is life, but hate and human destruction seems to be more in our nature. But the best things in life—love and attention—are free. So there's plenty of hope for humanity and human nature. Every time a mother loves a child as most mothers do, it shines the light on the glory of love and on the glory of man's spiritual nature.

Dual Nature

Man is born fully with an animal nature, more animal than human. It takes about ten years for him to fully develop and cook his first food. But make no mistake about it, from the day of his birth he fights to transcend the bondage of his animal nature and to reach his full human potential. He works hard for his daily bread and seeks knowledge. This dualism of nature does

64

nothing but cause confusion. He becomes so confused he brings self-hate and scorn on humanity.

Most adult pour scorn on the wild animal-like ways of babies. The biggest scorn on man's created nature is by some religious people who say that man is born a sinner with a sinful nature. They maintain that man's purpose in life should be "Every man for himself." They believe man must save himself from sin and make himself righteous.

Because of dualism and confusion in human nature, self-righteousness is the biggest cause of human-to-human destruction.

At the innermost part of our being, our animal nature is driven by an instinct for survival. But also at the innermost part of our human nature lies a weeping soul that longs for love, redemption and salvation.

Looking at human nature, we see not only confusion of dualism but we see also many self-defeating ways. For example, man's greed for money stifles his need for love, the breath of life. And suppressing his emotions stifles his need for the self-expression that lifts his self-esteem.

What is human nature? Is it to lie and deceive or is it to be truthful and honest? It sometimes seems as if every man is two people in one. Does that mean that every man is a victim of a split personality? Is every man's personality split between ego-centeredness and soul-centeredness?

Human nature is the only place in creation where we find sin and all kinds of evil. If we want to be sinless and do no evil, we have to go back into our animal nature, back to the place where we were born. However, the ego-centered part of our nature pours contempt on the part that is animal nature.

So what is man that God makes him a little higher than the animals? Is man an animal-like human or a human-like animal?

Whatever mankind is, we know he's split within himself and split against himself.

There will be no peace on earth until mankind unites himself within himself and that unity is a unity between body/flesh (the material part) and mind/ego (the mental part) on one side and spirit/soul (the Godly part) on the other side. Peace on earth, goodwill to all men will come only when we solve the problem of dualism, a split, with soul on one side and body and mind on the other side. Peace on earth will come only when inner unity and harmony enables the spiritual side to take the sword out of the hand of the ego and replace it with a light so bright that it will take all of human nature out of the darkness of spiritual separation and make every human whole.

The Kingdom Of God
"The kingdom of God is within you," Jesus said. That means God is deep within the soul of man. The expression of God in man is his expression of love, spiritual love, the divine love that exposes him to brotherly love. The essence of this spiritual love is man's only reality in life. So every man who has lost total connectedness with the grace of God lives in the illusion of darkness and is like a living dead.

The soul is the kingdom of God in man. Many books have been written saying the kingdom of God is only for those who **believe**. Every human soul represents the kingdom of God in man. The man who has lost his soul has lost intimacy with God and has lost intimacy with the innermost part of himself. Only babies have this complete intimacy with God and at the same time, babies have complete unity and total integration within self and with the universe.

The kingdom of God is in every baby in the crib.

The "Monkey Syndrome"
Man looks at the monkey and is totally perplexed. The monkey's nature is very close to the human infant. When Charles Darwin came out with his theory of evolution, all hell broke loose. Religious leaders got angry. They asked, "How could it be that

66

man is descended from monkeys?" Only man is created in the image of God. Man is created to worship, serve and obey God. Man is created by the hand of God." They poured scorn on monkeys, saying a monkey has a dumb animal nature while human nature is close to God.

If you think about it, the theory of evolution and the theory of creation are not mutually exclusive. God created every monkey as well as every man. We didn't need Darwin to tell us that we're close relatives to animals. It's foolish to think that mankind is more Godly than the monkey.

God is love righteous and divine. All the evil and destruction in history has been done by man, not by monkeys.

If mankind would cease to be ashamed, cease to pour scorn on his monkey nature and instead start to embrace it, some of the monkeys' kind and loving ways might rub off on him and he'd cease doing so much evil and do more good. Then there would be peace on earth, goodwill to all men—and to all monkeys as well.

One religion or another has started most of the wars in human history. People who believe in God or gods. If monkeys cannot believe in God and cannot start wars, then let us pray that we can be more like monkeys and also be more like little babies who are filled with the grace of God but cannot believe in God and cannot start wars.

That mankind pours scorn on animal nature gives us the obvious reason why man is afraid to look at himself when he was lying helpless in his crib. Lying in his crib, he was more animal than human. He crawled on his belly before he could walk. He couldn't talk more than to say "wa-wa-wa" as animals do, and he couldn't pray or worship God. Still, he was filled with the grace of God long before he could read a Bible.

The man who rejects his animal nature rejects the grace God in him. It does not matter how much he claims to worship and serve God, he has alienated himself from God.

The Ego
Animals live within the spiritual laws of nature, and they do it without having any religion. Why can't man be the same? The answer is easy. Animals have no egos. All men do. From the weak to the strong to the super-ego, mankind is blessed with egotism in the morning and cursed with it in the night. And as long as the ego remains dominant in man's psyche, ego-centeredness will motivate mankind to praise and worship God in the morning and kill off his fellowman at night.

The choice for man is either ego-ism or God-ism.

Creation Without Evolution
Every human is created. None was made by him or made by another human. The evidence of the animal nature in humans and of human nature in animals is so overwhelming it's very difficult for any person with sound reasoning to deny it.

World-renown scientist Carl Sagan wrote about the roots for the human species. In his book, "Shadows of Forgotten Ancestors," he gathered plenty of evidence of the astonishing similarity between animal and human nature. According to Sagan, there's nothing unique about human nature. There's nothing we do that some other species doesn't do in some minute way.

Here's something very important about Sagan—he didn't believe in God. So it's safe to say, he did not believe in creation either. But with every bit of evidence he had, not one drop of it proved there is in no creator.

When someone once asked him if he believed in love, he did not say no. I say, God is love and the love in every man is the God in him. Mankind needs only faith to believe in God. And he needs only to look at the scientific evidence to believe in creation. Mankind's best hope to save this world from total destruction is for all religions to unite with science within the essence of the spiritual gracefulness of God in little children.

The aim is a religion of Spiritual Humanism.

FOUR

SPIRITUAL HUMANISM

Spiritual Humanism is a devotion to advance the cultivation and proliferation of the spiritual essence of humanity so human kindness will bring peace on earth, goodwill to all men. We promote love as the foundation of all life fulfilling experiences. Man's experience with God brings inner peace, unity and harmony within self—body, mind and soul. This is the source of love that transcends all human-to-human experience into the virtue of human kindness and brotherly love.

At the core of every human being is an eternal soul that abides within the body. The body is the temple that houses the soul. The mind is our consciousness of light as it radiates from the inner spiritual soul. At the same time the mind is the consciousness of the dim light, and sometimes darkness, that comes from the outside world of sin and shame.

There's no human alive that's totally void of this inner light we call God. And since God is love, love is the source of living for every man.

Spiritual Humanism is a movement to start a revolution of faith, hope and love in the heart of every individual, by

promoting spiritual significance as the foundation and fulfillment of life.

The aim of Spiritual Humanism is to start a revolution that will move mankind from the darkness of ego-centered living into the light of a soul-centered consciousness. In this light, each man will seek to build his self-worth, not in the illusion of selfish materialism but in the reality of spiritual love.

Spiritual aliveness fills the life of every man whose life is fulfilled. It is the spirit-emotional life that fills the body with feelings of joy and keeps the body free from feelings of stress and strain. It is spiritual energy that keeps the mind free from worry and faithlessness. It is the opposite of spiritual emptiness or spiritual brokenness, which fill the mind with feelings of fear, loneliness and self-doubt. It is a vibrant inner spiritual energy that bubbles in the soul, giving us inner peace and the harmony of happiness, the harmony and unity of body, mind and soul.

Mind And Soul
There's an inner light that shines from the soul of every human creature. It shines through the prism of the mind into the collected soul of all of humanity. The soul is like the sun, the source of spiritual light, and the mind is like the moon reflecting this light into our consciousness.

The essence of our humanness and spiritual humanism is an inner spiritual light. It is pure and holy, and it shines from the soul of every living person. But we feel meaning and life fulfillment only when this light shines onto our consciousness.

Faith is the spiritual virtue in every person that keeps us in the light of hope and frees us from the darkness of despair. A contrite heart and a crystal clear mind reflect the light of faith and hope in the world around us. With this we feel loved, we love the world, and the world loves us. We walk by faith and not by sight. We walk like an innocent child. The sun is the light unto our feet by day, and the moon a lamp by night.

For he who walks by faith, there is no darkness.

70

The heart of mankind: A spiritual pump.

The heart is the special place inside all humans where spirit meets flesh and is coupled by the soul. Because spirit and flesh cannot mix, the soul is the coupler that gives spiritual life to the body. Love is the spiritual lubricating oil that mixes with oxygen and blood. As it pumps through the heart, man becomes a living soul.

A heart void of love soon will be broken. Any biological defect in the heart causes us to get sick. The heart stops, and we die a physical death.

Physicians of the physical heart can perform open-heart surgery or give medicine for a heart with biological defects. But what is a broken heart and how do we mend one? What about a heart filled with the emotion of love that's filled with joy and beats in harmony to the rhythm of life and in tune with the universe? What about when fear comes to conquer the soul and a frightened heart beats too fast, raising blood pressure and pulse rate? What about a worried mind that causes anxiety and psychosomatic stress on the heart?

What about when the heart is in perfect shape and the biological physician gives it a perfect bill of health, but still the dimness, meaninglessness and emptiness of inner life is felt? That's proof that the life of the human heart is one part biological and one part spiritual.

The soul is the inner life of the human heart. A satisfied soul pumps the life-giving source of spiritual love into the heart. This is proof that while the heart is the center of life to the body, the soul is the center of life to the heart. Spiritual Humanism is a dedication that pours lubricating oil into the soul that pumps the spiritual blood of life into the heart of every infant.

Spiritual Humanism is a devotion to the spiritual center of life in the human heart.

So what is man? Is his heart a biological pump as the scientist

71

and the evolutionist explain? Or is his heart a spiritual pump like the spiritualist explains? Is mankind a creature of faith or fact?

Can man live only by the facts of life for his survival or must he also live by faith for his salvation? **Is faith stronger than fact?**

Spiritual Humanism pours scorn on the ways of this world of selfish materialism. We believe man lets his obsession with machines and technology put him in the darkness of too many facts for survival and too little faith for salvation. Spiritual Humanism pours scorn on the ways of religions, which have failed to promote more brotherly love and peace on earth, goodwill to all men.

Spiritual Humanism is a devotion to giving every human creature a can filled with spiritual oil to fill the spiritual lamp that shines in the center of his heart.

Spirit, Natural Soul And Ego
The battlefields and halls of human history are paved with the blood and premature death of many individuals. Even entire cultures did not or could not have the wisdom and might to protect their material possessions.

Spiritual Humanism acknowledges the significance of life and fully understands that no life exists without material substance. The ego is the agent, the publisher and prompter of man's material self-survival. So we give some glory to materialism.
Mankind's deepest instincts for material survival are his animal-like, insuppressible hunger for food (for survival of the self) and his psychological impulses (that send him willingly or drive him kicking and screaming into sexual intercourse to prolong the survival of the species).

It's the ego's ways of power and glory that set mankind in a brighter and brighter light of material consciousness. But every material man is haunted by the darkness of spiritual emptiness. As long as this earth lasts, man's dilemma will remain a constant struggle for material comfort and consumption for his survival against a spiritual need for love and fulfillment for his salvation.

The struggle between ego and soul puts man in a dilemma that sometimes seems unsolvable. But the human spirit and the spirit

of human nature will be "Wherever there's life, there's hope." And hope and faith spring eternal in the human psyche of mind, ego and soul.

Throughout history, ego-centered man has sought some "spiritualization of the ego" by building institutions that we call religions. He has done this to practice and support spiritual holiness to save his soul from the wrath of God. At the same time, he's also had to promote "Spiritual Materialism" to protect himself and his people from the wrath of his fellowman.

SPIRITUALIZATION OF THE EGO is the Holy Book of God in one hand.

SPIRITUAL MATERIALISM is the mighty Sword of God in the other hand.

One Religion Of The Soul
What this world really needs is an **ego-less religion**—one universal religion that labors for the fulfillment of the human soul. The Spiritual Humanist religion seeks to nurture and cultivate the spiritual nature of man, as it's found in the crib, whole and holy. But this may be too much to expect. In this world of selfish materialism, sin and shame, man's ego seems to be his only weapon against the wrath of his fellowman and against the hazards of nature.

The Spiritual Humanist goes to the crib to see God and to behold creation. He does not open a book or walk into a holy building to read about creation. Every time he loves a baby, the experience draws him closer to God. Faith, hope, gratitude and humility also glow with every loving experience between mother and child.

The Spiritual Humanist looks to the experiences of brotherly love and compassion as experiences with God. These spiritual virtues brightly light the pathway, like floodlights brighten the path of spiritual love as man walks with God—with or without a

73

religion—every step of the way from the cradle to the grave.

The Spiritual Humanist seeks to destroy sin, shame and any kind of unrighteousness. Not because of the joys of heaven or the fires of hell in the afterlife, but to free mankind from the terror of fear and to give him the freedom to live in the spiritual bliss of love.

Culture Of Spiritual Consciousness
Mankind is a creature of bright consciousness. Vivid self-awareness is his most unique quality. But in us there's a material self that is so week and feeble that it demands the most of our consciousness. The spiritual self is eternal and so powerful; it needs much less of our attention.

But man ignores his spiritual self at a high price because he must have some spiritual activeness to find fulfillment in life. The human dilemma is we rarely find enough time to fully satisfy both our spiritual need and our material greed.

Some men give all their attention to making money and find out too late the loneliness of spiritual emptiness. Other men give all their attention to spiritual activities and live with the shame of material poverty. So what's a man to do? Must we feed the ego—the material agent—and starve the soul—the spiritual agent? Or should we starve the ego and feed the soul? Should we first seek material love or spiritual love? Can man find the perfect balance of spiritual and material significance for happiness?

Man's spiritual source and supply comes from the infinite source of creation, a gift of life. All we need to do is open it. But we must work to supply our material needs every day. Our spiritual significance is a fulfilling need. The trouble is our material significance is a bottomless need for consumption.

With this bottomless need for material consumption, it's difficult for all men, except the very righteous few, not to give all their attention to feeding the material monster. All great societies built their greatness by building material might. They built their greatness on material weapons and financial greed, and they used them to conquer the outside world.

But history also shows that a society that neglects to build a culture of high spiritual consciousness will be defeated by the enemy within—spiritual contamination and social corruption. Eventually, the conqueror from within replaces its outside conquerors.

This is why all great cultures fall and all great men fall. It's true, simply because man can never find the perfect delicate balance of spiritual and material consciousness. He cannot find harmony of inner peace or spiritual harmony of body, mind and soul. In addition, the arrogance of envy and greed prevent his finding material harmony with his fellowman.

Dynamics Of Arrogance And Greed

Spiritual Humanism does not intend to suggest a naïve kind of policy about materialism. We fully understand that egoism, greed and envy are the motivations that keep mankind from reaching the full potential of his humanness. We who live in the USA are lucky to be living in the greatest country in the world. It's the greatest because of military might, financial might and power, plus the freedom to have any religion and freedom to have no religion.

If we say the American people are filled with greed, arrogance and envy, let it be. The human spirit is free in America, free to fly like an eagle or free to walk like a chicken.

Spiritual Humanism does not ignore all the evidence of evolution. Nor do we seek to deny the power of faith working in creation. We have no conflict with creation or evolution. That mankind was evolved or created is not the central issue to us. In addition, belief in God or no God or many gods is not the central issue to us. Religion or no religion is of little significance to us. What's most important to us is that every man is born a spiritual being filled with the spiritual grace of his creator. This spiritual grace is an expression of love, and any person who experiences love experiences God. It doesn't matter to us what he believes.

75

Man's first and deepest nature is to express love and every expression of love is the expression of spiritual life inside of us.

But any suppression of love becomes the suppression of our true nature and at the same time, a suppression of inner life.

If material man suppresses his true nature to love and seeks to live only in the consciousness of his material self, his ego will take him on a trip of miles of rope with wealth and prosperity. But somewhere along the way, he will find the length of the material rope is just an illusion. Then he will come face-to-face with the reality that a faithless journey will put him at the end of his spiritual rope. His body will begin to tremble, his soul will weep, and fear will grip him. His mind will be confused with words and thoughts that are meaningless, and his heart will cry out, "I want to live, I want to live."

The Institution Of Man Is Created
Spiritual Humanism has become a non-religious, sectarian advocate that builds cultures to advance the spiritual nature of mankind. We seek to promote the spiritual essence of human nature. Bt we don't advocate building more manmade institutions to glorify the nature of God or gods. Instead we treat every man as an individual institution. We promote the glory of love and cultivate it in every corner of man's world, as gardens of human kindness, and as places where the spiritual part of human nature blooms and grows. *We call this Spiritual Humanism.*

Every human is an origination—body, mind and soul—that is created.

Every human is a creation, no man has every made himself.

Every time a child is born, the bells of heaven ring and angels sing, "Glory to God in the highest for unto us a child is born." Cuddled up on its mother's breast, a child is the most glorious fulfillment of creation.

To behold human nature in its fullness and completeness—to see human nature in its holiness and wholeness—we must see man at the dawn of his creation. Man is in the paradise of spiritual bliss and innocence only when he's in the cradle, before

he can walk and talk. As he journeys from the place of his birth, he must leave behind innocence and spiritual bliss.

God creates the institution of man. But every individual institution must journey into a world of adults that's filled with sin and shaped in iniquity. All must journey into a world filled with manmade institutions that try to save man from the sin and iniquity he gets into.

First, last and always, man is a spiritual being. Any experience of love is the manifestation of the innermost part of his existence. The core of human nature is the inner world of soulfulness that bubbles with emotions of love and flows into his heart. The expression of love is the deepest and most fulfilling expression of his nature. The baby crying and screaming for mother's milk and mother's comfort is very frightening, but still the deepest expression of human nature is crying for life. The mother putting the baby on her chest—her breast in the baby's mouth—and saving a life is the most endearing answer to the call of human nature.

Cultures Of Conflict

It's been said, man is a social animal. He must build and live in cultures, communities, societies or tribes that enhance the satisfaction of his social needs. No man is an island, and no man can stand alone. He must walk with his fellowman, and he must walk with God.

Some say if there were no God (or gods), man would invent one. He'd build his own god or imagine a God or gods in the corner of his mind. He'd do anything to give his devotion something to worship and adore. Every human must believe in a power higher than himself. Deep feelings of isolation can be so terrifying that they can drive a man to drink, drive him into self-destructive behaviors and even end his life.

In the history of the world, mankind has never been able to get it right. Every culture or tribe he has ever built to satisfy his social longing seems to come into conflict with his true nature. The true self that is a spiritual being living in a social and material consciousness.

The Social Animal

It's fully understood that man is a social animal. All living creatures are social animals, social birds or social insects. All living things that move and breathe live in communities, groups, herds or flocks. It seems the deepest and strongest instinct in these creatures is the instinct of socialization. If we don't socialize, we don't survive.

The instinct of socialization in all creatures can only be understood beyond any biological explanation. Sure, every living organism needs food for the survival of its own organic body. But if isolated, even a creature that has all the food it needs will look for company or it will die.

There's something in the psyche of living things that says, "Give me company or I'll die." Every living thing is driven by the social instinct for living that goes beyond the organic biological need. There must be some kind of psychological, sexual or social interaction, or there will be no life on earth.

Human nature at its core is the same as the nature of all living creatures. But there's a big difference between human beings and all other living creatures. The biggest and sharpest difference is that the human baby after its birth needs about ten years before it can support its own life. It's safe to say the human creature is born ten years premature. Social interplay and acts of human kindness are what keep the human alive. Every human stays alive because it's part of a social community. The organic body can survive only if it has sexual, social or psychological interplay with other humans.

I'm writing all this in order to build my case against Selfish Materialism. Whether it's a selfish man that rejects social interplay or the material man that lets greed and envy cause him to look out only for his own material consumption, he will destroy his own innermost nature. "He is a man against himself."

Cultures Of Selfish Materialism
The cultures of Selfish Materialism we're building today—with bigger machines and more and more technology—at best suppress and sometimes even destroy the delicate whole, holy and innocent innermost part of human nature as it is found in little children. The cultures we have today around the world—democracy, socialism, communism, religious theocracy and fascism—all have a common thread that runs through them. That common thread is egoism.

Ego Trip
Everything that is manmade on this earth—every religion, every social institution and every political party—is built through the lens of man's big ego. Every one of them is built to satisfy and express his ego nature of thoughts and ideas.

In all these cultures the soulful, spirit-emotional innocent human nature has suffered suppression in the crib. Every man must leave his soulful nature behind and let his ego take him on a trip in some social revolution to build cultures of human soulful nature suppression and ego nature expression.

Cultural Spiritual Expression
Religions take up the task of promoting spiritual expression in mankind. Some religions, such as Islam even build cultures founded on the Holy Book and the life and teachings of holy men. The failure of all religions is that at the fullest of man's nature and the fullest of his spiritual nature, his spiritual expression can neither practice nor comprehend a religion.

The essence of man's spiritual expression is created, not manmade. The only way for man to maintain full spiritual expression is for every kind of culture to do a much better job with more unconditional, tender loving care that starts on the first day of birth. In other words, if religions want to champion the spiritual expression of human nature, the only place to start is with much more tender loving care of little children.

79

Spiritual Humanism has no organized institutions and no social or political parties. It's a movement of spiritual humanism that lives in the soul of every individual human. It's a movement to honor and encourage all the soulful expressions of humanism in little children. Spiritual humanism is a movement against the suppression of human nature in the crib and against suppression by ego-centered self-righteous adult.

Suppression For Survival

At birth mankind is more animal than human. He cannot walk, cannot talk, and crawls on his belly. Modern man cannot survive his human journey if he acts like an animal. After all, he has to plant and cook his food, he has to learn to read and write, and most of all, he has to build a big house with a bed and pillow to lay his head and a toilet to do his waste business. Emotionally, the baby must be taught to control his feelings by suppressing emotions. He must be taught how to be disciplined, to meekly wait and not cry.

Strict discipline and suppression of emotions go against the true nature of the child. Most modern adults pour scorn on this childish expression of human nature. Some self-righteous people even call it evil. Every child who survives childhood in this world of technology and information has to suppress the natural part of the innermost self. The child is born filled with spiritual aliveness, filled with self-possession, filled with spiritual self-expression.

Because a child has little or no self-control, ego-centered adults are convinced that he or she must be domesticated as quickly as possible. If not, they think, the child will never make it in this world, where hard work, super knowledge, and a college degree are the only ways to prosperity.

Modern man has failed to nurture and shelter the spiritual holiness and spiritual-emotional nature of man as found in little children. In the name of material survival, we've suppressed the innermost core of human nature and put it in spiritual bondage.

Expression For Salvation

"I want to live, not merely survive. " These are the words of a hit song by Frank Sinatra. In some ways animals are luckier than humans because animals don't have to suppress part of their

nature to survive. Animals don't have to plant food, build big houses and send rockets to the moon to live out the true potential of their nature.

Man is the only creature that willingly suppresses part of his innermost self. He does it in the name of survival, but in the name of survival, he loses his salvation. He lost his salvation when he lost his self-love and turned to destructive behaviors toward his fellowman and toward himself. He lost his salvation when he worked very hard to get all the material things for his survival, but took his own life because he was spiritually empty. A human is the only creature who will take his own life.

Spiritual Humanism is a movement to start a revolution against man's suppression of his spiritual nature. This kind of deep suppression is the cause of too much human suffering.

We know that all the great religions practice and promote spiritual growth, but all also are too ego-centered. Every ego-centered man pours scorn on the soulful, undisciplined, spirit-emotional aliveness in innocent little children. Self-righteous adults think the child is being rude. They can't stand the little innocent child bubbling up with spiritual and emotional high energy, jumping up, down and around with joy and laughter.

If religions really want to work for the total salvation of all humanity, they must reverse the trend of scorn in the crib. They must cease the self-righteous "divide and conquer" mentality, rid themselves of any dogma that conflicts with brotherly love, and take the most righteous people on earth (children lying in their cribs) and nurture and shelter their innermost human nature with twenty-four hours a day and seven days a week of unconditional tender loving care.

Concept Of Spirit
Scientific theories of DNA and evolution offer mankind a very valuable understanding of his biological, neurological and

even psychological nature. But man is one part spiritual and one part material. We believe (and human history shows) that mankind's deepest longing is for spiritual significance.

History shows that man cannot live in a material consciousness alone. His need to feel loved and the high self-awareness of his own mortality put him in psychological chains and mental strains, if he neglects to keep in his consciousness a bright light of his spiritual self. Man needs not only keep consciousness of spirit, but he also must keep the consciousness of the good spirit, the Holy Spirit. If not, the consciousnesses of evil spirits will invade and torment his soul.

Witchcraft, voodoo, Satan, hell's burning fire. These are some of the dark spirits that invade the soul the moment man neglects to work hard to keep his spiritual self-consciousness. Spirit is an integral part of human nature. It's the essence of the soul, seated in the psyche.

The aim of Spiritual Humanism is to promote the cultivation of good spirit as a fountain of love flowing from the soul into the heart of every man, giving spiritual life to a stress-free body and a mind free from corrupted thinking.

Man's consciousness is so high it can take him far beyond the boundaries of his material world in dreams and in his imagination. It can take him far into myths and wonders of heaven and hell, and of angels flying all around, ghosts, or fairy tales of flying elephants or fire-spitting dragons and much more.

Man is a spiritual being who lives in a material body with a spiritual consciousness. It's not possible for any man to live totally void of a spiritual existence. He must ether seek the light of heaven and the good spirits of hope, faith and spiritual love, or he will plunge into the darkness of hell, hate, fear, terror and despair. The spirit in man is so potent it's divine, and he believes his spiritual essence is eternal. He believes in a life after death of this unholy body. His spirit was here before he was born, and it will go on after his body goes back to its mortal destination.

Spiritual Humanism takes the position that mankind must cultivate cultures that promote the essence of faith and spiritualism as mankind's only salvation. We cannot wait until children grow into adults to find a religion—it's too late then.

While the child is still in the crib, we must begin to cultivate more spiritual virtues in the child's soul. Mankind's only way to total salvation for all of humanity is tender loving care for every child. This loving care will save the spiritual gracefulness of the child and bring mother and child closer and closer to the love of God.

Motherhood
The experience of motherhood can be the most soul satisfying, the deepest and the widest expression of spiritual humanism. Loving motherhood offers the best hope for a world rooted in spiritual humanism. Tender loving care of little children is mankind's only hope of building a world of brotherly love, peace on earth, goodwill to all men.

History tells us about all the great men who have put hate and destruction on their fellowman. If we trace the beginning of their destructive character, it started with their days of a loveless, neglected or abused childhood.

Societies that don't emphasize the tender loving care of children pay a very high price in having every kind of human demoralization and dehumanization. Finally they build cultures with men of fear and anger, men who are bent on human destruction. On the other hand, societies that put loving parenting first, put love first and are able to escape the destructive ways of fear and selfish materialism and find the freedom and joy of humanizing spiritualism.

Soul Nature
A human being is a complete organism in three parts—body, mind and soul. The soul is the spiritual part of us, and the essence of the soul is the expression of spiritual love.

Each individual is a community of these three parts as well. In this community of self we can express the self in three different ways. First is soulful expression, second is mindful personality and third is body expression. The expression of the mind can be very superficial, with empty words and shallow thoughts. Also, the expression of the body can be just physical with pain or pleasure—no sorrow, no joy and no passion.

This threefold aspect of human nature also can be used to define a single person. One who does mostly thinking with very little emotional expression can be called a mindful person. A physical person is one who does little thinking and has limited emotions, but who expresses bodily aspects of self.

Of all the ways to define an individual, the deepest and most self-affirmed character is the passionate person. The personality most fulfilling with most complete self-expression is when passion flows, because it's only then that man fully expresses all three parts of the self—body, mind and soul.

The core of human nature is soulfulness. It is passion of love or even, sad to say, it can also be passion of hate. So any soulful expression is a passionate expression, and any passionate expression is an expression of the complete self.

Total self-expression is expression of body, soul and mind. It's the most fulfilling and the most meaningful. Body movements can be shallow and unfulfilling. Heavy thinking also can be shallow and unfulfilling. But any expression that comes from the soul is deep. It comes from the center of human nature, and it sends impulses to the mind and sensations to the body. It's the complete expression of inner life.

The Ego Nature
Man is born with little or no ego. In fact, the infant is said to be ego-less. It has no arrogance, no false pride, no greed, no envy, and no materialism. All these negative traits only appear with ego. In the few years after birth, the soulful nature of the infant rules its personality. Little children are soulful and joyful. You'll never see an infant ego-tripping. These are the days of innocence and l ove, the days of spiritual bliss, passion and

emotions. Hope and faith abound—*if* the child gets tender loving care.

But by the time the child learns to walk and talk, at about three years old, the soulful nature of the child is in suppression and subordination. The ego nature begins to rule the personality.

The ego is the consciousness of the mind, mental power and the intellectual, rational power of thinking and reasoning. These ego powers take many years to develop, as many as six to ten years for full development. But we cannot pour scorn on egoism or ego-centeredness because it's of utmost necessity to prosper in this high-tech world.

As the ego asserts itself into the personality of the child, soulfulness begins to be suppressed. Thinking begins to replace feelings. The hunger for love is suppressed and is replaced by the ego's ideals of materialism and hunger for power. The search for knowledge dominates the personality all the way to the grave.

Ego Dynamics Of Development
For the first three years after birth and up to six years, the development of the ego blooms. As it grows, it begins to dominate personality. Egoism is the mental power of thinking, reading and writing, and the power of words. It's also the self-affirmation to shout, "No" and at the same time, the boldness to gently say, "Yes."

The personality of the adult is greatly influenced by the different characters of the ego. **The weak ego** is one that gets easily out of control, characterized by a lack of ability to control feelings, little self-affirmation, a rush to fall in love, as well as rush to get angry and walk away from love. **The weak ego is a very insecure personality**.

The **strong ego** is one that has strong self-affirmation, good control of feelings, body, mind and soul, with thinking and feeling in union and communion. The strong ego is a person of strong mental courage and at the same time, one who has gentle ways of love. **The strong ego is the ideal personality.**

The super ego is the tough man. He's the rich man without a heart. He has strong courage and great mental capacity, and he's always in control of himself. He also may try to control everybody around him. His wife and children respect him, but fear him and there is little or no love. He has great ego-self affirmation and little soul-self. **The super ego may rule the world, but he has lost his soulfulness.**

Some Great Human Spiritualists

Jesus Christ was the father of human spiritualism. The four Gospels of Jesus are the greatest teachings of brotherly love, compassion and forgiveness. In every part of his teachings, he tells his followers, "To love your brother is the greatest love of all."

Jesus also teaches that little children are holy. He said, "If you go to the altar to make a sacrifice to God and remember that you have a conflict with your brother, leave the sacrifice at the altar and first seek redemption with your fellowman."

But Jesus' teachings against selfish materialism made people in high places angry. This included religious leaders of the time, just as it does religious leaders today. The laws given to Moses tell of a God with an angry personality, and religious leaders carry the Ten Commandments in one hand and a sword in the other.

Jesus teaches about the same God but with a different personality. He teaches about a God of unconditional forgiveness with no anger or revenge—a God of pure love. God's divine love in every human, according to Jesus, is what makes every man his brother's keeper. God says religion, class, race and ethnicity have nothing to do with it. **Jesus put spiritual love before religion**.

Sons Of Christ

History tells of many great men who were Christ-like, and I call them "Sons of Christ." The first is Mahatma Gandhi, a Hindu in India in the turn of the Twentieth Century. Gandhi had a picture of Jesus in his office and quoted the Sermon on the Mount.

86

During that time England was ready to give up occupation of India, and religious leaders of all the different religions started to kill off each other in a power struggle. Gandhi said he would fast until death or until the killing stopped. While Gandhi was on his dying bed, the religious leaders came to him to say, "We will stop the killing." Gandhi drank a glass of orange juice.

Other great spiritual men include Saint Francis of Assisi, The Buddha, Muhammad, and Dr. Martin Luther King Jr. I call them all "Sons of Christ."

FIVE

SPIRITUALISM IS BROTHERLY LOVE

Jesus Christ told his followers, "A new commandment I give unto you that ye love one another."

Jesus acknowledged himself as a source of divine love. But time and time again, he told his followers that everyone must be the source of human love to find salvation. Jesus was the greatest teacher of the virtues of brotherly love. He also said, "If you go to the altar with your sacrifice to the Lord and remember you have a grievance with your brother, leave the sacrifice at the altar and go make amends with your brother." Jesus put brotherly love before seeking God's love.

Personally, if I have the Ten Commandments on one side and the new commandment of Jesus on the other, I'll take the new one of Jesus.

Jesus promotes spiritualism using the laws of brotherly love so he comes into deep conflict with those who promote spiritualism with the laws of religion.

It's easy to give lip service to the devotion of loving God or gods, but when Jesus said, "No greater love has one than he who lay down his life for his friend." Only a very few among the saints can walk that walk. The man who shows brotherly love and compassion has the closest walk in the light of spiritual love. Loving kindness is the evidence of spiritualism.

Acts of human kindness are the most spiritual acts of all.

Man is one part spirit and one part flesh, but he was spirit before he was flesh. His spirit will last until eternity, but the flesh will quickly corrupt and rot. The flesh is just a mass of organic matter germinating into a short span of life, but it will grow and consume life in order to glorify the spirit.

Man is an inner spiritual, infinite source of oil.
The flesh is the wick that burns and consumes life till it consumes itself.

Each individual is the expression of an immortal spirit manifested as flesh in a mortal journey from cradle to grave. The essence of mankind is a spiritual source we call love. At the core of our humanity, we're the expression of an infinite eternal spirit. It lives in the outer layers of the self we call the flesh that's finite and mortal. Unlike a car with only one drive train, man is a complex being with three main driving motors—the soul, the body and the mind.

Spiritual Harmony
The body is physical, the soul is spiritual, and the mind is mental. The internal dynamic of the human engine can cause a pushing-and-pulling of spiritual conflict of anger and fear between body, mind and soul. Or it can be a sweet harmony of all three. Harmony of motion and unity of direction makes us feel loved. The passion of love is the joy of all spiritual fulfillment.

In today's world of machines and paperwork, too often we feel like work is boring and undesirable. But if our activities are with the passion of unity in body, mind and soul, the work becomes a labor of love. If we give with inner harmony, then giving is better than receiving because the act of giving itself is passion and pleasure. It becomes a journey of spiritual fulfillment.

Inner harmony is important even in our thinking. If we think good things of virtue and think positive, we feel the experience of love. Positive thinking uplifts the ego, enlightens the mind and comforts the soul.

If body, mind and soul are caught up in the beauty of nature and each step is taken in the glory of the moment, a walk in the park is a spiritual walk. We say, "I love to walk," and really mean it. With each step we feel happy every time we even think about walking. **Happiness is spiritual harmony.**

Any experience of love is a soul satisfying, spiritually fulfilling, and emotional experience. Love and spirit are one. That means any kind of love, not just divine love. Romantic love, brotherly love and parental love are also spirit-fulfilling and self-esteem-lifting experiences. Man is a spiritual being living in the flesh but in a spiritual consciousness. Any experience of love brightens our consciousness and increases our spiritual significance. Spiritual, not material, experience is the foundation of our self-esteem.

Ebb And Flow, Love And Hate
Hate also is an emotional experience of deep passion and unity of body, mind and soul. But hate is unity void of harmony. Instead of being a spirit filling, life fulfilling experience, hate is a spirit breaking, life ebbing movement in the inner self. It can be a very exciting, passionate feeling. But unlike love that's the passion for life, hate is the passion to destroy the meaning of life or to destroy life itself. Love and hate can be said to be opposite, but not equal because love is the flowing of life while hate is the ebbing of life.

Love comes first. We're born to love, filled with the passion of love. But this sinful materialistic world teaches little children to repress the passions of love. Empty of the passion of love, we learn to refill our souls with the passion of hate. An empty soul is a dying soul void of any passion. Fear and anger invade a soul in spiritual emptiness.

Love is a spirit-filling, life-fulfilling experience, while hate is the opposite. Hate is a spirit-emptying, life-emptying experience. If man doesn't work night and day to fill his heart and soul with love, an empty soul easily can be filled with hate. Everyone who hates was first empty of love. But any betrayal of love can be a life emptying experience that leaves an empty soul to be filled with hate.

You may ask, "If hate is so life diminishing, why do people love to hate?" The answer is, a loveless life that's empty of passion feels lifeless. It even can drive a man to take his life.

Consider the rapist. He comes to life in his act of hate and destruction, but in between his acts of destruction, he feels like the living dead. Every rapist is one who was unable to love. Somewhere in his childhood, any passion of love was ejected from his system. That's why he becomes a walking dead person, held in the grips of spiritual terror and fiery fury. But his hate can take him from the door of the grave into the land of the living dead.

The paradox of hate is that a man who loves to hate is filled with fear but is empty of love. Acts of evil, voodoo, witchcraft, demons and ghosts are spiritual experiences, but they are spirit emptying, not sprit filling.

EVIL SPIRITS
I do not believe there is such a thing as evil spirits. I believe it is the absence of the Holy Spirit that invites evil, and spiritual emptiness is a vacuum that draws evil into the soul.

Mankind is so absorbed in spiritual consciousness that he must be in the light of spirit-fullness or in the darkness of spirit-emptiness. Heaven is the place of spirit-full bliss. Hell is the place of spirit-broken terror.

Spiritual Love
Divine love is the infinite source of creation, and we call its infinite source of love God. Some call it the Holy Spirit. This God/love is a fountain of spiritual waters that flows into the soul

of every human being, filling the heart with emotions of love. The most spiritual action in human experience is giving the tender loving care to a baby that saves, nurtures and cultivates human life. Spiritual love is heavenly, but also the human source of love that nurtures life is heavenly.

The Spiritual Humanist
The Spiritual Humanist seeks experiences of spiritual bliss in each moment on earth and is not concerned about heaven or hell. "Heaven and Hell!" he says. "It's up to God or the gods to decide my fate."

Human life is a life of spirit, flesh and blood. Life is a soul filled with the grace of God inside a body. Little children live in the moment. Each moment of innocence is one of spiritual gracefulness, void of any consciousness of God, heaven or hell. Spiritual humanism states that the most spiritual people have no consciousness of God, heaven or hell. They live only in the consciousness of love.

The code and creed of spiritual humanism is not to dwell on mystic speculation about a spiritual, disembodied life in the after life. Neither do they dwell in the spiritual bliss of heaven or the spiritual terror of hell. We dwell only on the reality of love. We emphasize love in the morning, love at noon and love in the evening time. Love is always in the moment, with a feeling of spiritual joy.

If every adult could remember and could look at himself just after he was born, he would see a little child that needed only love. Well, let me tell you something. Your need is no different today than was then. The only difference is today you're better able to receive love as well as to show it.

In this modern world obsessed with money and machines, only the lucky few children get enough love to grow up as spiritually

whole adults. Most of us get so little love and attention that we feel a permanent spiritual emptiness. Even in adult life most of us still long for love and attention, just as we did when we were infants. This is simply because our souls were always empty of loving emotions and we never got enough love as children.

Spiritual Humanism is a force meant to bring more love to the cradle, to bring more love to the toddler and to bring more love to each man from adulthood to the grave. We're devoted to the glory of living, mortal though it may be, in this life in the present—in each moment, each hour, each day.

Happiness: An In-The-Moment Experience
A feeling of happiness is an in-the-moment spiritual experience. We feel pleasure as bodily sensations, but happiness rises above simple pleasures into the realm of joy. To feel love is to feel fully satisfied in the moment.

Imagine yourself standing in a moment of total and complete satisfaction—free from longing, free from hunger, and free from desires. "This is where I am, and this is where I want to be," you think. "I feel like a child eating ice cream and cake. This is the moment, and this is a place of love and happiness. Let me stay here forever."

Most of us don't know moments of blissful love. We long for it, we hunger for it, and we dream about it. We hope one day we'll find it. But we've never lived in a moment that makes us feel we're completely living.

Many people still will long to be near someone. Even when someone is near, some people can never live fully satisfied in the moment. Some lucky few can remember some childhood moments of bliss, but the bills and burdens of adult life have robbed them of their moments of joy and true happiness. Joy is a feeling that may come and stay for a moment, but happiness is a prolonged feeling of joy.

Spiritual Humanism is devoted to taking the journey of life with each step of the millions of steps in life's journey. It's devoted to

be one step in a moment of spiritual bliss, the bliss of love and happiness. Troubled moments of fear or sorrow may come but are short and infrequent. We aim to put aside, to throw out of our consciousness, all concerns for the sorrows of yesterday. We aim to put aside all the concerns about whether there will the joys of tomorrow. We try to put away all our thoughts of a heaven above or a hell below.

Most of the people who dream of heaven imagine a place where each moment is lived in the consciousness of the infinite spiritual bliss of eternity. The aim of Spiritual Humanism is to find heaven on earth, to live in moments of absolute spiritual bliss. We aim to do this by guiding mankind out of the darkness of obsessive material consciousness and placing each and every person in the light of total and complete spiritual consciousness.

Spiritual Humanism is happy to embrace a soul-centered philosophy that is deeper, wider and more fundamental than the ego-centered doctrines of religions. We look to creation (at the birth of every human) to find the spiritual laws, not to any holy book written by man. We will find the source of spiritual holiness.

The cradle is our starting point, and the book of love is our book of rules. The rules in the book of love are written on the wind that blows in every corner of creation. These are the spiritual laws of creation bold and bright. Man is the only creature that needs to read a manmade book about love because we're the only creature that sins and needs salvation and redemption.

In the crib, there's no sin and no shame. There's only pure love, innocence and grace. The soul of the child is seated in the tender loving care of the mother, father, brothers and sisters. The whole village embraces the birth of creation and raises the child. Tender loving care nurtures and cultivates all the spiritual virtues that mankind needs to the build strong spiritual self-affirmation that's the foundation for happiness.

Loving care of little children elevates parenting to the top of all human virtues. It builds faith, hope abounds, and loving soul satisfaction and humility grow. It chokes out the weeds of fear, anger and self-doubt in the garden of the child's soul.

Notice that the fundamental aim of all the great religions is to water the seeds in the adult of the same virtues that tender loving care lets bloom and grow in the child.

In the case of the child, the soul is filled with the grace of God. But in the case of the religious adult, ego is filled with the consciousness of God.

Aspects Of Love
Divine love is the source of creation, the grace of God in the soul of every living human. The human soul is the vessel that's filled with the source of life. But it's true only for those who have life's fulfillment. A meaningless life is only half full of spiritual life.

A soul filled with spiritual grace puts the whole person in the embrace of union and communion with God. In this state, man also has inner peace with self and union and communion with his fellowman and with all of creation. The human soul is the vessel that holds the spiritual waters of life in the body of every soul. The soul is also the vessel of the flowing waters we call human emotions.

The spiritual waters of life—the emotional flow from the soul into the heart—give man the inner peace and gracefulness that's the essence of divine love. We grow with grace from strength to strength when we're filled with the source of divine love. We have the strength of inner peace and the strength of peace on earth, goodwill to all men. We love the whole world and we feel loved by the world. We're free from sorrow, free from fear and free from sin and shame.

But just any vessel filled with anything is stagnant. If we're filled with spiritual grace, we can feel the closeness of the holy sprit that is divine holiness. But divine love is not an all-encompassing kind of love unless it flows in the circle of brotherly love.

Children are filled with divine love, but they're not mature and able enough to show brotherly love. So they seem selfish, narcissistic and self-centered. The more you love them, the more love they ask for.

What about adults who are obsessed with divine love? They say they put God first, but they act like little children, with the same spiritual immaturity. They have no flow of brotherly love. They're self-centered, ego-centered and narcissistic.

Little children can seem selfish and unkind from the outside, but they smile and feel lots of love flowing on the inside. But because this world of materialism measures love from the five senses, we walk by sight and not by faith. We love by words and not by feelings. We fail to understand that feelings, faith, hope, spiritual self-affirmation, and divine love are strong in little children, and what we see of them is just the outer layer of the their characters. Deep inside, they're more lovable than adults.

Any adult who claims to put God first but neglects to show love to little children fails to nurture and water the garden of divine love in the soul of little children and therefore, fails to put God first.

The foundation of Spiritual Humanism is to tilt the vessel of divine love in the souls of little children. As they grow, so will flow a fountain of brotherly love.

Life Is Love
Life is the proliferation of goodness. It's the triumph of light over darkness, as well as the cradle over the grave. Life is the triumph of spirit over matter. At the conception of life, spirit germinates, love becomes flesh, and man becomes a living soul. Every human life is a living soul and every living soul is the manifestation of love that becomes life, which is the **materialization of spirit.**

Any religion that claims to be the source of man's spiritualism makes an anti-life claim. They also make an anti-creation claim, because creation is the source of man's spiritualism. Sure, all the great religions seek spiritual fulfillment for their believers, but all

they can do is promote spiritual growth and redemption. They cannot create a spiritual source.

Any institution that fails to believe that creation puts spiritual holiness in the soul of babies at birth will be unable to avoid treating little children in a way that results in suppression of human nature. Too many religious people practice spiritual oppression of babies in the crib.

The paradox is that while some religions claim to promote holiness in man in order to wipe out evil, too often they do just the opposite. Their holy rules and regulations suppress the holy side of the child's nature. Children grow up feeling unloved and so have a greater propensity for fear, anger and self-doubt. Too many who were raised with strict religion rebel against it.

A little baby is holy and cannot sin. Only unconditional loving care can make holiness and spiritual life in the child bloom and grow. All the holy books that are written by man do little to promote unconditional love as the only rule to raise a child.

Brotherly Love
The source of human love is the proliferation of goodness, peace on earth, goodwill to all men. The fountain of brotherly love flows from the well of divine spirit. Sad to say, too many people who pray every day for divine love don't feel the need to be the source of brotherly love. They have the Holy Book in one hand and the sword to strike against their fellowman in the other.

But all the great prophets teach brotherly love, especially Jesus Christ, who is the father of brotherly love. The concept of brotherly love gives nurturing tender loving care to babies in the crib. And that tender loving care makes a world of peace and love.

When children are given love, they grow up to be loving adults. An adult from a loveless childhood is filled with fear and little self-love. Only brotherly love can wipe out hate in the world. I'm my brother's keeper, and when I love my brother, I feel loved. When I give to my brother, my self-esteem is lifted. When I love my brother, I see him as holy. I can hate his sins, but I cannot hate him. Every man is born to love his brother and if he feels loved, he will love with every drop of his power.

Romantic Love

Romantic love expresses the nature of mankind at its core. The love between a boy and a girl or the desire for romance between a woman and a man leads to the action of our deepest instinct of love. It's the deepest movement of our spiritual aliveness. The strong instinct of romantic love is understandable when we consider this is the action moving towards sexual intercourse and that's the reason for the procreation of the species. A kiss or tight embrace between a man and woman in love can be one of the most joyful feelings in heaven or on earth.

There's no more spiritually fulfilling, spiritually exciting and blissful feeling than sexual intercourse between a man and woman who are romantically in love—in or out of marriage. One reason the earth is such a loveless place is that people who are obsessed with religion (as my mother was) pour scorn on expressions of romantic love. She believed love should only be expressed to God, not even to little children. My mother got very angry if one of her children even sang a romantic song. Anyone who loves God but looks down on the virtues of romantic love has a narrow kind of love.

One of the best virtues of religion is that they all promote strong family values. The happiest people in life are those who grow up in a loving family. Self-love only grows in the homes of loving families, so we say, "Glory to all religions and to the way they promote marriage and family."

Poets, Songwriters And Romance

Let's give glory to poets and songwriters, who have given us some of the sweetest and loving words and sweet harmonies about romantic love. It's interesting to note poetry and songwriting are not manmade institutions. They're not from any organized entity of egoism.

Every poem and every melody of love comes straight from the soul or the imagination of someone who has felt the bliss and ecstasy of love. They come from someone who has felt the agony in betrayal of love, or from someone who's loved and lost.

Or in the words of one song, from someone who says, "Why can't I fall in love?"

But sad to say, in today's world of information and high technology, people have given the romance of their hearts and souls to hard cold machines. Words and melody of any deep loving essence are not so sweet anymore. Today's people give little or no meaning to the words of the song "People who love people are the luckiest people in the world." They give more and more meaning to the thinking that people who love machines are the luckiest people in the world.

Religions, Human Nature And Suppression
Self-expression is man's greatest virtue in life. Spiritual self-possession, intellectual self-expression and physical self-expression are the three parts that make a whole self. Only when we're able to fully express body, mind and soul are we free to express the fullness of our human nature.

Only when we are free to express our full nature are we free—free to love and free from hate, fear, anger and self-doubt.

When the ego represses our emotional spiritual life inside the soul, we become the prison master of our own aoul. We lose our true nature and live with just the superficial part of a false self. Complete expression of human nature is found only in babies. By the time we learn to walk, talk and read, adults see to it that we repress the true nature of our spiritual aliveness.

How long can little children laugh out loud, jump for joy, cry in sorrow, or show anger when adults offend them? How long can they be free with full self-possession and full self-expression, free to express the fullness of their human nature?

When self-righteous adults pour scorn on every playful, wild and free expression of human nature in children, the answer to both questions is "Not long." Not long when ego-centered, self-righteous adults see obedience to the golden rule as children's highest virtue.

Too many religious people use the Holy Book of rules to cripple the true human nature in their children. It's a well-known fact that children who grew up in strict religious homes too often become adults with little or no inner self-expression. As a result they have fear and anger inside and live a bottled-up life. Often they rebel on the outside, while on the inside, they suffer pain and sorrow. They live a life of spiritual emptiness, empty of inner life and empty of spirit.

I volunteer as chaplain at the Lake County Prison in Florida, and I'm surprised to see how many of the inmates come from preachers' homes. Many preachers like to lay down the golden rules but are not willing to give a child unconditional love. Some of these inmates are very angry, some have a lot of fear, and some are "people pleasers" who are afraid to express any true feelings or ideas. Their inner nature has been repressed. Some come from "do or die" religious homes. For a while, they cling to religion with every bit of ego willpower they have, but often slip onto the grips of violence and chemical addiction.

It upsets me to see that many of the most religious people care so little about tender loving care of children. I wonder if religions don't play the ultimate conman's game on human nature. They suppress spiritual aliveness, the core of human nature in children, and then use religion's holy rules of power and glory to **save** the adult's soul from spiritual unrighteousness. One could say when it comes to Spiritual Humanism, religions give and religions take.

Sublimation, Sex And Freud
Sigmund Freud, who's said to be the Father of Psychiatry, gave mankind the theory of sublimation. His theory states that mankind cannot successfully repress all of his human nature. When memories, feelings, thoughts, impulses and instinctive drives are repressed by the ego in one channel, they will rise again in another shape and form. Freud called this action **sublimation**. For example, the person who represses impulses of deep fear and anger may act with plenty politeness one day and plenty of violence the next.

According to Freud the sex drive is man's deepest, most demanding, and most potent instinctive impulsive drive. If the sex drive is left free to have its own way, Freud said, it makes man uncontrollable and uncivilized. Mankind has no choice but to do everything within his power to either chain or tame his sex drive.

Freud believed the sexual impulses in man are so dominating and so strong that they are almost totally responsible for shaping the personality of the individual. If a man is lucky enough to **tame** his sexual impulses in childhood, he will turn out to be a healthily man of peace on earth goodwill to all men. On the other hand, if the sex drive is chained or left untamed in man's development stage, he will live in hell on earth, with all kind of neuroses, emotional torment in his soul, and a soul filled with anger and fear.

The sex drive is at the core of man's drive to love and feel loved, because sex brings life and love nurtures and grows life. Man's need for sex and his need for love are the most significant parts of his animal as well as his human nature. Everything we do in life we do for love, and every desire for love has some sexual impulses riding along. At its core, the lust for life is driven by the desire for sex and love, because without love and sex there would be no life.

Let's make it clear that little children have sex drives, but no sexual desires. Drive and desire are two separate things. The satisfaction from sex, love and food are the only absolute fulfillments in living.

Religions And Repression
In their principles and practices religions have ways and means that inadvertently suppress man's overactive sexual nature. In their zeal to bridle man's sexual overdrive, they suppress the wholeness and holiness of man's nature. Any repression of any part of his nature puts man in the grips of anger, fear and spiritual brokenness.

The nature of man is manifested in his hopes and dreams and in his longing to find intimacy with God. He longs for a divine love, and for a union and communion with his fellowman (brotherly love). He cannot live without religion. It's what gives him the enlightenment and the holy words of wisdom to find his strength in God and to find an inner peace with the love of God. Religion gives him spiritual self-affirmation, glory and inner peace and strength.

But what happens? The same religion that gives man the inner strength of divine love uses that inner strength to destroy brotherly love, replacing it with oppression and holy wars against his fellowman.

Freud was anti-religious, for many reasons. I believe one of the reasons was that he saw clearly how religions work to suppress the true and loving freedom of emotional expression, especially in innocent little children. I believe man's escape from the freedom of inner emotional expression is the reason for most human destructiveness.

Freud had many patients who suffered with neurosis, and he believed that every case was the result of repressed sexual impulses (libido) in childhood. In other words, when mankind represses the inner core of his nature, he goes insane.

He also believed that society's way of raising children represses children and teaches them the art of repression of instinctual drives. According to Freud, these unconscious and irrepressible drives in the psyche of every man are vital to man's sanity as well as his survival. They control man's lust for life.

Freud's theory of sublimation implies that the dilemma of human nature is that man's willingness and ability to repress the life in him puts him in bondage. But there's something in the dynamic of the human psyche of mind and soul that bubbles and pushes until his drive for living finds a way to sublimate out into life. Sublimation causes repressed memories of traumatic events that are buried in the unconscious. They rise and come to life in dreams and fantasies, daydreams and impulsive behaviors.

They also rise up to liberate man from the self-imposed imprisonment of his nature.

I believe Freud was a little too obsessed with core sexual libido. He neglected to explore the wider aspect of human nature, which is love. He also overlooked the tender loving care of little children, the only weapon against man's freedom to love, which will set man free from emotional torment and mental psychosis in adults.

Sigmund Freud's great achievement was restoring the understanding and virtues of human nature to its original state of wholeness and unity. He was a spiritual humanist, although his work was dressed in the coat of psychiatry. He gave mankind an invaluable understanding of human nature, as well as man's desire, hunger and longing. He helped man understand the lust for consumption and the need for sexual gratification.

Religions make a big mistake when they are too obsessed with the study and understanding pf the nature of God, while they neglect to comprehend the nature of mankind. Religions need to spread the news that the nature of God and the nature of man have a common foundation. That common foundation is **love**.

Divine love creates life, but human loving kindness is the salvation of life.

Without human loving kindness, every baby would die immediately after birth. Man can live and love without the consciousness of God. Little children do so because they're filled with the grace of God. But no human can live outside the consciousness of self and self-love. Until modern man returns to studying and understanding every corner of his true nature, until he takes off where Freud left off, there will be no peace on earth. The demise of self-knowledge is the demise of self-love. It's the demise of brotherly love and the demise of peace on earth goodwill to all men.

At the beginning of his creation, mankind is imbued in his heart and soul with divine love. He's a vessel of God's love. At the

104

core of his nature is a spiritual well of love. But love cannot be a vessel of spiritual stillness, it must also be the spiritual expression we call brotherly love. Love is only potent when it is a constant moving flux, a flowing spiritual emotional impulse. Love is the wellspring of life that flows from God, in and out like a river, into the heart of humanity.

Religions also make a big mistake when they are so obsessed with the nature of God's unconditional love, yet neglect to unselfishly work hard to fulfill mankind's holy salvation of brotherly love. The flow of brotherly love is one of the most spiritually fulfilling experiences one can have, especially when it provides the tender loving care of little innocent children

Freud: Nature And Nurture
As I said, Sigmund Freud is considered the father of psychiatry. He gave mankind the most valuable information to date about human nature. He gave us information about conscious and unconscious instincts, information about the ego and the id, and new information about internal drives and desires of human nature. He started his studies in medicine, physiology, zoology and biology as a young man, but more and more the problems of peoples' psychosis and neurosis confronted his consciousness. His investigation into the causes of every one of those psychosis shows they all are rooted in conflicts in early childhood development. He said that these conflicts developed in the infantile stage of life.

But the findings of Freud's investigations were **too heavy on nature and too little on nurture**. Freud fell into the error of believing firmly in the authority of parents over children. He was a victim of the conventional attitude at the time by religions and the culture as a whole that parents are pillars of wisdom. Since they adore their children, parents cannot be the cause of any conflicts in childhood development. In other words, if a child is hostile to the parent, it's due to the nature of the child. The child's hostility couldn't be caused by neglect and the lack of tender loving care by the parents.

Until this world does a better job of nurturing human nature

105

in infants and stops oppressing it, there will be no peace on earth good will to all men.

Jesus Christ said, "Ye must be born again, be like a little child to enter the kingdom of heaven." But he was crucified because he talked against the laws of religions that conflict with brotherly love. Throughout human history it seems only primitive tribes had the time and the wisdom to put raising children as their first priority. Sadly we must say to all the children of the world today, the road from caveman to high tech man must be unburdened by not putting your tender loving care first.

Isms And Ologies

Psychology, theology, science, and philosophy and the cultures of socialism, communism, capitalism, and imperialism—shamefully all are the culprits of pseudo-child abuse. They also are guilty of a conspiracy of silence on the issue of raising children. They fail to sincerely and vigorously promote the tender loving care of children.

Let me explain some of the high prices we pay for the neglect of tender loving care. First, it causes spiritual emptiness and emotional torment. It also causes stress on the body and social conflicts.   People are unwilling to show love and so are unable to feel loved. People have lost faith in themselves and lost faith in their fellowman. Hopelessness and despair drive people to God, saying only God can **save** me. The insecurities and anxieties of hate and fear drive humanity into wars and rumors of wars.

A New World Order

The Spiritual Humanist seeks to build a new world order, a world free from spiritual emptiness. We want to build a world that abounds with the spiritual fulfillment of brotherly love and is free from the bondage of selfish materialism. We want to build a world where every man is free to fully express his human nature and live up to his full potential. We envision a world where every man is willing and able to be his brother's keeper. We want to build a new world where every child is loved and feels loved and

106

every adult sees love as the only reality in life because he or she is in love.

We want to build a world where people are in love with God, in love with self and in love with their fellowman, because love is the only absolute reality.

SIX

SPIRIT, MIND AND BODY

The spiritual dimension of the mind

To feel whole, every man must be united in body, mind and soul. Emotions from the soul resonate into the consciousness of the mind and send sensations to the body that make man feel passionately alive. Thoughts in the mind—positive and negative—can pull or push emotions into ego-consciousness. Thinking also can push painful emotions into a place where they cannot be felt. The sensations that radiate from the mind regulate the physical movement of breathing in and out that keeps man feeling alive.

The human being is the interplay of emotions, when the soul interacts with neuro-electrical impulses from the mind to stimulate the movement of the body. That's what makes a person feel wholly and completely alive. The soul is man's agent of love, and our nature is to love. Love is the essence of life and the will of the creature.

Happiness is found in a holistic way of life, being gracefully and emotionally free in spirit, physical health, mobility, and rational and intellectual reasoning. To fill his life with meaning, every man must seek within him the unity and harmony of body, mind and soul. A healthy soul is filled with love, while a healthy body is free

109

from stress and disease and a healthy mind is active with positive and rational thinking. If this situation doesn't exist, man will feel separated and alienated, weak and empty. He never will feel completely whole and alive.

A healthy mind pulls emotions of spiritual love into the consciousness, which brightens the path to love. When a person feels loved, body, mind and soul harmonize with each other to give the whole personality an attitude of spiritual joyfulness.

In our world today where machines are more treasured than people and technical information is more treasured than self-examination, man has lost the unity and capacity to reason and love. He has lost the inspiration and imagination of his mind—the wings that could let him fly into the spiritual realm of angels among the stars. Man's fascination with material things saps his spiritual energy and dims the light in his spiritual consciousness.

More and more man is building his intellectual power. Unfortunately, he's using that power to understand and build machines as part of his romance with material things. He's lost faith in the spiritual world of inspiration and imagination.

Children go to college today to study machines. Even physicians study more about how the body reacts with medicine than they study about how the spiritual sensations of the mind could have a healthy effect on the body or how a tormented soul causes an unhealthily body. The mind is a very complex instrument. One part of the brain is used to think with strong intellectual and mental power. But the spiritual portion of the mind, the ego, deals with love or fear.

Evolution has given man more and more mental capacity. His ego uses this mental strength to repress emotions of fear that bring painful feelings into consciousness and give him feelings of isolation. The bad news is when man represses one emotion, he represses all emotions. He represses the emotion of love and clips the wings of the spiritual dimensions of his mind.

There's a downside to man becoming super mental and too

110

intellectual. It's the danger of becoming less spiritual and becoming strong on the facts of machines but weak on faith in himself. The mind has infinite power, but it's not mental or intellectual power. It's spiritual power—the power to dream, hope, and imagine. Most of all, the mind has the spiritual power of moral positive impulses to send down into the kingdom of the soul to bring into man' conscious joyful emotions of love.

Love is mankind's only absolute reality in life. He will find that reality only when he stays in the spiritual dimensions of his mind, so he can think, imagine, dream, and walk in the consciousness of spiritual love.

Man's consciousness is in his mind (or head), while his sub-conscious is in his body. His thinking is in the realm of consciousness but perceptions are in his sub-consciousness. In a quick flight of fear or even love, he'll act before he has time to think. That action is driven by perceptions in his sub-consciousness. His sub-consciousness is the ocean while his consciousness is the ship that floats on the ocean.

A strong mentality with rational thinking is like a ship with plenty of diesel power, moving fast and steady toward its destination. But with a weak and feeble mind, the ship loses its power and drifts on the waves of the subconscious mind. The saying, "Mind over matter," could mean man's thinking dominates his experiences in his material world. What about, "Mind over emotions"? This means his thinking dominates his emotions, and how he feels is dominated by the way he thinks. Positive thinking brings positive feelings, while negative thinking brings negative emotions.

Within the human being, the physical body is contained within the boundaries of the self. The strength and significance of the body is finite, the weakest part of the self. The body's demand on the self is too strong—it consumes, consumes and then consumes some more. The body's need for comfort and repair makes life a burden.

Only the virtue of a strong mind and strong mental courage can fight off the despair, especially in old age, caused by the demands and disease of the body. Only these virtues can make life feel worth living. A strong mind with high mental strength and an infinite and bright spiritual consciousness are the makings of a progressive human living.

Intellectual arrogance is a man who has gone to college and gotten his big degrees and centered himself only in the intellectual power in the windmills of his mind. He has become so ego-centered that he's narrow-minded. He's unable to enter into the spiritual dimensions of his mind. The super intellect deals too much in the world of fact and little faith. His power of knowledge and reason has captured his power of vision and inspiration.

Vision and inspiration are the spiritual dimensions of the mind. Throughout history these creative forces have lifted great men to scale infinite boundaries and influence humanity to higher heights in human potential.

The prescription for intellectual arrogance is wisdom mixed with humility because it gives man the double power of mental and spiritual potentialities. There's no man who can be greater than one who's a great thinker and is also a great visionary. He has the virtues of all human potentialities.

Dreams And Imagination
When we're asleep the ego consciousness is removed from guarding the gates of the mind. The psycho-spiritual waves in the mind are free to wander off, leaving the vast boundaries of the subconscious world and into the universe. I believe every dream is a revelation of an issue in the subconscious mind that is given expression only in sleep because the ego-consciousness had forbidden it to surface while awake. A dream is a spiritual journey into images of the material world. **The ability to dream is one of mankind's deepest spiritual virtues**.

In the darkest night and deepest despair, a dream can take man on a spiritual journey to heaven to shake hands with his angels and see his creator. On the other hand, in the brightest light in

112

his greatest glory a dream can take man on a spiritual journey into hell to shake hands with his demons and to see the devil.

The spiritual side of human nature is fascinating. It has a way to brighten man's darkest days and a way to darken man's sunniest days. Dreams give mankind the power to visit heaven to see his angels and also the power to visit hell to see his demons.
Imagination is also man's gift to travel into infinite spiritual boundaries. He opens his eyes and sees his physical world and worries about his mortality. But if he closes his eyes and opens the imagination in his mind, he can see a spiritual universe and be glad about the immortality of his soul.

Mental Health, Spiritual Hell
Good mental health is when neuro-electrical impulses and psychological impulses work well together. This keeps the body stress-free and in good physical health with a sound and rational mind. However, a man still may go insane and take his own life even when his mental ability is in perfect shape. I believe this can only happen when someone has traveled to the limits of his mental ability and must take his next step into the spiritual dimension of his mind to keep his sanity. There's nothing there, so he falls into the abyss of a bottomless pit of spiritual emptiness. He loses his sanity so the pain and terror of living becomes worse than the fear of death.

Mental sickness is when something is wrong with thinking or the neurological wiring from the brain to the body is messed up. That compromises freethinking and free movement. A man with mental sickness may not feel any pain because he's not spiritually broken. He has a dysfunctional mind and body, but his soul could be blooming with spiritual wholeness. **Mental sickness is a dysfunction in the head.**

Emotional Sickness
Emotional sickness is different from mental sickness, even though one dysfunction has a way of causing the other. The foundation of emotional wholeness is love. If man feels emotionally whole, he has the full human capacity to love and feel loved. Every person who is emotionally sick has lost some

113

capacity to love. Every emotional dysfunction is a spiritual dysfunction.

Emotional sickness is very painful. In fact, it can be more painful and deeper than any physical pain. A person in physical pain wants to live and will struggle to live with every drop of courage he has. But emotional pain easily can cause terror, sap courage and physical energy, and cause depression. If there's a heaven and a hell, emotional wholeness will put you in heaven, and emotional sickness will put you in hell. Emotional sickness is a soul, mind and body function or dysfunction.

Emotional traumas are the most painful feelings on earth. They include feelings of rejection, terrifying fear, or an anger that drives you insane, perhaps making you kill somebody or even kill yourself. Emotional traumas also include the emotionless feeling of spiritual emptiness and feelings of "nobody-ness" that can drive you into the fear of living, a fear that can be deeper than the fear of death.

Thinking And Feeling
There's a distinct difference between thinking and feeling. Feeling is emotional sensations flowing from the soul into the heart and sending those sensations into a bodily consciousness of pleasure or pain. Everyone has had these good or bad feelings many times in life.

When the soul weeps, the body trembles because negative emotions cause painful sensations in the flesh. A person who has plenty of feelings is said to be a soulful person. Passion is a soulful experience, so a person who has a passionate lust for life lives a vibrant and fulfilling life. But everyone also can have moments—even once-in-a-lifetime moments—when emotions of love and passion burst into the consciousness and cause a sensation of spiritual bliss.

Thinking is a disembodied intellectual and mental experience. Thinking is the duty of the mind while feeling is the duty of the soul. Thinking is an experience in the head that easily can dominate man's personality. So much so that man's thinking is used to repress emotions and give him a feeling of spiritual emptiness inside.

We've seen too many highly intellectual people who think too much and cannot *feel*. But they feel the inner emptiness and the loneliness of living an unfilled, passionless life. Modern man glorifies high technology and information, while computers require him to think less. Sadly, his thinking less with a machine also diminishes his emotional activity, stifles his imagination and dries up his inspiration. As technology increases, passion and enlightened thinking decrease, turning mankind into a dehumanized slave to his big machines.

The Great Escape
In today's world of selfish materialism, man has little or no emotions for love. Little children are taught very early that it's rude to have emotional outbursts, whether negative or positive. A child must be smart and learn not to cry, nor laugh too loud. With the child empty of love, emotions of anger, fear and hate invade its soul. These are very painful, negative emotions and if they appear in man's consciousness, we think they must be repressed. As a result, modern man is on a treadmill, constantly running to escape his inner self.

This great escape that modern man has planned for his way of living alienates him from his inner soulful aliveness. It takes strong mental power and energy to keep the body and mind in good enough shape to keep running away from himself and his inner painful emotions.

Belief Kills And Belief Cures
Faith is the key to a belief system that can cure almost any kind of sickness, simply because the loss of faith can cause such sickness. Surly everyone will agree that actions of faith are taken within the spiritual dimension of the mind. Faith could not be in the mental or intellectual dimension because we've seen men with Ph.D.s and men who are great thinkers but have no faith who can never find meaning and fulfillment in their lives.

Faith is much more than positive thinking.   It's a positive attitude in life. Too many people have positive thinking in the consciousness but in the sub-consciousness, they have an attitude of fear and doubt.

All the great religions promote faith at the foundation of their practices. They all have a strong belief in a spiritual power much greater and higher than themselves. And for everyone who has this strong attitude of faith, it works. In the spiritual dimension of the mind, faith is stronger than fact. A strong belief in the unseen holds a deeper reality for the person of strong faith than anything that he can see. The facts will tell you how to move a mountain, but faith can move mountains. Belief in a God that cannot be seen has infinite power over anybody's God or gods that can be seen.

If any man could truly believe in love (this is almost impossible in our selfish materialistic world), love would be his only reality. The spiritual essence of his soul and of God, the creator of his soul, would be his only reality. In the spiritual dimensions of his mind, this material world would be just an illusion, "Here today and gone tomorrow." If man truly believes he is eternal because his soul is eternal, he shall live forever.

The belief system is definitely found in the spiritual dimension of the mind. It gives man the almost infinite power to face death while embracing the celebration of life and to face life's most celebrated moments trembling in the fear of death. Such infinite sources and such infinite forces can be found only in the spiritual realm, and man can feel an eternal glow in the body of a mortal flesh only in the light of spiritual consciousness. When all the facts in his material world tell him hell is his destination, man can believe in heaven only in the light of his spiritual consciousness.

The most powerful force on earth is the belief in God, and the facts of the material world have little or no significance to he who stands firm and deep in that belief. His faith tells him to live for God, and he will *die* for God and will *kill* for God. Man's flesh has the same basic makeup—DNA and brainpower—and many other similarities to all other creatures.

116

The only uniqueness of humanness is the spiritual source of the human soul, coupling into the spiritual dimensions of the mind and the body. Scientists who don't believe in spiritual essence will easily believe mankind is the same or just a glorified version of this world of creatures.

Little children are filled with the grace of God without having any **belief** one way or another. They're also free from any ego concept of God and free from any ideals that conflict with brotherly love. Children are free from any **words** from God that tell them how to think and how to fight a holy war. They live only for love.

There are some spiritless people who believe only in material things, but they must live an unfulfilled life of spiritual emptiness. A person who is spiritually broken gives up on ever finding goodness in the world. He is imbued with such negative thinking that any positive thinking or emotion drives fear in him. So he slips into a bag of negativity and can never escape.

A spiritually broken man is contaminated in body, mind and soul. He thinks the world is a bad place and all people are bad. Anger and despair corrupt his thinking. His faithless beliefs put stress and every kind of sickness in his body.

Mankind has infinite power but he'll find joy and fulfillment only if he lives in the spiritual dimension of his mind where he can walk in the light of spiritual love. In the material realm, he's finite and feeble with a body that's just a bottomless pit of accumulating and consuming.

The Ego
The ego is the psychological part of the mind, the venue of conscious thoughts and emotions. Self-awareness, self-affirmation, and self-control are the ego's duty. The development of the ego comes into full bloom at about six years old. The ego is more an intellectual than an instinctive drive. It seeks to glorify the social and material side of the self, rather than the soulful side of the personality.

117

Tender loving care from one to six years old is the foundation to a wholesome and holy childhood development. The ego and the soul form a union of love, making it possible for the person to journey through life in love with life. Only the child who receives tender loving care has a high capacity to love. This means he will go through life living a soul-centered life of love.

But in this world of selfish materialism, very few children are given enough loving care. That's when the ego, unable to embrace love, becomes an agent of fear. A subconscious layer of fear is the reason beneath every ego-centered personality.
The ego is the gateway for thoughts and emotions that come up into consciousness. The ego very much likes to express positive joyful thoughts and feelings while it represses all the painful negative ones. But what if the soul is contaminated and the mind is corrupted? Then the sad ego must use all its energy to repress bad feelings and play the "blame-and-complain" game with the outside world.

Mankind has but two choices—living with his soul embracing love or his ego fighting fear.

Dynamics Of The Ego
The strong ego is the making of a lovable personality. Tender emotions rise up into consciousness, and ego and soul meet in a dance of love. Spiritual self-affirmation abounds as does faith, hope and forgiveness. Body, mind and soul are in union and communion.

Tender loving care in childhood creates an adult with a strong ego. The strong ego is strong self-possession in the soul, strong but tender self-control in the ego, and a strong, stress-free body. The strong ego doesn't always face conscious tender emotions. However, it handles emotions of fear and anger with integrity, holding things under control and making a personality of strong self-control and strong self-expression. These are the makings of a happy person.

In this world of high technology self-love decreases and love for machines grows greater and greater. People with strong egos become few and far between. And children are neglected, which weakens ego development.

In the chaos of working and shopping, everybody is stressed out. They're too busy to take time out for body, soul and ego to harmonize with each other. **Faith** is the foundation on which a strong ego is built. Tender feelings give a child faith in himself and generate good moral thinking and reasoning. Finally, a system of joyful feelings builds faith and strengthens the ego.

The Weak Ego

Within the human psyche the soul is spirit and emotions, while the ego is thoughts and other conscious sensations. During childhood development neglect or abuse can cause rebellious emotions of anger and fear to invade the tender ego. Ego strength and integrity is stifled, self-control and self-expression is compromised, and the integrity of the self is compromised.

The weak ego makes a weak personality. The person who is very insecure with little self-affirmation laughs too much and cries too much. He is weak with love but strong on resentment. He needs love badly but is unable to handle the give and take of intimacy with another person.

The weak ego is a person with a broken spirit and a feeble mind. He can be very sentimental but he's also very fragile. He can be very kind and loving but love can be very unkind. The weak ego also needs lots of self-examination or a lot of prayer and praise to God. That's all that can remove the anger and fear that fights against the ego and brings back emotions of love into a life that once was in love with self and in love with the world.

The Super Ego

Evolution has seen to it that humans have bigger and more powerful brains. This stronger ego power could be used to express deeper emotions of love, but that doesn't happen in this world of selfish materialism. Modern man uses his strong ego power to repress emotions of love, because love is seen as a weakness in a selfish world where power is king. On the other hand he uses the same strong ego to repress the anger and fear that result from the repression of love.

Power is the aim of the super ego. Power to repress the spiritual life of the inner self, power to escape from the freedom of a soulful self, and the power of self-control and strong willpower to conquer the outside world. We've seen many religious leaders with the power of a super ego. With the Holy Book in one hand and the sword in the other, they're ready to divide and conquer with salvation and oppression.

People who grew up with strong egos are those who were given plenty of attention and adoration but little love in childhood. Their self-esteem is high, but it's only the esteem of the ego-centered self. These are strong military men, strong dictators, men who rule with an iron fist and conquer the world but cannot surrender to the call for love inside the soul. All these man are super egos. They get plenty of respect from their wives and children but little love in the family.

Expression And Repression
The saying, "Belief kills and belief cures," is very real in life. Negative thinking will **pull** negative emotions into man's ego consciousness. It will bring loneliness and distress into body and mind. If a person believes the world is a bad place, he'll find that people in the world are bad. On the other hand if he thinks positive (the world is a good place), he'll find his world is good. As the saying goes, "So I think, so I am."

Every depressed person is in a bad mood of negative thoughts. Depression is a complex issue because some depressed people can appear to be the most positive thinkers. Little do we know the depression is caused by a faithless, deep, negative unconscious attitude that hides under the shining mask. A negative belief system is the symptom of a soul in distress and it results in an up-tight stressful body.

The character of the super ego is the development of a strong mental power. It's the strong power of will that represses all emotional feelings—both negative and positive—of the soulful

SPIRIT, MIND AND BODY

self and has almost total expression in the ego mentality of the self.

Why would anyone of sound mind desire to kill off all the inner life of the self? Well, the super ego is an agent of fear because he's unable to love. Man's deepest terror comes from a love-starved soul crying from the pain of spiritual emptiness.

The super ego triumphs over internal fear. It's the paralyzing of the soulful expressions of the self and the triumph of ego-centered expression of the self. Fear is an emotion that easily drives a person crazy, so the super ego is developed to repress fear, while expressing courage and hope to have a sane and sound mind.

The super ego is always a positive thinker. He conquers the outside world with his positive super intellectual power, and his emotions never get in the way of his progress. The super ego is the quintessential "Pusher Man." He pushes all his emotions—negative and positive—into repression and pushes people around.

But with all his power of control the super ego has a high price to pay. He's pushed all his spiritual aliveness into isolation and has alienated and isolated himself from the love of his family and community. The super ego seems to be the desired way of life in this selfish materialistic world where people seek to substitute the joy of love with the excitement of power. The social character of selfish materialism is that spiritual love is weak, while social, economic power is strong. And only the strong survive.

Don't blame the super ego for his uncaring ways—he's just looking out for number one. Don't blame him for his super mental courage and strong mental power. He's worked very hard to develop this mental toughness. Just remember his tough heart cries out for love. He's given up trying to *feel* and his thinking is his only salvation.

The strong ego is the ideal. It promotes positive thinking and pulls positive emotions into man's ego consciousness. The mind lives in the sensation of beauty and love, and the body feels totally alive and stress free. What a wonderful feeling to wake up in the morning feeling loved, all because body, mind and soul are in resonance—united with self, united with God and united with fellowman.

It's difficult for me to remember ever waking up with such a wonderful feeling of joy, because I have a weak ego caused by too many emotional storms during my tender years of ego development. My weak ego is unable to repress all the negative emotions, so they haunt my dreams at night, and negative thinking gives me bad feelings when I awake in the morning. It gives me an angry and sad disposition.

But I don't wish to be a super ego and be the master of repression and suppression. I don't wish to be the pusher man. I'm working every day to be the strong ego pulling emotions of love into my consciousness and to pull people into my life with ways of loving kindness.

Infinite Dimensions
The brain is the mass of the mind with its neuro-electrical impulses sending information all over the body and giving conscious thinking and feelings. But the boundaries of the body are finite and so give man finite significance.

But the mind is capable of spiritual dimensions that are infinite. This is to say, each man has within his being a power that's infinite because it's capable of expression and imagination into the whole universe. This infinite power is in the spiritual dimension of the mind. It's the power of imagination, the power of dreams and the power of hope.

Mankind has the power to sit in his room, close his eyes and travel to the ends of the earth. It's the power to go to sleep in despair and dream he's in love and feel the spiritual bliss of love. He also has the power to be a material pauper but hope to be the world's richest man. The richest man who is void of any spiritual dimension also can feel like a pauper.

Man is a spiritual being, and in his soul he is pure spirit. His mind is a physical mass that radiates into the spiritual dimensions of the universe. His body is flesh but needs the inner sunlight of spirit-emotional life so the flesh feels vibrant and stress-free. Only this inner spiritual aliveness can make man feel fully alive. Even when he's totally full with biological food, he feels only half full if he's spiritually empty. And if he feels totally spiritually empty, he feels totally worthless.

Infinite Spiritualism
If an infant child could talk or write a book it would tell of the ecstasy of inner spiritual aliveness. Filled with spiritual self-possession and spiritual self-expression, the infant would tell of emotions of love bubbling up from the soul into the heart and filling the whole being with the light of spiritual consciousness. Babies, who cannot walk by feet but can run by faith, could sing of the light of spiritual love.

Unfortunately for every child born in this world of selfish materialism, this strong faith will bloom and grow or wither and die on the condition of tender loving care from adults. If written by an infant, this book would be more spiritually potent than the Bible, the Qur'an and the Torah put together. Unfortunately books can only be written by ego-centered men who lived for many, many years with learned knowledge who cannot remember when they were in the spiritual paradise of sucking on their mother's breast.

All creatures great and small, except mankind, obey the spiritual laws of nature. No other creature needs to read a book to give loving tender care to their young, because they all move and live by their instincts of creation. But humankind soon after his birth walks into the glory of his ego, which spiritually separates him from the grace of his creator and eliminates his holiness. It's the fate of man to write Holy Books to enlighten his understanding and guide him back into his lost inner city of holiness.

Spiritual Dimensions Of The Body
It's fully understood that the human house, like all houses, are three - dimensional entities. The house we live in has a

foundation, walls and a roof. A human being also is a house—the foundation is the soul, the walls are the body and the roof is the mind. But in the human being the spiritual foundation of the soul is connected to all three dimensions of the house.

As one journeys through life the soul is the foundation of fulfillment. The mind covers the soul and body with wisdom, and intellectual and spiritual consciousness, but the body consumes more and more.

The body is the substance of life, not just a biological organism. The flesh must have feelings running through blood and veins to *feel* alive. We call this flow of feelings spiritual aliveness. At its most life-fulfilling level, emotions of love flow to carry the source of life from the soul into the heart. Every part of the flesh is joyful, stress-free, vibrant and free. This puts spiritual lubrication into the blood and oxygen, causing an easy flow of love and life. Love is the body dancing to the music of the soul. Human living is a house made with emotions pouring spiritual life into the flesh.

A Broken Spirit
The day the spirit is broken is the day the music dies. With a broken spirit the soul weeps, the mind worries and the body trembles. Trembling is fear, which tightens up the body making it ready to fight or take flight. Everyone has short moments of anger and fear and with a strong will, everyone can take flight or fight.

But a broken spirit is a broken *will,* a sour disposition that's set up in the mind, body and soul, causing it to tremble in fear of the world. The broken spirit feels trapped. He has given up the fight but is unable to take flight.

Spiritual wholeness is the inner source of spirit, the soul flowing into the spiritual dimensions of mind and body. A broken spirit is when the spiritual source is dried up or stormy and the outer dimensions are battered by the storm.

In our society today of high technology—the age of information—

we've built a culture of selfish materialism and a culture of selfishness. People put material *things* before even their children. Children with broken spirits are the rule, while children who are spiritually whole are the exception. The symptoms of a broken spirit are many, and afflictions are deeply rooted into the person.

The reason for a broken spirit is some kind of neglect, abuse, or too much punishment in early childhood development. Put another way, a loveless childhood gives man a broken spirit. Any kind of psychological trauma, in childhood or in adulthood, will give man a broken spirit.

The state of America in 2007 is surely a "**Culture Of Broken Spirit.**" All the people have a broken spirit. Broken spirits are on the rise, and we have little understanding of what it is and even less of an understanding of how to repair it. The best virtue about the American culture is its freedom to have religion and freedom from religion at the same time.

Culture Of Broken Spiritualism
Today America is the greatest country in the world because we've built a culture of democracy where the roots of capitalism grow deep. We have a culture with religious freedom but it's not rooted in religions. God bless America, a culture where the human spirit is free to be whole and fly like an eagle and also be free to fall like an eagle with broken wings.

But we've made a big mistake by making capitalism the end of our destination. We've gotten into the path of selfish materialism as the only means to that end. And a culture of selfish materialism is sure to be a culture of broken spiritualism. A broken spirit is a breakdown of body, soul and mind. It's a psychosomatic-spiritual breakdown, a spirit-emotional dysfunction that affects body and mind.

In the history of humanity religion has been the institution that has taken on the task of building repair shops to fix mankind's broken spiritualism. As broken spiritualism grows, so religion grows because we need more shops to do the fixing. Every church, every mosque, every synagogue, and every temple is a shop to repair broken spiritualism.

As the story about Adam and Eve goes, since the day they were thrown out of the Garden of Eden, mankind has not been able to fully embrace spiritual love. Since then in every culture, no matter where or when and no matter what the ideals and ideologies of a culture, all of mankind has fallen victim to a culture of broken spiritualism.

Anyone who doubts the spiritual dimensions of the mind and body and doubts its paralyzing significance, consider this. A person may have a broken spirit because he's going through a divorce, and suddenly he has frequent visits to the doctor. The doctor gives him pills to calm his mind and combat depression— pills for high blood pressure and pills for back, neck, stomach and chest pain.

An even more dreadful result of divorce and broken spirits is the little children who live in the haunted house of the divorcing parents and are dragged through dark boulevards of broken spiritualism. When they grow up to be adults, these children most likely will be taking the same pills for their spiritual broken hearts that their parents started to take during the divorce.

The Dynamics Of Spiritual Wholeness
Spiritual wholeness is an expression of pure love and also the expression of life. Love is the creator, a nurturing and propelling agent of life from beginning to end. **The end of love is the end of life**. The lust for life is the passion of love at its purest and holiest, and only babies experience it.

Pure spiritual wholeness is only for the infantile innocence in the Garden of Eden before the infant has knowledge of good and evil. Spiritual wholeness is a team effort of body, mind and soul at the top of their game, each one passing the ball to another and running to the goal to score. That's the passion of life.

The source and expression of spiritual wholeness is also seen in tender emotions rising gentle into the dimensions of the mind and putting a smile on the face of a stress-free body. It is emotions free from the oppression of anger ant fear, free from the demons of materialism, and free to express spiritual love. If the mind is free from contaminating and corrupting thoughts, it's free to think free and clear only about things of moral virtue. With a love that's pure, and a consciousness that's pure spirit, there's no room in the inn for any words, thoughts or deeds that come not in the name of high moral virtues.

Every mass in nature is of three dimensions—length, width and height. The spiritual essence of human nature is the same. The soul is pure spirit, the body has a spiritual dimension, and the mind also has a spiritual dimension. In man's quest for happiness, he will find only fulfillment and meaning if the spiritual passions from his soul flow into the spiritual dimensions of body and mind and make him feel spiritually whole.

WHAT IS MAN?
If he must feel whole and not fall to pieces
If he must walk and not feel abandoned
If he must talk and not feel unfilled by his words
If he must work and not blame and complain

If he must give and not feel misused
If he must have a lover and not feel unloved
If he must eat to a belly full and not feel half empty
If he must gain the world's riches and not feel like a pauper
Then: he must labor tirelessly in the vineyard of all
the virtues of **Spiritual Wholeness.**

Meditation
Meditation is a very good way to attain spiritual wholeness. The Buddhist religion has a long tradition of deep meditation. Today Christians and some secular people also are coming to realize the virtues of mediation. It's a very good way to still the mind and still emotions. It's also a good way get in touch with the presence of the Holy Spirit.

127

In this world where everybody is obsessed with working and shopping, the whole world should have a mass movement I call, "A Revolution of Silence," in mediation. In our capitalist society obsessed with material consumption people stay on the go. We don't have time for inner stillness and silence, because our whole culture in built on progress and prosperity. Every man must run away from himself to stay afloat in the ocean of material consumption.

The Buddhists who have perfected the art of mediation may be the people with the most inner peace today. Meditation can include mind-pushing emotions, mind-pulling emotions or mind and emotions in union and communion with spirit. If the Buddhist monk can use the power of the mind to push down and **still the storm** of unwanted emotions, he'll find inner peace. But it will be a peace without any joy.

Mindless meditation is good. But we must be careful that it doesn't lead to soulful-less or we can become numb and emotionless. On the other hand, if we can use the power of the mind to calm the sea and bring tender emotions to unite mind and soul, then joy will come and absolute victory will be won.

Meditation is a very good way to put a person in the experience of spiritual love. It's safe to say in today's world, people are too busy for true love. We can experience true spiritual love only with inner unity, along with a calmness and stillness of mind and emotions.

SEVEN

PARENTING: CULTIVATING PERSONALITY

Human nature is an innate organization of instinctual desires, drives and habits. It's body, mind and soul moving with a unity of purpose to exalt and promote life. To the extent that man is just another creature of creation, the nature of man in its earliest and purest form is closer to animal than to the fully mature, developed human.

Human nature as a created entity is only true to itself in babies. In adults the truest essence of human nature is repressed, lying buried in the dark corner of the soul. Therefore, any attempt to define human nature can be truly accurate only if the spotlight is turned on the crib where babies lie.

In the cradle babies are egoless, wordless, innocent, and sinless. Their flesh is filled with emotional, spiritual life, and their breathing is deep and wide. Growth enzymes are at their best, as are self-expression and self-possession. All the virtues of human nature are at their best in babies lying in the cradle.

At the dawn of creation, human nature is pure spirit, an eternal mountain of soulful emotions bubbling from the top of the mountain and flowing like a mighty river into the ocean of life.

There at the dawn of creation, life is so alive that all human nature needs to bloom and grow is a warm and tender place on a mother's breast, sucking mother's milk, the holiest food in nature.

With every deep breathing in and out, mother's milk fills the belly, wind fills the lungs and the grace of God comes to fill the soul of this innocent creature of pure spirit with pure love. There on mother's breast, the baby knows paradise. He's in the Garden of Eden, a holy place of spiritual bliss.

If this is all there is to human life, then man was born to run away from his true nature. He was born to run from this egoless place of powerless crying—tears and fears— where he cannot talk, walk or think. As soon as he can walk, he runs. As soon as he can talk, he runs. As soon as he can think for himself, he runs. Most important, as soon as he can cook his first pot of food, he runs and runs.

He wants to escape from his "Puppet-on-a-string" self. He wants to escape from the commands of people and parents, who always seem to give so little love and so little attention. Man's only hope for salvation, it seems, is to escape from his true nature just after birth. He must run from his unintelligent creature nature to acquire knowledge, work hard, and love much. He must be "Born Again," back to the place of his birth, to be reunited with the inner core of his blissful self, a self that's full of grace and holiness.

Born holy but dumb, man must journey to escape from himself. He must walk, talk, and acquire enough wisdom, knowledge and enlightenment to light his pathway back into the kingdom of his soul. He must go back almost into the womb, to be a baby, but one who needs no parenting. This time he will feed the little child within the man, to find his true self. He must go back to be reunited with himself and with his creator to find peace and unity with his fellowman.

All religions claim to be the source of man's spiritual fulfillment. But mother's milk was the source long before any written words were heard. At the dawn of creation, parenting is responsible for the growth and character of human living. Parenting is the most significant occupation in human living. Parenting cultivates the spiritual essence of living, along with the human body, mind and soul, into the human personality.

In the history of humanity, shamefully little significance and glory have been given to parenting. With very few exceptions, adults who easily find happiness and fulfillment have tender loving parenting. But if you go to a drug or alcohol rehab center or a prison, you'll find that almost all of them had a loveless childhood. Parenting failed them.

Parenting is the land where human nature is created, but it's also the garden where the human personality takes root and starts to grow. With tender loving parenting, the roots of the personality grow strong and deep, but with neglect and abuse or too much punishment, the roots of the personality are weak and insecure.

Man is a created creature and those who believe it will say God is their creator. But to those who say they put God first, I say, "Parenting waters the seeds of creation from the womb to the breast to the tomb." Were it not for parenting, the creation of humanity would not exist.

Parenting—whether loving or loveless—keeps man alive for the first twelve years of his life. He may have just a small window (until he's about twenty years old) then he most likely will be a parent himself for many, many years. If he's lucky enough to live a long life, someone will have to be a parent to him in his old age. As the saying goes, "Once a man, twice a child."

For all those wonderful people who say, "I am saved from sin, and I am going to heaven," please remember that if it were not for parenting, you would never have walked the earth, so you could never think of heaven.

Pure Spirit
If we could fully understand man's nature, we would see that pure spirit (spiritual significance) is at the core of human nature.

131

The human being is an origination of body, mind and soul that's separated one from the other unless there's a spiritual unity and harmony within the self. Separated within the self, man feels alienated from his inner core. Feelings of spiritual emptiness make him feel worthless and alone. The soul is the source of spiritual energy but that spiritual energy must be connected to the body and mind or else we lose significance. Man must have spiritual significance or he feels insignificant.

In the consciousness of pure spirit, the human is centered fully in his creature nature like a child, innocent and holy. All he needs is food for his survival and love for his salvation. Little children are a jumping body of spiritual joy. Their bodies, minds and souls are filled with the grace of God. Children are free from contamination and corruption of mind and soul.

Most of all, if they receive loving care, they're free to love. They're free from anger and fear, the enemies of spiritual fulfillment. Deep in the soul is the lust for life, and it's expressed in desire and a drive for spiritual love. The more lust, the more love, and the more love, the more lust.

Too many self-righteous adults ask, "If the child is so righteous, why do they kick, cry and scream?" I have good news for you. The child's same bubbling lust for life demands that it kick and scream when its life support is compromised. At first babies only cry when something is wrong with their life-support supply or when they're in discomfort or pain. The baby will cry for no apparent reason if the mother's eyes are cold or if her body is not tender. The baby can feel unloved even in the embrace of the parents.

When we study the lives of primitive people, we find they live much closer to their true creature nature. They're closer to God than modern man. They live in a brighter spiritual consciousness and have a deeper unity and harmony with their own nature and with Mother Nature.

However, evolution and creation demand that man live in triumph over all other creatures. After all, we have the potential of

132

intellectual and inspirational power to build pyramids and even send rockets to the moon. As man walks away from the spiritual garden of his inner nature, he gains the world but loses his soulfulness. At best, he will become an ego-centered adult of spiritual materialism and at worst, he will be a biological mass, walking spiritless like the living dead.

So what is man to do? Stay in the Garden of Eden where he can nurture his pure spirit nature and never have to know sin and shame? Where he never has to cover himself with fig leaves, never has to work hard by the sweat of his brow to eat bread, and never has to know the spiritual bliss of sending a rocket to the moon? Should man just hunt, fish, eat, drink, have sex and be a good parent?

It seems mankind is destined to be more than just a created creature person. He must cultivate his human personality to his full potential and be a creature of sin and shame, joy and laughter, and heaven and hell. He needs to pray every day for the serenity to accept the fate he cannot change, a fate of sin and shame. He needs to pray more and more that his moments of sin and shame are few and far between. His moments of joy and heavenly bliss are present in every step he takes.

Uprooted
 Mankind has freedom of choice. He can uproot himself from his pure spirit creature nature— spiritually separated with a disintegrated body, mind and soul—and be ejected from the Garden of Eden. Or he can transcend and seat his soul in a spiritual garden—with a fully, harmoniously and spiritually integrated body, mind and soul—but let the spiritual wings of his soul fly into his mind. With all the psycho-spiritual impulses of his imagination and his inspirational and his intellectual wisdom, he still must uproot himself into a world he built for himself. He can transcend into a world that extends to the extreme boundaries of all his human potentials, a world that frees him from the self-destructiveness of a palace where he is uprooted from his pure spirit nature.

133

Molehill To Mountain

Body, mind and soul are whole and pure spirit at birth. The flesh is at its peak of spiritual aliveness. The mind roams wide and free in all the corners of its spiritual dimension, and the soul—the source of all spiritual energy is pure Holy Spirit—free from corruption or contamination.

At birth the mind is strong in its spiritual capacity but very weak, with very little mental capacity to think and reason in the intellectual human capacity. The body is flesh, weak and feeble, but imbued with live emotions, live and jumping with spirit. The whole being is filled with innocence and grace.

In his infant day's, man is a spiritual mountain, but a physical midget and a mental molehill. The essence of man at the core of his being is not biological. It's a spiritual essence. The baby lying on its mother's chest soaking up love with each deep and wide breath. Its heart pumps strong, giving the flesh plenty of blood and oxygen for rapid growth.

At the seat of creation lies the innocent infant, as true as any human can be to nature. It lies on mother's breast centered in her creature nature, in pure spiritual consciousness. If you gave him all the riches of the world, he would reject it just for one tender hug from his mother, just to embrace one moment of spiritual love. All he lives for is the milk from the breast and to feel the spiritual bliss of every moment in the embrace of spiritual love.

The infant's lust for life is manifested in the lust for love and the grace of God. As the infant goes, so goes the man. Inside every adult person is an infant child that lusts for life, love, and the grace of God.

Man is not born lusting for religion, because he is born at the "Spiritual Mountaintop." It's only after he loses his spiritual holiness and moves into spiritual separation that a still voice in his soul keeps repeating, "You must be born again. Its the only way to be free from the terror and fear of spiritual emptiness and spiritual brokenness."

134

All the great religions became great because they offered believers the enlightenment to free the soul from sin and shame, terror and fear, while giving salvation and redemption. At birth the soul is a mountain of pure spirit but the mind (mental capacity) is just a molehill. The mountain of spirit is the tower of strength for the molehill of mental incapacity. The infant's action is influenced more by emotional feelings than by rational thinking.

The mountain of Holy Spirit of love carries and protects the infant until its feeble feet are able to walk, its feeble voice is able to talk, and its feeble hands are able to coordinate with the feeble mind to cook its first pot of food.

A close look at this infantile state of being shows a mental capacity. Like a midget who has lost all his teeth and has no ego strength to repress and hinder the expression of man's true nature. This is the only place where we have true and full and true self-possession, and total expression of the spiritual self. These are the days before spiritual separation.

But these also are the days of mankind's greatest opportunity to grow into a person who lives up to every drop of the glory and ecstasy of human potential. However, these also can be the days of missed opportunity. If there's no love, the human spirit is paralyzed and can never find its full potential. These also are the days when a mental molehill can be turned into a mental mountain.

At about three years of age, ego comes into full bloom. The child learns to read, write and have analytical thinking. If the home has plenty of love and good discipline, self-esteem blooms and grows. If parents provide plenty of inspiration, faith and hope abound. The child's search for wisdom and knowledge makes the adult a spiritual and mental mountain—free to live in spiritual bliss and in the light of spiritual consciousness.

Human Nature
Any successful attempt to look at and understand human nature must start at the cradle. If not, it will wind up in obscurity. True

human nature isn't visible very long after birth, because it soon becomes separated from true inner self. Influenced by the world around him, man is quickly on his way to building his individual unique personality.

The truest existence of our nature exists before man can walk and talk, when he's rooted more in his creature nature. The adult human long has been separated from the spiritual essence of his created nature. Fundamentally he lives in the consciousness of a learned personality. The roots of human nature are a spiritual essence of pure love, free from the painful emotions that cause spiritual emptiness.

Many psychiatrists in the Nineteenth and early Twentieth Centuries studied childhood development in order to understand man's behaviors—his desires, drives and habits. These included Freud, Erickson, Jung, Reich and many more. Along with many social scientists, anthropologists and theologians, they studied human behavior and man's nature with relation to God or gods. Each focused on different aspects of humanism to answer the question, "What is man?" But they all failed to adequately study and understand the deep and wide effects of tender loving care on childhood development and how it shapes the individual human personality.

Born Again
At the core of his created creature nature, man is a spiritual essence of pure love. If the adult human is true to this nature, he must seek to free himself from his cultivated ego-centered ideals and desires of materialism. He must do this to return to the spiritual place of his birth and reunite with the inner core of his created nature and become spiritually whole again.

He has to seek first, last and always to nurture and cultivate this essence of spiritual love in children so that every human tree will bear the fruit of pure brotherly love. How can any student of human nature understand the essence of pure spiritual love when he himself lives in the consciousness of an ego-centered materialism?

136

The day a baby can write a book about human nature will be the day man will be free to embrace and understand the nature of his true self. Then and only then will he be free to express his true self and free from the ways of all the self-destructive personalities of humanity.

We've said that primitive humans lived closer to their spiritual creature nature than modern man, but primitive man had little or no control over his own nature or Mother Nature. The fate of man is not to be primitive but to live with the power of knowledge and power to control himself and control the world God gave him.

The perfect way for man to live is for each individual to create within himself a new person by cultivating his own new personality of peace and love and struggle to perfect it every day of his life. In modern societies where the human soul must dance to the music of machines, true human nature is buried in the dark unknown of the human psyche. Cultures are not rooted in the created essence of human spiritualism but in the cultivated consciousness of ego materialism.

What is man? We can only find accurate answers where babies lie. We can only find the answer if we look at babies before they learn to walk and talk, before they learn the knowledge of good and evil, and before unholy parenting suppresses their innate drives and desires. Before unholy parenting gets a chance to reshape and cultivate the personality.

Primitive Man
Born a spiritual mountain and a mental molehill, primitive man was likely to die still centered in his true nature. He remained a spiritual mountain but a mental molehill because all he had to do was hunt, fish, have sex and parent his children.

The same is not true for modern man. We need knowledge and inspiration. We need to know the ecstasy and spiritual bliss of victory and the agony and fear of defeat. We must know the joy of sending a rocket to the moon and the terror of using chemical weapons to kill thousands of people.

From primitive days to modern days, man has learned to repress most of the instinctive drives of his inner nature of pure love. He has learned to cultivate a mental capacity that increases his mental ability as he climbs up to the mental mountaintop.

But what has man gotten from this long and winding road that has lead him to this modern day of progress and prosperity? On the top of his material mountain, without his spiritual safety net, man looks down and sees himself falling. The fear of falling makes him insecure with trembling anxiety.

Sure, he's living with more comfort and convenience, and his material wealth and medical inventions diminish his anxiety and insecurity. But if he compares his day with a day in the life of a primitive man, is he really happier? Is he more spiritually fulfilled? Which man feels more insolated and alone? Who suffers the inner fear caused by having material plenty but spiritual emptiness? I believe it's safe to say modern man has gotten much from his industrial and technological revolutions. But he has become a victim of his own success and so, a victim of spiritual emptiness.

Although today's man holds an empty victory cup, we cannot turn back to primitive days and primitive ways. We're programmed to move forward from victory to victory and to go fast and faster. We build bigger and bigger empires and highways, but each mile forward is another milestone running away from our inner self of spiritual unity, harmony and wholeness.

What would our primitive ancestors say of us now? I believe they would envy us because we have it all and we have it easy. Little would they understand how we left behind with them the glory of our spiritualism. As we run into the glory of our material abundance, each day draws us closer to the day of total destruction, the day the materiel monster rises up and devours us all.

Primitive man dreams of a modern day, while modern man dreams of a judgment day.

Created And Cultivated

"We hold these truths to be self-evident that all men are created equal, that they are endowed by their creator with certain unalienable rights, and among these are life, liberty and the pursuit of happiness." These words are from the USA "Declaration of Independence." But some of the men who wrote and signed the document owned slaves and treated the slaves as if there was no such thing as equality.

The theorist of evolution denies the theory of creation. Just like the theorist of creation seeks to deny the theory of evolution. When man became an ego-centered creature, he lost his attitude of unity and harmony. He seeks conflicts to divide and conquer or to destroy another's theories and possessions.

I believe the evidence for evolution is almost too strong to deny. I also believe every man is created, and at the core of each man's being is a spiritual essence called spiritual love. This is a divine infinite power of faith, hope and compassion that's much greater than evolution. And man's needs give me enough evidence that all men are created equal, which means there must be a creator. These needs include man's life and death search for God, his search for spiritual significance, his life and death need for love, and his need to love and be loved.

I also believe strongly that all men are created equal, just as it says in the Declaration of Independence. But all the men who wrote that document had long been removed from their created place of spiritual wholeness and were living in an ego-centered consciousness of materialism.

There's strong evidence of equality in creation. Put together babies at the dawn of their creation and there will be nothing but total equality in the crib. They will be equal in the consciousness of love, and they will think and act as equals. Even if they're of different races, different creeds, different classes, and different genders. And even before they have a chance to **LEARN** any racial, religious, cast or class prejudices.

Created equal
Every human nature is created equal to every other human nature. But for each individual, there is a unique quality and quantity to the cultivating and nurturing of each individual's creature nature. Parents, the community and society determine this difference. Within the very same family with each child born in the same condition, each child's personality is unique. Each grows up with differences in personality, and even some brothers and sisters feel unequal to others.

Cultivated Unequal
Evidence shows that all men are created equal, centered in the spiritual harmony of body, mind and soul. While humans are equal in nature, we are anything but equal in our cultivated personalities.

Look at the human race. Every baby's personality is equal and the same, given the same quality of tender loving care. But as man grows up and begins to think for himself and parents begin to teach each one differently, man no long wants to be equal. He takes pride in being different.

Every creature that learns to walk on two feet wants to walk differently, and every creature that learns to talk wants to talk differently. The equality of mankind in the spiritual essence of his creation is a reality. Some take pride and even boast about the inequality of mankind. But after man is separated from the garden of creation and enters into the land where his personality is cultivated, equality is an illusion. There's equality only in creation—there's no equality in cultivation. Man finds equality only in things of creation. Anything manmade, such as religions institutions, Holy Books, and political, social or economic originations, has no equality.

The study of human nature just after birth cannot find any significant inequality. All the innate instincts, desires, habits and drives are basically the same. As the "Declaration of Independence" states, the pursuit of life, liberty and happiness is equal at the core of human **created** nature. But if we look at the **cultivated** personality of adult humans, it seems the pursuit of

140

liberty and happiness is the exception. The pursuit of human destructiveness is the rule.

If the slave masters were living centered in their created human nature, it would not have been possible for them to embrace the sins of inequality and own slaves.

AT THE CRADLE IS CREATION
Some men go to the book of Genesis in the Holy Bible to read about creation. But the words they find in Genesis are some of the most violent words ever written. Genesis, like so many religious documents puts a "Holy Spin" on violence. Come and let us go to the cradle to look at creation. We see creation in the cradle, we see no conflicts, and we see no violence. We see no envy and no hate. What we see in the cradle is pure love.

We see mankind centered in the spiritual bliss of his creature created nature before this world of sin, shame and inequity. He cultivates and shapes his creature nature into a human personality that embraces knowledge of good and evil.

Transformation And Separation
Every adult has gone through a sharp transformation from creature nature to human personality. The adult has also gone through a spiritual separation from a unified self, mind and soul, to a divided self, alienated ego from soul.

All other creatures remain true to their created natures throughout life. A day or two after birth, some animals can walk and eat grass. The human creature nature is the most helpless of all. Mentally and physically, he needs rapid change to grow to be a mature person.

Parenting was meant to be twelve years of spiritual bliss for parent and child. Unfortunately, when humans lose the capacity to love and need to work very hard to make a living for themselves and the child, parenting loses the spirit and the bliss.

Human parenting can be the most burdensome task in living. It can be more than twelve years of hard labor. But there is nothing on earth more important than parenting. Why does the most important occupation on earth have the potential to be the most burdensome? Why do children need twenty-four hours a day and seven days a week of undivided attention? They kick, scream, cry and must have their own way. They need plenty of food, warmth and comfort, and they get sick and become a pain, while parents have to work to feed them, love them and also work to pay other bills.

Why did the creator give humans such a long, long time to reach maturity? Why do some children need more than fifteen years before they stop needing the help of somebody else to stay alive?

The answers to all these questions become clear only when we look at the glory man has over all other creatures. Man in his glory is a co-creator. He can be born again and reinvent himself. He alone can feel the highest ecstasy of love and the spiritual bliss of praying and singing praises to God. Man alone can dream of heaven and believe his soul is eternal and lives forever.

At the same time man alone can feel the terror of hell and the torment of sin and shame. We are created creatures but only in the way we're born. The journey from cradle to grave is a journey from being a created creature to being a cultivated human with potential and personality.

What is man that his creator sees fit to offer him a journey of one hundred years, transformed above all other creatures, from cradle to grave? Why does his creator offer man a journey walking in the spiritual bliss of love, his spiritual consciousness bright as the noonday sun? Why is man allowed to walk with his creator, his faith moving him to pray, praise and worship in the presence of his creator?

Most adults block out the memory of their infant created creature days, especially if they didn't have enough tender loving care. Memories of crying and screaming are not good ones.   Humans in that situation cannot wait to outgrow their creature natures. They're eager to walk on two feet, to talk, to read a book or even to write a book. They can't wait to get the good news about God and his love and can't wait to fall in love or plant a tree. Most adults cannot wait to grow up, to be separated from this creature, separated and transformed from animal nature to human personality and human potential. They can't wait to spend their own money, something no animal can do.

Personality: Culture And Community

Man must live his life rooted in the essence of his created being, in the spiritual image and in the footsteps of his creator. Man is a spiritual creature, but the substance of his life is the material flesh. Man's dilemma is the conflict in his duality of body and spirit. If he can cultivate a unified self with a non-dual personality, he will find inner peace and happiness.

But if he fails to keep spiritual unity, he has to live with a split personality. If he fails to build unified communities and a spirit of unity through his culture, he fails to live up to all the glory and honor he was created to be. If he lives too much in his spiritually created consciousness and neglects his substance of life, he lives with physical pain and a short life. On the other hand, if he is too materialistic and neglects his spiritual essence, he feels an inner aloneness. He's isolated and alienated with a life not worth living.

In light of his duality of human nature, man has to take on the challenge of cultivating two different crops in the same garden at the same time. Two different crops with two different needs and two different types of nourishment at the same time. One crop needs more sunlight while the other needs more rain. So when it's raining, he prays for the sun and when it's sunny, he prays for rain.

The gift of life is a created creature living in grace, driven by the instincts of the creator. When man lives rooted in his created instincts, but is not centered in them, he's separated from them soon after he's born.

Parenting, family, community and culture reshape the created soul into every human personality. A strong community of people who love people and don't put machines first—people who put loving children over spending money on them—build a culture of inner peace and peace on earth goodwill to all men.

Every adult in today's world of selfish materialism, as long as he lives, must be rooted in his created soulful nature. He also must center himself in the ego-centered personality that's cultivated, shaped and molded by family, community and society as a whole. The best things in life are still free, but it doesn't seem that way in a culture obsessed with material consumption. When we put more significance on material consumption than we do spiritual fulfillment, we live in the darkness of an illusion.

After all, how much of the material can we really consume? We can only sleep on one pillow at a time, only wear one pair of shoes at a time, and only eat one plate of food at a time. The man with a million dollars has no more material significance than a man who has only ten thousand dollars. Between the ten thousand and the million dollars, it's money spent without any real absolute significance. It's money spent just to get the excitement and the satisfaction of material desires.

Passion And Personality
"Follow your passion," the saying goes. Passion is the fuel of life. It's the difference between eating a sweet juicy orange and a dried one. It's the difference between doing something half-heartedly and whole-heartedly with a joyful heart, mind and body. Passionless people get bored easily. They have a flat personality, and they walk, talk, play and work in a very lifeless fashion.

Love is the passion of life and the lust for life. It's the heart and soul sending emotional life into the body to make a person want to dance, jump and sing. Passion is like a river flowing into the sea. Passion makes a person work with joy and love.

Each child has a very deep, passionate personality. It's an innate part of human nature and the instinctive drive that lusts for life. If children were left to follow their passions or guided and encouraged to find and follow their passions, we would have a much happier world today. We'd have a world with more love, more joy and more passionate personalities. People's lives would be filled with more meaning and deeper fulfillment.

Unfortunately, this passion of joy and fulfillment is not to be. Passion is a soulful emotional that flows to unite body, mind and soul into a total expression of life. Little children are experts at passion until their ego-centered parents teach them to suppress feelings, think smart and get rich. Those parents have long lost their passion because this technological world pours scorn on it.

Ego-centered parents push their children into religions and visions of fame and fortune. They kill the children's passion, and the children grow up feeling the emptiness in life. These children are unable to find passion. They're alienated from self, alienated from parents and alienated from the rest of the world.

If the richest man in the world lives a passionless life, he's a sad and lonely fellow. He must be born again. Before he can live a life centered in the ecstasy of passionate love and passionate labor, He must return to the place of his youth to uncover the flame of passion buried in his soul.

Spirit And Passion

At the core of his being, man is a spiritual creature. An infinite fountain of spiritual water flows from his soul into his heart, giving emotional life to the flesh and giving psychological tranquility and harmony to the mind.

Love, work and knowledge are the three-dimensional quality of life that puts man in the driver's seat. It allows him to celebrate life and move full speed ahead on the highway of life and full throttle with passion and spirit.

A life without passion is like eating potatoes without any meat or gravy. It's like eating a dried up fruit without any juice. It feels like everything you do in life is with a dull spirit and heavy boredom. A passionless life is not worth living. Passion means experiencing love and experiencing heaven. It means experiencing every drop of the wine of living, from the brim to the dregs.

Anger also is a passionate experience, but the passion of anger is only to defend the passion of love when it's denied or betrayed. The most passionate child for love will be the most passionate child in anger if refused loving care. The passion of anger in a healthy child lasts but for a moment, until the obstacle to love is removed.

But what if the obstacles to love, like neglect and abuse, are permanent? Then the anger becomes permanent—it gets frozen. And the passion of hate can be just as wide and just as deep as the passion of love. The passion of hate also can be very exiting. That's why people who have lost the passion to love get their kicks from hate and love to hate.

Hate is frozen anger.

All parents need to be conscious that they are responsible for the growth of their child's passions. Whether passion blooms and grows or withers and dies is up the delicate mix of love, discipline and self-affirming guidance that parents give the child. There are seeds of passion planted in every child and those seeds will only grow if watered with emotional expressions that spring from the innermost parts of the child. Let every child grow, find and follow his or her own unique self-affirming passion or passions.

Every parent owes it to the child to help the child find the path to passion. It's the same path to the child's happiness.
.

EIGHT

THE ART OF PARENTING

Parenting is an instinctive action for all creatures great and small. The tool kit for parenting comes with life itself, because it's the reason life exists. Man's deepest instinctive drive is to incubate, nurture and cultivate life. Once the creator breaks his mold and life begins, the hands of man must keep it alive.

Except for man, most creatures become parents within a few years after birth. Normally, it takes the human about fifteen years to become a parent. Every man was born with parental potential, but it takes so long before he actually becomes one that he loses his instinct for it before he's able to use it. In addition, his own parents may not have nurtured him with tender loving care, so he may have lost the innocence, grace and love he was born with.

How can he give tender loving care when his inner capacity for love has been suppressed? And if parents have lost the instinct for parenting, how can they be ideal parents?

The problem is childbearing and child-raising take too long. They take too much time and require too much loving and caring. Maybe we should do away with parenting and build a machine to change diapers, feed and burp the babies.

To do it right, man needs to study the art of parenting. And since love is the foundation of everything he does in life, he must have a deep capacity for love before he can be a good parent.

Art And Instinct
All creatures, except mankind, parent their young by instinct. All obey the spiritual laws of creation and do not neglect or abuse their instinctive code of parenting. None except man needs to read a book or study anything to follow the golden rule.

Only man needs to teach the young how to talk, how to read and write, how to plant food, or how to make a fire and cook food. Only man has to teach the young how to think intelligently and suppress feelings, and more important only man has to teach the young how to worship, praise and pray to God or gods.

So it's man's fate to sin. It's his fate to transcend his instinctive living and center himself into artful living. To live up to the full potential of his humanness, he is destined to shake off the shackles of his creature instinctive nature. He must spiritually separate from his creator and isolate himself from his fellowman. While this may make him a creature of the highest glory and virtue, at the same time he becomes a creature who needs to spend most of his time, "Doing, Learning, Teaching, Being, Receiving, and Giving."

Parenting
Man can escape a meaningless life and live free in celebration of life only when he stays rooted in his instincts and grows in the art of parenting. And only when religions, politics, science and educations begin to treat tender loving parenting as the most spiritual and the most important occupation in life can mankind be free from the proliferation of sin and shame, free from every other kind of human destructiveness.

For those who doubt that parenting is the most important part of human living, just remember this. If it weren't for parenting, the human race wouldn't exist. To take this further, tender loving parenting is the salvation of mankind. Those who receive tender loving parenting in childhood will be saved from the unholy sorrows of anger, fear and self-doubt. But those who did not get

148

tender loving care—or got too little of it—will travel through life in the darkness of fear and self-doubt. Or they will seek the light of salvation through some kind of religious devotion.

As tender loving parenting diminishes in human culture, the need for religious activities increases. All religions offer enlightenment and salvation to those who are spiritually empty and spiritually broken by a lack of or too little tender loving parenting. You'll find in life people who had TLC have a smaller need for any religious activities. Religion is man's cry to God, "Save me." While instinctive parenting is for the survival of humanity, the art of tender loving parenting is the salvation of humanity, the art of living, and the art of happiness.

Parenting: Rooted, Uprooted, Transcended
Rooted parenting is governed by the spiritual laws of creation, which are the incubator and cultivator of life. All creatures great and small—except mankind—must live by these laws. The creator gives man a choice: to stay rooted in these instinctive spiritual laws of nature or to uproot himself from them.

To stay rooted is to be rooted in the holiness of creation. It's a journey from cradle to grave. First, we're babies who receive loving care from our parents. Then, we're adolescents living in the consciousness of soon becoming parents and for many years, we are parents. Finally, we're grandparents and even great-grandparents. It's a lifelong journey of holiness and love. But only if we stay rooted in our instinctive inner self of spiritual love.

In our world today parents teach their children how to be smart, how to get a big education and how to get rich. We teach them very little about the virtues and responsibilities of parenting. If self-preservation is the first law of nature, parenting is the opening chapter of this book. But we've failed to teach our children that parenting is the first law of creation and we've failed to love them as if parenting is the first law of creation. Children of today grow up rich, but they feel an inner spiritual emptiness and live a life that feels meaningless.

Humans and all mammals are born rooted in the instinct of parenting because it's the instinct at the core of life. Mammals must suckle their young to keep them alive. They're born rooted.

But how do humans stay rooted in their instinctive selves? The journey starts from day one with tender loving care from parents. From day one, a baby's instinctual behavior is more like an animal than human. From day one, he must be fed with unconditional love and breast milk every moment he needs it, all day and all night. Any parent who feels scorn for these animal-like ways will inadvertently teach the child to suppress his instinctive nature and stifle the child's instinctive maturity. The child will become uprooted from the natural instinct of living in the consciousness of parenting.

Only the child who receives consistent tender loving care, without any neglect, will stay rooted in the loving consciousness of parenting on life's journey from cradle to grave. Only the child who receives loving parenting is ready, willing and able to be the best loving parent.

If you want your children to love and care for you in your helpless old age, you must be a loving parent to them in their helpless young age. Every time you hear a parent complain about how their child doesn't love them, it's safe to assume it's because the parent failed to first love the child.

Uprooted
To be uprooted is to be separated from the spiritual essence of our creation. To parent a child is a long journey of more than fifteen years. It takes a lot of unconditional love, patience, tolerance, humility and human kindness to raise children rooted in the glory of parenting. Lacking all these virtues of good parenting, each child will grow up uprooted from the instinctive nature of loving parenting. If the child feels unloved, chances are the reason is he or she feels an inner emptiness and an emotional disconnectedness from the parents. It's not easy to make an accurate evaluation of the true character of children, as to whether they feel love or unloved. The rule is if the child feels unloved, something went wrong in parenting.

Children of rich people often feel unloved, and this is very perplexing because rich people's kids usually get lots of adoration, lots of material comfort and lots of glory. The truth is they get the best of everything but love. So they grow up feeling unloved, uprooted from the inner self of loving parenting and uprooted from inner peace and human kindness.

Adults who have been uprooted from the inner instincts of parenting wind up not really ready, willing and able to be good loving parents themselves. Unfortunately, the sorrows of uprooted-ness are passed down from generation to generation.

The essence of BE-ing is to live and experience the highest quality and virtue of parenting. One must live and embrace the essence of BE-ing. That is to say, one must first live rooted in the core of the self. "I am myself, and I have no desire to be something or somebody else."

The essence of BE-ing is one who is rooted in the true self, and one who is not running away from his true inner self. The essence of BE-ing is the possession and expression in the core self, with spiritual affirmation. It is living centered in the soulful self of created instincts and emotional aliveness, strong and bubbling with self-expression.

Only children who have gotten tender loving parenting become adults rooted in the essence of **BE-ing**. A happy loving child will **BE** the best happy loving parent. A happy loving parent who gives adequate care to the child will automatically pass on the love and happiness to the next generation.

In human history we see that the super-achievers—people who want to conquer the world—win the Olympics and want to be the best they can **BE.** They're never rooted in the virtue of parenting. They have no time to BE—they're constantly in the having mood.

To experience love, one must "**BE in-the-moment.**" In the moment that the mother gives loving care to the child, the mother is in a moment of spiritual bliss. In the same moment the child who receives loving attention is in the moment of spiritual bliss.

One moment of spiritual bliss can live forever in the soulful memories of every mother and child relationship. But the reality of living is a selfish materialistic world, where neglect, punishment and abuse destroy the happy moments of parenting.

Tender loving parenting is the most life fulfilling experience. It's an unselfish spiritual experience. But in this world of selfish materialism, most of us must live uprooted from the inner true self and uprooted from the virtues of loving parenting. The world goes on from generation to generation, passing down bad parenting, and selfishness.

Self-esteem. A man with low self-esteem, who can't simply BE himself, often must have *things*, such as money, fame or glory from others to feel safe. It's a sure bet that he was uprooted from the inner spiritual core of the self in childhood. He didn't receive the best tender loving parenting and as a result, he feels terribly unloved.

One day, I met a lady in the bookstore who said she was looking for a book on self-esteem. Without thinking, I said to her, "If we were able to love children as we should, we wouldn't need any books on self-esteem."

Today in our world of selfish materialism, children who received tender loving parenting are the exception. Neglecting to love children is the rule. Parents tell their children that the most important thing is a college education, while they fail to give their children plenty of love and attention. Evidently, parents today don't know that a good education starts with good self-esteem. Without self-esteem, the best education is of little or no value. It will not give meaning and fulfillment to life.

Transcending Instincts
If man were to live only by instinct, we would still be in the Stone Age. All that human potential would go to waste, and the industrial and the technological ages would never have been.

The fate of mankind is to transcend his instinctive nature and walk and talk with intellectual reasoning. The fate of mankind

152

also is to live and have his being in the light of a cultivated personality with a high spiritual consciousness.

Walking in the light of a super bright spiritual consciousness is the quality that makes us most uniquely human. In that light, we transcend our instinctive created nature without being uprooted. We become a living soul, still filled with spiritual grace, still walking side-by-side and in the consciousness of our creator.

The glory of mankind is that we are the only creature who is able to live in the heavenly bliss of prayer and praise to the creator. Mankind's deepest, strongest, and most significant instinct is parenting, because it's the source of life itself. Sex is at the core of this parenting instinct because sexual intercourse plants the seed for life.

But mankind cannot live by instinct alone. It's the fate of humans to move out of the garden of an instinctive paradise. We must escape or transcend the spiritual essence of our BE-ing and move into a place of ego-centered living. We can no more live by our created creature nature but must **learn** the "*Art of Living.*"

Sexual intercourse and parenting are two of the most spiritually significant virtues in human living because these two instincts are about life itself. But as man moves out from the essence of his instinctive self and into an ego-centered self, we've made a big blunder. We've lost the free and holy attitude towards sex. And we've lost the spiritual bliss of sexual intercourse and the spiritual fulfillment in tender loving parenting.

As a result sex has become the most conflicting and most perplexing issue in our society. As we move to fulfill our deepest instinctive drives, the pleasures of sex have been integrated with sadism and masochism. The fulfillment of parenting has become diminished.

From the day we're born, our personality begins to be cultivated, shaped and molded by parenting. But parents in our society are too modern and too ego-centered. We pour scorn on the playful, wild and animal-like ways of children—babies cry too much, they

153

ask for too much attention— and every child is taught to quickly move away from childish ways of living. They must grow up quickly because parents are too busy and have to work too hard.

Children must do all of this because adults in a selfish materialistic society have long lost the tender loving caring attitude. They've been left with little or no tender loving capacity for parenting.

In the laws of creation, parenting is ruled by the essence of BE-ing. The fate of humanity is to escape our essence of BE-ing and learn the art of living, But first he must learn the art of parenting. or his living will only be in vain.

The true reality in this modern world is by the time an adult is ready to be a parent, he or she has lost that inner instinctive source of tenderness and love that's necessary for tender loving parenting. It's the soulful essence of loving parenting that babies need to feel loved, and not the ego-centered attitude of wealth and prosperity.

Let me say ego-entered prosperity is good for living. Man cannot live by love alone, and we must **work** hard to buy material things and comfort for the whole family. Wisdom and knowledge are also necessary needs for good parenting, to enlighten and inspire the child to live and celebrate life to its fullest glory. Discipline is also a necessary component of good parenting. Good discipline gives the child strong self-confidence and strong integrity of self.

Parenting Is Love
Good parenting, be it instinct or art, is rooted in love and without love, parenting is bound to fail. It will fail to build a loving relationship between parent and child and fail to give the child strong spiritual self-affirmation.

When it's rooted in love, parenting is a labor of love. Without love parenting is just boring labor. For parents it's sweet labor pouring love into a tender vessel, filling the infant's heart and soul. Parents are the fountain of love that pours living waters of faith, hope and human kindness. It builds self-esteem and causes it to grow high and higher.

No adult is totally void of parental instincts because parental instincts cannot be totally suppressed. They're alive even through ages of grandparents and great-grandparents. This is the logical plan of nature because if we totally lost the desire for parenting, the human race would end.

Some people have lost the capacity for love, but the instinctive drive for sex and parenting is still vibrant inside them. It's the instinct for life in the face of any danger at any cost. Parenting rooted in the instinct for life is manifested in the emotions and actions of love. When parenting is at its highest virtue, parents put the life and well being of their child before their own. No religion comes before the child, and neither does politics. No golden rule that conflicts with the nature of the child is held in honor.

When parenting is rooted in unconditional love, it's easy to discipline the child. But when love is absent in parent-and-child relationships, any attempt to discipline the child is bound to fail. Any child who feels unloved will rebel against his parents and everything the parents believe in. There's no deeper sorrow than a child who feels deeply unloved. The two edged sword in the hands of every rebellious person is the pain of self-hate, low self-esteem, deep anger, and fear.

Parents need to know that the instinct and lust for life in the child is stronger than the one in the parents. They need to know that instinct drives the child to every kind of disruptive behavior, just to get life-saving attention from adults

Unlucky is the child who has parents who are self-righteous, religious, arrogant or egotistic adults. By virtue of their inability to feel compassion for the infant's tender feelings, these people inadvertently always go wrong, even with the best of intentions. With the book of manmade golden rules, they fail in their duties of loving parenting. These parents are unable to understand that nature, not the writer of some book, writes the rules for parenting.

Lucky is the child whose parents are humble, forgiving, and hard working. Lucky is the child whose parents have plenty of wisdom and knowledge by virtue of their ability to listen to the child's inner feelings. They will see any rebellious actions of the infant as a call for love and a call for life, and they will tenderly answer every call of the child.

The quality in the virtue of parenting can only be measured one way—whether the child feels loved. If the child feels loved by the parents, then and only then, we can say that parenting was done perfectly right. Every parent will say, "I love my child." It's an instinctive reaction. Most children will say, "I love my parent." Again it's an innate desire to want to feel loved or even to hold on to an illusion of love. However, the evidence of love is not found in fancy words or innate desires. The most satisfying feeling is to *feel* loved.

If man feels deeply unloved, he will feel worthless. But he will suppress the consciousness of unworthiness and tell himself the reason for his terrible feeling is because people are no good. "If people are bad, then it's me against them. I have to fight my way through life." Anytime you see someone fighting their way through life, it's because of feelings of low self-esteem.

Evidence of a child who feels loved is one who has strong faith, hope, and spiritual self-affirmation. Any child who is free from anger, fear and self-doubt is evidence of a deep-seated quality of love. The evidence is a child who grows up to be a kind and loving parson, and most of all, a **kind and loving parent** and a kind and loving grandparent.

It's strange but true. Parents work very hard, long hours a day to buy things. They buy the best of everything in order to say, "I love my child." Rich people have plenty of money but still spend very little time with their children. Many parents don't seem to know that every moment away from an infant is a moment not loving the child. It's a moment not filling the infant's most important need.

Unless the infant is sleeping, he or she needs to be in the arms of or in sight of a parent, until the infant has the blessed assurance and faith that love is always available. Every infant needs faith and assurance that life itself is destined to bloom and grow, not wither and die. The infant will feel loved in the celebration of life, or feel unloved in the fear or life. Only tender loving parenting can give an infant the assurance of love and celebration. All religions are in perfect harmony and total agreement in the garden of parental love.

Egos, Religions And Parenting
Parental love flows at the seat of creation, where infants, fresh from the womb of creation, have only one reality. That reality is love and only love. Filled with the grace of God, the cradle is a place of no ego but pure spirit and pure love. I go to the cradle to embrace, to hold and behold creation. I don't have to read about it in the book of Geneses with all its violence, human conflicts and human destruction.

Take all the leaders of all the different religions of today. *If* we could've put all of them in one room at two years of age, we'd have nothing but pure love in that room. The soul of every one of those infants would've been filled with the grace of God. Every infant would love each other without any conflicts, without any prejudices, and without any idealism.

If we could put all the adult religious leaders of today in one room, and *if* we could find a way to remove everybody's **ego**, the grace of God in everyone's soul would be free to flow. With ego removed, each man would be "Born Again." Each would become like an infant, and every man in the room would form one religion of *pure spirit*, one religion of *pure love*.

In a world of pure spiritual love, there would be no holy wars, no images of God or gods. All of humanity would be free to love God and love self. Every man would love his fellowman. With only one religion of pure love, every man would be free to be his

157

Brother's Keeper. Children would be free from neglect and abuse. Every child would be born free and could live free to feel the spiritual bliss of tender loving parenting. There would be peace of earth goodwill to all men.

There's a place of pure spirit and pure love in this world, and it's in every cradle where the fountain of human kindness flows into the seat of creation. It's a place where the wellspring of parental love flows into the holy immortal soul of an infant child. It gives life to every beat of the heart and to mortal flesh.

The spiritual laws of creation decree that sex, eating and parenting—the seeds and cultivators of life—are the most life fulfilling experiences we can have. If we follow these laws, we'll love from the bottom of our hearts, with kindness in our minds and with our souls seated in peace and tranquility. The flesh is tender and free from stress, and the mother's eyes shine with joyful radiation. Paradise on earth is the smile on a mother's face when her baby suckles at her breast. The mother is the garden of paradise while the infant grows in the Garden of Eden.

Enemies Of Parenting

Today's man must work by the sweat of his brow, because he must earn money to eat. Not just one but both parents must work to pay all the bills in our society that's obsessed with material consumption. That's the biggest enemy of loving parenting. This world of material plenty leaves children with empty spirits.

For as long as I can remember, people have been growing more and more selfish and materialistic. The "Me First" mentality started in the sixties and has steadily increased. Individual rights have become the first birthright of every citizen. "Me First" started with the Civil Rights Movement that caused every black person to want a big job in a white office and the biggest house in a white neighborhood. This led to the Women's Liberation Movement and the Gay Rights Movement. Then it went on to "Be the best that you can be" and get the best things for yourself.

Even in the church today, materialism is promoted before spiritualism. The "Me First" rights have taken root. The rights of one or two homosexuals, for example, is put before the moral foundation of the universal laws of nature that govern loving children and building strong families.

All these movements have done a lot of good for individual rights, but they've turned out to be the enemy of family and the enemy of tender loving parenting. The right of every individual to be the best he can be and to make as much money as he can has been placed ahead of the ethical and moral good of society. It's also been put before the moral birthright of tender loving care of children.

Materialism is a very strong enemy of parenting. Of course, man must work to make a living and provide food and comfort for his children. But in this culture of materialism, people are obsessed with working and shopping. There's very little time left to tend to the loving care of the child.

Materialism is a bottomless pit of desire. Materialistic people hold fast to the illusion that happiness is the satisfaction of every new desire, but all the satisfaction they ever get is the excitement that comes with every new desire. Materialism provides no real joy to people's lives.

Sure, every child needs food and material comfort, but these material needs are only secondary to the need for love and tendered. Parents who work too hard and too long are tired and stressed out. They may buy the **best**, most expensive material things for themselves and their children. But they're doing harm to the children because what the children need most is love, not things.

The sad part of this big mistake is that when the children grow up, they don't remember the expensive things they got. Instead, they remember every lonely moment when they didn't feel loved. The parents are perplexed, unable to understand why their children are ungrateful and unhappy. They say, "I did so much for my child and the child cares little about me." They truly can't understand the problem.

159

Materialism is an enemy of parenting. It's an enemy of families, and it promotes greed, selfishness and distance among people and families. Children from materialistic homes either must break the shackles of materialism by seeking a renewal of spiritual consciousness or live their lives in loneliness and emptiness.

However, the "Me First" mentality, along with the materialism and selfishness it promotes, is not the disease. It's only one of the symptoms of a culture that has lost its collective soul and the tender instinctive touch of loving parenting. "Me First" is a culture of children who grow up feeling spiritually empty, so they build a new kind of culture where machines are easier to be with than people. We build a culture where mothers would rather spend the day in a room filled with IBM machines than in a room of loving children.

There's an unavoidable trait in innate human nature—we hunger for what we feed on. As we feed on material desires, we hunger more and more for material things. Our hunger for loving people and loving children subsides. In a materialistic culture, people work long hours, shop long hours to buy fancy things and go to church to praise God for all the good he's done for "Me." But who will love the children, if all our love is only for God, the one who loves "Me First?"

The American dream is the ideal of having a bigger car and a bigger house. But this dream is for more wealth and prosperity, not for more love and happiness. If America follows this dream to its highest ideals, we have less time for children and less time to spend with family. The dream could turn into a nightmare for the spiritual integrity of children and families.

A Parenting Revolution
For the past half-century, we've had many mini-revolutions in America. We've had the technology revolution, the civil rights revolution, women's liberation and the gay rights revolution. We have many revolutions of individual rights. This is what makes America great. Individual rights are even guaranteed in the Constitution.

As a black man I'm thankful for what the civil rights revolution has done for my people. In fact, I say let us declare victory for all the revolutions we've had in the past fifty years. Individualism and materialism have won.

But victory, oh victory, where is thy ecstasy? Where is thy sweet passion of love and happiness? Where is the sweet passion and spiritual bliss of children in the arms of love? Where is the sweetness in children when parents are too busy, too tired and too stressed out to give children tender loving care?

In some middle-class neighborhoods everyone in the household has his own car. Every member in the family, including the children, is separated from early morning till late evening. People don't have time to be with other people. We have more and more single parenting, a high rate of divorce, and two parents who must work hard to pay big bills. Everybody looks out for self. It seems the victory of individual rights has made a victim of the spiritual quality of parenting.
 We need a brand new revolution, one that will take parenting onto the holy ground on earth. We need a revolution to put the rights of children to be loved unconditionally before individual rights.

I dreamed I was walking with every citizen of the world and the revolution was on the move. People carried big, bold signs exalting the most endearing human rights for all. They praised the rights of every child to be loved unconditionally. Citizens of the revolution equated human rights with parental rights to love every child in the village. People shouted, "This is a revolution of faith, hope, and peace on earth goodwill to all men. Give kids the world, and let every citizen of the earth be a parent to every child in the world."

I dreamed of a new world and a new world order, with no more hate, no more wars, no more prisons, no drug addicts, and no alcoholics. The only reason why is because loving, spiritually whole children grew up to build this new world order of love. Love of God, love of self, and brotherly love have become the first order in this new world.

I dreamed I was in a church, and the silence was frightening. I listened and listened, and all of a sudden, a voice from the pulpit shouted the praise of parenting. A little child stood up and walked from the front door towards the pulpit. People praised God for the holiness of little children. The kingdom of God has come. Everyone shouted, "I am in the kingdom. I am the spiritual parent of every little child on earth. Every time I love a child, I go to the Kingdom of God."

The same dream took me to many temples, to many mosques and to many synagogues. In all, I heard people praise God by loving children.

Pure Spirit, Pure Love

If we would abide by the universal spiritual laws of creation, we would build our cultures rooted in the deepest instincts of our true creature nature. At the core of our true self is the instinct for parenting, for motherhood and for fatherhood. The instincts of parenting are rooted in the experiences of pure spirit and pure love, but only for those who haven't been spiritually separated from the inner soulfulness of the self.

The essence of our being is pure spirit and pure love, and the true significance of our being is in the reality of pure love. The only time we feel total fulfillment and meaning in life—the only time we feel totally alive—is when we love or feel loved. If we will not or cannot love, we feel worthless and spiritually dead. The glory and exaltation of our humanness is that man is born in this high consciousness of pure spirit and pure love. Man's spiritual consciousness pits him above all other creatures.

At birth our pure spirit consciousness is very immature. It's very vulnerable, very tender and very fragile. Only tender loving parenting can bring it to full holy maturity. At birth the flesh is weak and demanding for material consumption. The mind and mental capacity also are undeveloped. The spirit is the guardian angel that embraces and watches over the mind and the flesh.

But this guardian angle is pure spirit and cannot save the flesh. The flesh is a bottomless pit of material demand and consumption. From birth all through life's journey, parenting is the foundation of spiritual wholeness.

Tender loving care from parents gives the person a journey through life in the consciousness of pure spirit and pure love. We walk in the light of faith, hope and happiness. We see the light at the end of every dark tunnel. In every valley, we can see the mountain, and in every stormy sea, our anchor holds. Faith and hope set us free.

On the other hand, if parenting isn't tender or if it doesn't provide love, our life journey will be dark. If parenting is filled with neglect or abuse or too much punishment, our journey through life will seem to be a journey of one long and dreary dark tunnel. In the darkness one is separated from the consciousness of inner light, separated from the soulful essence of pure spirit and pure love.

In the darkness every footstep echoes with fear. Demons and ghosts seem to be coming to capture your soul. In the darkness you lose the reality of spirit and love. In the darkness what keeps you alive are the illusions you built by virtue of a strong ego and the courage you have of a strong mental willpower.

Let this be a warning to every adult. Parenting is the most spiritual, self-affirming experience on life's journey. Parenting in your childhood, parenting in adulthood, and parenting in your old age. **Parenting is the cultivator of mankind's inner peace and human kindness**.

Parenting: Soul And Ego
The art of parenting is to let loving care satisfy and fulfill the soul. At the same time it lets wisdom, knowledge and reason cultivate a strong ego. Any kind of childhood trauma or a loveless childhood will produce an adult with a wounded soul and a weak ego.

This is a formula for a life of emotional pain, fear and self-doubt. The personality with a wounded soul and a weak ego loses the integrity of the self, loses self-possession, and loses self-control. This personality loses any real chance of true happiness. People with deeply wounded souls and very weak egos too often wind up addicted to chemicals or in prison. Later you find them in a church praising God for saving them from self-destruction.

Parenting: The Child Inside The Man
Mankind is an origination of body, mind and soul. Happiness is unity and harmony within the origination. The body is the temple and at the altar, the mind and the soul give inner light and spiritual life to the body.

The soul is eternal and divine, and it never grows old. At the end of life, even after a hundred years, the eternal soul is the same age and form as when man was born. Throughout life the soul remains the "Little Child Inside the Man." If one must live in total self-affirmation, one must live centered in a self of soulful childlike humility and gracefulness. If ego dominates the center of living, however, that childhood humility and grace is suppressed. One must live separated from the essence of the true self.

It's all up to parents, in the duty and glory of parenting. Love is the foundation that gives the little child a chance to live forever in the soulful light of spiritual bliss. Every adult is a guardian to a little child inside. If the little child is happy and free, so is the adult. But if the little child inside is tormented with fear and self-doubt, then so is the adult.

Fate, Fulfillment And Responsibility
Man is born in love to love, and he's only true to himself when he experiences love or travels the path to love in the spiritual consciousness of love. Parenting is the experience of love that says life must go on. The creation of life puts the deepest virtue of life in parenting.

Those who travel through life on the path of love will find that parenting is the most fulfilling experience. Life itself is a gift. We find much excitement and fulfillment as we unwrap the gift. Each ribbon we untie makes us feel the gift of love, from love to love. As we hold and behold the gift, our fate and responsibility is not to hoard the gift of life but to share it. We give in order that we may receive happiness through life's fulfillment.

Mankind can feel whole only in the experience of love. That's because love and the fulfillment of life are the same. The most fulfillments in life are those activities that are the salvation and the survival for life. If you survive for the first twelve years or more on life to become an adult, parenting is the reason for it. People have been kind to you, so kindness must be your way of life. Even if the care was loveless and uncaring, if you survive childhood, it's because of parenting.

One must fulfill his or her responsibility and travel life's journey to its fateful end. Then one must be a parent. I don't mean to say that everybody should be a parent because some people cannot handle the responsibilities of taking care of a child. But let it be known, he who missed out on parenthood has missed out on one of life's most rewarding fulfillment.

The virtues of human kindness are most fully expressed in parenting. If man must fulfill his responsibility for the gift of life, he must be a parent because parenting nurtures life. Parenting teaches him how to be humble, how to be unselfish, how to be forgiving, and how to merge himself into the unconditional experience of the love. It takes love to raise children. A man who has been there and is able to wallow in the virtue of tender loving care of a child surely has experienced heaven on earth.

NINE

THE VIRTUES OF LOVE

"A new commandment I give unto you that ye love one another," are the words of Jesus. He acknowledged himself as the source of divine love, but time and time again, he told his followers that to find salvation, they must be the source of human love.

Jesus was the greatest teacher of the ten virtues of human love. All of the great prophets—Martin Luther King Jr., Gandhi, the Buddha, Jesus Christ and Mohammed—achieved their greatness by promoting the only totally fulfilling life experience. All of these great men taught mankind how to open the pathways to love, such as faith, kindness, humility and forgiveness.

The kingdom of God is a pathway to love open to little children. The source of life is a wellspring of spiritual energy that flows from the soul of every man; filling his heart with the thing we call love. The divine grace of love in our consciousness is a state of spiritual bliss and the source of life itself. That may be why a broken heart and a soul that's empty of love precede every suicide.

The spiritual source of life is a spiritual fountain that flows into an emotional experience. Our heaven on earth is an inner emotional state of spiritual bliss and our hell on earth is a state of emotional pain and terror. Newborn babies in their innocence have the greatest capacity to experience this spiritual, emotional bliss because they're filled with the grace of the Holy Spirit.

But the state of spiritual bliss in the infant lasts only as long as the child is given tender loving care. Any kind of neglect or abuse causes the child to suffer spiritual brokenness and fall into the **dis**-grace of fear and sorrow. The experience of love is the fulfillment of life itself. Love is the way, the truth and the light— the only path to righteousness. Love lives on faith, and he who walks by faith will never stumble in the darkness.

If we're void of love we live a life of spiritual emptiness. A life of spiritual emptiness is a life that's open to sin and sorrow. Too many people give Satan credit for sin, but the devil has no power. Sin is the result of a soul empty of spiritual love that becomes a vessel for sin, sorrow and corruption.

When a child is born, his soul is filled with spiritual love. But he's born into a world of selfish materialism, a sinful world shaped in iniquity. The child is born whole and holy in the loving grace of the creator, but his sinful world quickly corrupts the soul of the child. Too many people mistakenly conclude that the child was born unholy and corrupted.

The Ten Virtues Of Love

1A---SPIRITUAL MATURITY
2A---KINDNESS
3A---HUMILITY
4A---SELF-AFFIRMATION
5A---WISDOM
6A---FORGIVENESS
7A---TRANQULITY
8A---FAITH
9A---GRATITUDE
10A---REALITY/TRUTH

168

For every one of these ten virtues, there's an opposite, and we will use from one-to-ten Bs to describe the opposites later. Each one of these ten opposites is a roadblock on the highway to love, and each—fear, arrogance, anger and selfishness, and others—is an enemy to love. Each of these enemies puts man in a place of spiritual emptiness, a place that makes a man his brother's competitor, rather than his brother's keeper.

But let it be known that each of the opposites is a call for love while each one of the ten virtues is an answer to the call for love.

Aspects Of Love
We've talked about the ways of love, but what about the aspects of love? Love is an emotional experience manifested in waves of impulses we feel. Any feeling that promotes life can accurately be called love. Love is the miracle of life. It's something we give away in order to receive, also known as sharing. In the experience of love, every man is a magician because the more of it he shares, the more of it he has.

Spiritual love is the source of life. It's a wellspring of infinite spiritual energy that flows in the soul of every living person. Imagine the glory of man. He has within him a soul deeply rooted in the infinite power of all creation. Life only exists by a desire to live, and the love of life is the source of that desire. Any life empty of that desire has the ability to and will destroy itself. Void of the desire to live, life becomes self-destructive.

Evolution And Creation
Carl Sagan was one of the greatest scientists of the Twentieth Century. In his book, "Shadows of Forgotten Ancestors," he said that life is a three-letter word—the **evolution** of DNA, a combination of physical mass and chemical formulas. But what about a DNA scientist who kills himself because he feels rejected by love?

On the other hand, the spiritualist says life is just about the word became flesh in **creation**. But what about the spiritualist who

169

claims high spirituality but has over a million dollars and winds up in prison for stealing money?

I believe there's some truth in the theory of evolution and also some truth in the ideology of the spiritualist. Every man is created, and every human life is an evolution of DNA. I believe love is the answer to the origin of life. Evolution and creation are both rooted in the foundation of love. The evidence of all human life shows that man's deepest instinct is his hunger for love, and any life totally void of love will lose its desire to live and will self-destruct. So let's say it loud and clear, spiritual love is the source of life.

Spiritual love is the fabric of the human life. The threads of the body, mind and soul are integrated to form the fabric of each individual's life. When body, mind and soul are aligned and in synch, man can experience the bliss of spiritual love and live in celebration of life.

But when man's soul is contaminated and his ego dominates his personality, then the mind sides with the flesh. We become prone to selfish materialism, and we are plunged into an inner civil war. Ego sides with the body (flesh) against the soul, and the freedom of inner peace is destroyed. We experience a loveless life that we come to feel is not worth living.

THE SPIRITUALIST...**THE SOUL**
THE PSYCHOANALYST...**THE MIND/EGO**
THE SCIENTIST...**THE BODY**

Every one of these virtues is vital to the achievement of human wholeness, and wholeness brings inner peace and happiness. Harmony of body, mind and soul offers man a heaven on earth where he can live a soul-spirit-centered life. But total *dis*-harmony is hell on earth.

When man is in a state of inner *dis*-harmony, his ego separates from his soul and takes on its own agenda. His life becomes an ego trip, and his flesh also has its own agenda of material desires. He lives a life centered in selfish materialism, and his soul is left contaminated and unfulfilled. He loses his way and loses his soul. From the pathway to love and righteousness, he drifts into the path of evil.

If the scientist, the psychologist and the religious hierarchy could come together in harmony, mankind would find harmony between creation and evolution. He would find harmony between emotions and thinking, as well as harmony and balance between materialism and spiritualism.

All that harmony would bring a world of inner peace in each man and that inner peace would translate into peace on earth goodwill to all men. That would further translate into a world without wars, racial prejudice, and religious prejudice. The world would not be filled with so much selfish materialism. The world would become a place where every man is his brother's keeper. The cry throughout the would be:

"I am my brother's keeper. When I love my brother I feel loved.

This world would be a better place, especially for the tender loving care of children. Children who are given tender loving care grow into adults with tender loving feelings. An adult with tender loving feelings has high self-esteem, and he is the most spiritually fulfilled man on earth.

The man who is totally spiritually fulfilled sees love in everything. He walks in the light of a spiritual rebirth. His body, mind and soul are in the unified harmony of a spiritual consciousness. He sees love in everything and love in every person.

If he's a Christian, he walks the Christian path to salvation, the Christian path to love, truth and light. If he's a Buddhist, he walks the Buddhist path to love and truth to the other side of the river to his salvation. If he's spiritually fulfilled, with or without any religion, he will walk the path to truth and light. The man who is totally spiritually enlightened and fulfilled is filled with the grace of God. He sees every other man filled with the grace of God, regardless of any religion, and regardless of whether he's a scientist or a psychologist.

The Spiritualist: The Soul

Man's deepest hunger comes from his soul. He hungers for both spiritual love and human love. Man's deepest fulfillment in life is in the satisfaction of his soul. His deepest experience of pleasure comes from his soul, but his deepest experience of terror also comes from his soul.

At the core of the being lies the eternal soul, pure and holy in infant days but contaminated and corrupted as we become adults. The soul is rooted in the infinite spiritual source of all creation—flesh without a soul is dead. Because the soul is the strongest, it's the power of the personality. It is divine power.

Man is born with an innate longing for God that stems from a deep hunger in his soul. It's his hunger for life itself manifested in his hunger for love. At birth his soul is ageless and divine, rooted into the infinite, absolute power of all of creation. A baby's cries say, "I am my soul. I need love, so love me or I'll die."

Religions grow and flourish out of man's deepest hunger, his hunger for spiritual love. The **spiritualist's** work and passion is to seek a pathway to find food for man's soul. The spiritualist also seeks to open a pathway to man's most fundamental freedom, the freedom to love God or gods and to be loved. Human history is filled with religious wars, which shows you can mess with man's food for his belly and you can mess with his mind, but don't mess with the religion that provides food for his soul.

This is why most of the mass killings in human history have been done with man taking his personal religion (his God or gods) on the battlefield with him.

This also is why the spiritualist, with all his religious and other spiritual activities, shows that man's hunger—in his soul—for spiritual love is the most important and the deepest hunger in his existence. When man is born, his soul is filled with the grace of

172

THE VIRTUES OF LOVE

God. But when ego develops, spiritual separation and alienation from God plunges him into the darkness of sin and shame. In his darkest hour, he cries out, "God, God. Where are you? Save me, save me!"

The scientist in his lab with his vial of DNA may not cry out for God, but he cries out for love. It's the same thing. Because God is love and love is God. **This is evidence to show that man's hunger for spiritual love and his hunger for life is one and the same.**

So tell the scientist and the psychoanalyst that without the spiritualist, man will find little or no fulfillment in life. He must have spiritual food to feed his soul because without it, his gift of life will become lonely and worthless. He will feel as if life is not worth living.

Spiritual love—man's soul filled with the divine grace of God—is the most important possession for inner peace and happiness. It's true even for those who do not believe in God. The spiritual essence of mankind is not in what he believes.

At the core of every man is a spiritual fountain of love flowing into creation. It fills him with the desire, the will and the courage to live. It doesn't matter what he believes. Even if he becomes totally detached and alienated from the spiritual source of life, and even if he walks around like a living dead or runs away from the grave, it doesn't matter what he believes.

The Scientist—The Body
Scientists say life is nothing but chemical energy, physical mass and energy. DNA is flesh, bone, blood and neurological impulses. They say evolution is the only way to explain life.

I believe the theory of evolution has virtue in it, and science has done many, many good things towards the growth and pleasure of human life. Medicine is the most important of these. Thanks to medicine, man lives longer, with less pain, more pleasure and more convenience.

173

Less pain and more pleasure are very good, but there's more to human life than pain and pleasure. All the animals in life have

that. But we're humans and the essence of our humanness is to feel the ecstasy of spiritual bless. Humans have a higher consciousness of love than all other animals.

Scientists cannot explain every human's ability to descend below the pain of his body and experience hell on earth when he feels deep despair with fear and terror in his soul. Scientists also cannot explain man's ability to feel the ecstasy of heaven on earth when he experiences a fountain of spiritual love flowing from his soul and filling his heart.

The Psychoanalyst—The Ego/Mind
Psychoanalysis seeks to analyze and understand human behavior in terms of mental capacity and emotional feelings. Another discipline called psychobiology looks at the field of psychology from a biological point of view. It studies how the nervous system interacts with emotions and the body to cause chemical imbalances. This is where psychiatrists come in. They believe every kind of emotional and mental disorder should be treated with medicine.

A long time ago, I heard a doctor on the radio talk about practicing medicine for more than thirty years. He said most of his patients had one problem in common. He called it "a hole on the soul."

Sigmund Freud, the father of psychoanalysis, discovered every one of his patients had emotional conflicts or trauma during their childhood development. He believed those childhood experiences were responsible for the patients' problems.

I believe the cure for most adults' emotional dysfunctions is simply to treat children with tender loving care. Love is the cure for most of the sickness we have today. If we love children and make them feel loved, they grow up with body, mind and soul in harmony and inner peace. Inner peace brings a stress-free body, with no anxiety and stress to tighten up the body and cause disease. The mind also is free from negative thinking. If we could achieve this, we would have a healthy body, healthy mind and a healthy soul.

Psychology, science and religion—all three disciplines are vital to man's freedom from pain and his material survival. They're also key to the fulfillment of man's spiritual joy and happiness.

The trouble comes from man's ego. Our religions are ego-centered, which makes them instruments of a kind of self-righteousness that pours scorn on science and psychology and so, never the twain shall meet. The scientist, the psychologist and the spiritualist all suffer from the same kind of ego-centeredness where every man wants to be better than the other.

The world will be a much better place when all three disciplines sit together at the table of humility and brotherhood in one accord and mutual regard. When all three consider man as an individual, in the wholeness and harmony of mind, body and soul.

Human Love
Divine love—the source of spiritual love—is the source of life. But the source of human love is the nurturer and the keeper of life. Every one of the ten ways of love is a necessary ingredient to live a life in the fulfillment of love. Imagine a baby in his crib. Even if you put food in his hand, he cannot put his hand to his mouth. It's surely the source of human love

Parental love is the most important aspect of human love. The instinct of mother's love is the deepest, most powerful and most fulfilling part of mankind. In this world of selfish materialism, shameful little is said about parental love, the tender loving care of children. That's because selfish materialistic people have too little time to love children. Instead, they spend their time looking for romantic love, making money and going to church on Sunday to praise God for all their material prosperity.

There's a soulful spiritual aliveness in tender loving parenting. It

175

was meant to be the most life fulfilling experience an adult can have. But because most adults today have lost their inner soulful spiritual aliveness to ego-centeredness, the passion for parenting has diminished. Parenting has become a call to social duty, rather than to fulfill the duty of love and life.

Parents today need to understand that little children are born the most spiritual people on earth. If you refuse to give them unconditional tender loving care, however, they stand a very good chance of rebelling against you, against your God and against the world they live in. Go into any prison in America, and you'll find almost every inmate was a victim of living a life of rebellion before they committed the crime or were arrested. Too often the most self-righteous people turn out to be the worst parents.

We live in a world where many people say a good education is the best thing you can give your child. Let me tell every parent, a good education starts with high self-esteem, and high self-esteem starts with giving the child tender loving care and good discipline.

Parenting—a mother's love and a father's love—is the most important thing a man or a woman can do in life. The experience of being loving parents also can be the most life fulfilling experience of all.

Romantic love is the deepest inner pleasure man can feel, because romantic love leads to sexual intercourse that makes life. Isn't it interesting that romantic love, the thing that makes life, is the same thing that offers mankind the deepest pleasure?

But most times, romantic love is too self-centered. The jealous lover who kills his beloved shows how often romantic love betrays all the virtues of love. Listen to all the loving romantic words of poets and songwriters—it's all about self-centered glory.

Also, romantic love is focused from one person toward another person. We say, "I love you so much. I live for you. I'll die for you." It's true that romantic love is deep and wide because it moves toward sexual intercourse that plants the seed of life in the womb of a woman. Life itself is in the motivation of romantic love, and a betrayal of romantic love can be considered to be a betrayal of life itself. Creatures live for life, they will die to make life go on and they will kill for life.

Romantic love leads to marriage and plants the seeds of life and family.

Romantic love can be the sweetest thing on earth. However, when it's lost, betrayed or denied, it also can be seen as a rejection of life itself. Romantic love can be strong and free only when it's rooted in self-love and individualism wrapped up in unselfishness. This enables man to give of self without losing the integrity of self.

Despite his dependency and insecurity, man will move with every bit of energy towards romantic love. However, in the face of the intimacy of romantic love, he often becomes frightened. Many times, people look for love but are unable to hold on to it. They may get burned so badly that they stop looking and bear the pain of loneliness. Unfortunately, they may find someone they cannot love or someone who cannot love them.

Brotherly Love
Brotherly love is the most significant happening that could bring about world peace. Every other kind of love is easily used and abused to promote selfishness. Even spiritual love—the love between man and his God—can't do it, because some of its most ardent prompters are some of the most selfish people on earth.

Parental love often means, "looking out for my child first," and some of the best parents are racist and religious separatists.

Brotherly love, on the other hand, covers every area of love because it's rooted in human kindness. The great redeemer, Jesus Christ, was the biggest teacher of brotherly love. In every

177

part of his teachings he proclaimed man's love for his fellowman as the greatest love of all.

But look what happened to Jesus. The religious hierarchy crucified him because his message of brotherly love came into conflict with their religious dogmas and ideals. The creed of brotherly love is peace on earth goodwill to all men. That means goodwill to **all** men, not just to some men.

With brotherly love, every man in the human race is in a soul-centered place of equal significance of every other man. All are equal as one—one spirit, one creation. The soul of every man is intimately tied to the soul of all men. No class, no religion, and no social or economic class separate us.

Brotherly Love, God And Religions
Every man is the keeper of every other man. Brotherly love is the only thing that can remove every kind of injustice, every kind of prejudice, and every kind of war in the human race.

He who stands on brotherly love stands on holy ground. He's filled with the grace of God. With this grace, he can't hate anyone and he can't condemn other men as unholy. He sees holiness etched in the soul of every other man. He loves equally all the people of his religion, those with no religion and those of every other religion.

Brotherly love is the divine essence of all creation. It's "ground zero" if we want to live and be united as one, with peace on earth goodwill to every man and to all men. Brotherly love is holy ground.

All religions seek a spiritual consciousness for their devotees. However when religious men use their heightened spiritual consciousness only to focus on God and use the spiritual power of God to war with his fellowman, it does nothing to promote peace of earth goodwill to all men. Also with this power, many spiritual people become self-righteous. They become self-made saints with the Holy Book in one hand and a sword in the other. They cry out to God, "Save me, save me."

We'll have world peace only when all religions focus their spiritual consciousness on brotherly love and love their neighbors as themselves. We'll have world peace only when every man of every religion—and every man of no religion—unites.

Brotherly love is forgiveness. It's also compassion and humility. It never judges or condemns, and it doesn't separate saints from sinners. Brotherly love believes no man is so sinful that he doesn't deserve love and no man is so saintly that he doesn't sin.

Only the infant child is sinless, innocent and holy. Unfortunately they're caught up in their own helplessness. They're strong with inner peace and spiritual love but unable to show brotherly love.

If ever we have a world where every child is given adequate tender loving care, every child will grow up to be his and her brother's keeper. Then brotherly love will spread throughout the world. We'll have one religion, the Religion of Brothers Keepers.

In this world of high technology and selfish materialism, very few people are filled with the full capacity for love. Today, people who are truly loving, such as mothers who stay home to give tender loving care to their children, are considered out of touch with what's going on.

Love is an inner stillness, an inner peace and tranquility. People who cannot sit still but are always running to do things are running away from themselves and running away from love. Love is an "in-the-moment" experience. It's an "I am where I want to be, doing what I want to do at this moment" experience. But very few people experience many of these moments. Wherever most people are or whatever they're doing, they want to be someplace else or doing something else.

Instead, we should take time for love. Spend time doing nothing, just to be with God or just to be with someone you love. Or even better, spend time with yourself in mediation or in solitude. Take time to feel the inner movements of the self.

TEN

THE TEN
VIRTUES OF LOVE

Ten different ways to experience love

Love covers every corner of our lives. Everything we do is for love and if it's not love, it must be a *call* for love. Life is a highway of love with ten different lanes to travel. Every lane is easily interchangeable with every other lane, but there is no need for a conscious decision to switch lanes. You could be driving with humility when things get slow, and all of a sudden love takes the steering wheel. Without realizing it you switch to gratitude and then to kindness.

Love is not just for romantics. Love is motherhood, fatherhood, brotherhood, and sisterhood. Love is the essence of unity in one humanity, and it's truth and faith. All these things and more promote life. All these things we call love.

The Ten Ways Of Love Are:

> 1A—Spiritual Maturity
> 2A—Faith
> 3A—Humility
> 4A—Self-Affirmation
> 5A—Wisdom

6A—Forgiveness
7A—Tranquility
8A—Kindness
9A—Gratitude
10A—Truth/Reality

Love has many virtues, and in this chapter we are going to describe ten of them. Each one is necessary to fulfill the experience of love in a different way. If I have faith in my brother it's easy to show him love, even in my moments of conflicts with him. But if I have no faith in him, then it's just as easy to pour contempt on him with every little disagreement we have.

A faithless person has an inner doubt and insecurity that gives a feeling that something is wrong inside. But the pain of inner conflict is repressed, so the faithless person always blames the outside world for his displeasure. A faithless person is always blaming and complaining, but with faith there is always a light at the end of the tunnel. My faith helps me live with love and happiness.

Humility also is one of the ten ways of love. I believe humility is one of the most underrated of all human virtues. If I have great humility, I will try to use kindness to help a brother in his moment of weakness. Humility helps me strengthen my brother.

But without humility I am filled with arrogance, and I will use my arrogance to pour contempt on my brother's weakness. That weakens my brother more. So you see with humility I show kindness in the face of someone's weakness, but without humility I show contempt. Faith and humility are two key components in my journey to love.

Spiritual Maturity
On the day we are born the soul is the only part of us that is fully mature and fully developed. The soul is ageless, eternal and divine, and imbued with the spiritual power and wisdom of all creation. At birth even our emotions will easily explode out of control. The body is crippled and immature, and the mind is a blank slate waiting for this unholy world to write on it.

The root of man is his soul. It is the soul that roots us in the soil of creation from cradle to the end of life. The soul also is the core of the self. If the roots are deep and strong, soaking up plenty of spiritual nurturing, the tree will blossom and flourish, like a tree that is planted by a river of water.

The fully developed human takes about twelve years before he can cook his first pot of food—twelve years to become fully matured. This shows how feeble, weak and vulnerable the human species really is.

But we are born with the divine and eternal strength of the soul. Man is born a spiritual giant but with a crippled body and an animal instinct and mentality. We are born more animal than human. The newborn child has a long and dark journey as his soul takes his body and his mind into development as an adult human being. Notice it is the soul that is the root of the self.

A man who has lost his soul has lost the roots of himself and his spiritual maturity withers.

This journey can take about twelve years before the child becomes mature enough to take care of himself. In these long and dismal years, body and mind are developed. Emotions are stabilized, the crippled body becomes agile and strong, and his mind grows stronger and stronger in mental capacity. That's when the ego comes of age.

But man's ability to love, the vitality of the soul in those developmental years, is suppressed in order to fit into this material world. When mind, body and soul develop in one accord, unified and in harmony, then man arrives into adulthood with what I call **spiritual maturity**. Spiritual maturity means having no emotional outbursts, when soul, mind and body are in perfect harmony. We are is in a state of inner peace and tranquility as the spiritual, the mental and the material part of the self are in perfect synch with each other.

Life does not get any better than this—the roots of the soul are strong, the body is in love with the soul and the ego is aligned with the body and the soul. With spiritual maturity, the ego develops in the spiritual consciousness of love, and the journey through life is traveled in the lighted path of love.

The Ideal Spiritually Mature Person

Many pages could be written to describe the ideal spiritually matured man. But it's safe to say in one sentence, "The spiritually matured person is one who understands that love, work and knowledge are the wellspring of his life and he has the good fortune and good wisdom to let all three virtues govern his life."

Love is food to fill the soul, work is food for a healthy body, and knowledge gives wisdom, stimulation and inspiration to the mind. So you see, the spiritually matured man lives in the glory of a holistic life. He is blessed with the **harmony of body, mind and soul** and the inner peace of self-love. He has love and goodwill for the entire world.

The word harmony is worth repeating.

In this selfish materialistic world we live in today, it is close to impossible for anyone to reach this ideal of full spiritual maturity. We all suffer from spiritual separation and fall short of the glory and ecstasy of spiritual love. Spiritual maturity is a life-long journey from cradle to grave.

The journey starts the first day the child is born. I have often said, "A man never lives long enough to outlive the desire to be mothered." Let me also say, "I have no scientific evidence to back up my theories." I don't believe I need scientific evidence because I write from purely a philosophical point of view.

From our infant days long before we can remember, most of us lost our spiritual wholeness. From childhood it takes a long journey of extreme tender loving care and good fortune to get to be an ideal spiritually manure man. And that assumes the child is blessed with loving parents, something that often is not the case.

184

The first three to six years of life are the most crucial. During the first year the child requires twenty-four hour/seven days a week attention. Every time the baby cries he should be picked up and hugged and cuddled. This hugging nurtures his vital spiritual growth and maturity.

Any kind of neglect or any punishment will blight the baby's spiritual maturity. Please remember the child has no rational understanding of the outside world. For about the first eighteen months the child understands and lives for only one thing— unconditional love and tender care from caregivers.

At birth the child is an emotional volcano, exploding one moment and calm and smiling the next. Emotions are strong but fragile, tender and vulnerable. Any kind of long period of neglect or trauma will damage emotions, sometimes beyond repair. The child will grow up an emotional cripple, feeling unloved and spiritually broken. And he won't even remember the scene of the crime.

The years between one and three are called the formative years. They are the most important years of the child's life. Emotionally, spiritually and psychologically everything about the infant is marked fragile and tender. Maximum tender loving care is a must in these formative years in order for the child to grow up to be a spiritually matured adult.

I cannot overstate that tender loving care is a must to avoid a wounded soul, with emotional damage and psychological impairment. In his first three years, the child is very vulnerable to all these internal, sometimes irreversible, damages that can last for the rest of its life.

At about three years old, the **ego** comes into its own, and the mind becomes an instrument of rational thinking and reasoning. The child begins to understand the power of words, saying "Yes" and "No." He runs and plays and the roots of high self-esteem are nurtured. With self-love, all the love and glory of human excellence comes into play, between the years three to six. This is the time when discipline can be mixed with love, the years when wisdom and understanding begin to take root in the personality. Words and inspiration begin to take form, and skills in communicating with people are learned. Even reward and punishment disciplines of right and wrong can be applied tenderly when necessary.

If the child is given plenty of love to feed the **soul**, plenty of milk, vegetables and meat to feed the **body**, and plenty of intellectual inspiration to stimulate the **mind**, then he is on the right road to a life of full spiritual maturity. He is on the pathway to a life of inner peace and happiness, and peace on earth goodwill to all men. To love and be loved is the manifestation of spiritual maturity.

Let me send out a warning to all parents, especially to those who have to work too hard and have little or no time to love the child. If the child **feels loved,** then everything will be fine. But if the child does not feel loved by you, then something will be radically wrong in the child's growth and development. Every time you try to discipline your child, you will have a rebellious child on your hands. And to make matters worse, a child who is starved for love and attention will quickly learn how to use negative behavior to get attention.

There is no deeper hell on earth than a rebellious child. Just go to a prison and you'll see them, addicted to every kind of chemical. Go to church and you'll also see them—praising and thanking God for saving their lives.

In the years from six to twelve, the personality begins to take shape and take roots. Plenty of tender loving care is still required and if given, high self-esteem and high spiritual self-affirmation becomes deeply rooted in the personality. Between six and twelve all the virtues of spiritual maturity take root.

Self-possession, self-control and self-expression boost self-confidence. Then a hunger for love and knowledge dominates the personality. At about the same time the whole personality is formed, and then comes the dawn of spiritual maturity.

The adolescent living in the light of **spiritual maturity** has

186

embraced all the ten ways of love. He has the inner harmony of body, mind and soul. He lets the proper balance of love, work and knowledge govern his life. He lives a soul-centered life, and his desire for material things is holy, with the kind of material desires that will never come to the point of greed, envy or selfishness. At about twelve years old, he comes into spiritual maturity.

Living in the light of total self-love and total self-affirmation, the spiritually mature person has no need for a college education or any kind of fame or fortune to make him feel important. He already feels a total sense of high self-esteem in the dawn of his teenage years. His desire is to feel love—brotherly love, family love—and to gather more knowledge and wisdom as he seeks the benefits and inspiration of hard work.

His self-hood is strong because it is rooted in the strength of a spiritually mature person.

The ideal spiritually mature person's thinking is positive, sound and holy. Any kind of thinking that would corrupt his soul causes him grief and quickly disappears. Any kind of material desires that would defile his body or any vanity that would corrupt his soul also causes him grief and quickly disappears.

He is free from hate and free from selfish materialism. He is humble and kind, and he is always calm, cool and collected. He is emotionally strong and has a strong power of will. The ego is aligned with the soul. The spiritually mature man's faith is strong and his soul is pure and holy. He may or may not live in the consciousness of God, but one thing is certain. He has the grace of God in him.

The spiritually mature person has all the ability to get angry and will do so to defend himself, but he will not hate. He is too forgiving to harbor any hate.

The spiritually mature person is his **brother's keeper**. His self-love is manifested in showing love for his brother. He or she is a good loving father, a good husband, a good mother and a good neighbor. To sum this all up, the spiritually mature person is everything that is the essence of love and one brotherhood of man.

Faith
Faith is a belief in something without the benefit of evidence. In the reality of human living, faith is stronger fact. The scientist who reduces mankind to a source of mechanical mass and chemical formulas is trying to deny mankind the wonderful virtues of faith.

All the great religions are founded and flourish to fill the need of mankind's deepest hunger, the hunger from his soul for meaning and fulfillment. Faith in an unseen, immaterial power is required for feeble mankind to have a meaningful life. Faith in his fellowman is also required for man to love and feel loved. Faith in the source of human love is a vital source of living, simply because it is the source of human love that keeps man alive from the baby in the crib to the sick and very old who have become "once a man but twice a child."

In this selfish materialistic world most adults have little faith in human love and so have lost faith in life itself. Faith, hope and trust in the goodness of humanity is required to live a life of love that is filled with meaning and high self-esteem, a life that is free from fear, self-doubt, despair, and even ego-centered selfishness and arrogance.

Looking at human history and the history of man's religions, we see that faith, religions and mysticism play a much larger and far more meaningful role in man's life than science. Thank God for that. The faithless man will always stumble in the dark, but with faith there is no darkness.

Our relationships with people are our most important relations in life, and good relationships require faith. The faithless man who has little or no trust needs to see evidence of love face-to-face in all his relations with people. But the man filled with faith and trust, even in the face of hate, fear and despair, will keep a positive disposition that keeps hope alive, because he always believes love is just around the corner. His faith in his fellowman gives him inner peace, love and goodwill to all men. Faith is stronger than fact. We can have all the facts telling us how to move a mountain, but faith can move mountains.

Too many faithless people worry about things they cannot change. Sometimes even in the evidence of positive facts, a faithless man will ignore the facts and keep on worrying. This is evidence that faith is stronger than fact.

We either live in the light of faith or in the darkness of fear.

Humility
The story is told of the man who, when his neighbor's dog messes on his lawn, goes to his neighbor angry, blaming and complaining. He gets into a fight with his neighbor and creates an enemy. Another man, after seeing his neighbor's dog mess on his lawn, gave a sigh of annoyance but silently went and cleaned up the mess. The first man is an arrogant man, and he makes an enemy. The second man is a humble man, and he makes a friend.

Humility is certainly one path to love. In this unholy world we live in, too often the ego takes control of the personality and life becomes one long journey of ego-tripping. The ego-tripper is on a mission to glorify his image. He is arrogant and self-centered. You see him often selling his soul to get attention and gain acceptance from the world.

But the humble man is a soul-centered man who gets acceptance from his world by giving love and attention to people. Every religion teaches humility simply because, only with humility can man find the inner peace mixed with peace on earth goodwill to all men, the inner peace that is vital to every man's soul salvation. The man without humility pours contempt on his brother's weakness. But the humble man pours kindness and understanding on his brother's weakness.

189

Self-affirmation

Before man can have self-affirmation, he must have self-awareness, self-expression and self-control. He must have a deep consciousness of self, and he must understand what's going on inside of him. His feelings and all his emotions are vibrant, his thinking is clear, and he is free to express the way he feels and thinks. Self-control is to express actions, thoughts and emotions with discipline in the right place and the right time.

Self-affirmation is what we call self-confidence. It's a self-confidence that goes deep down into the very soul of the personality. Self-confidence affirms the integrity of the self. It promotes high self-esteem and gives meaning and spiritual fulfillment to life.

There are some sad things known to man, but there is nothing sadder than a man who cannot express how he feels. He becomes a "people pleaser," and he has no opinion of his own. He loses the integrity of the self and lives in the fear that people will reject him if he disagrees with them.

There also are people who seem to be self-affirmed but the reverse is true. They build up a big ego-affirmation but deep inside they have a trembling soul. True self-affirmation is a spiritual expression of the true self. Self-denial promotes self-depreciation.

The Ego-Centered Self Vs. The Soul-Centered Self

Self-affirmation in an ego-centered self is not a virtue. It's a vice that too often leads into the path of narcissism and selfish materialism. The same thing goes for self-love. Some people claim to be in love with self, but it's just ego-centered narcissism.

All the great religions teach denial of an ego-centered self and at the same time they teach self-affirmation of a soul-centered self as the pathway to inner peace and happiness. But sometimes religions that teach denial of self fail to distinguish between ego-centered and soul-centered self.

Feed The Soul And Starve The Ego

The root of man's existence is his soul, a soul that is deeply rooted in the spiritual infinite source of divine creation. If he wants to be strong in himself—strong with faith, hope and self-affirmation—he must be deeply rooted in the spiritual integrity of his soul. The integrity of self is in the strength of the soul, and in the trinity of body, mind and soul.

The flesh is only an instrument of consumption—it's too feeble and weak —while the soul is an instrument of fulfillment. The mind takes lots of work and lots of years to become strong with intellectual reasoning. It goes astray and is filled with corrupted thoughts.

But the soul is ageless and divine, and at birth it has the spiritual wisdom and strength of all creation. A soul-centered person lives a life filled with meaning and the absolute power of all creation.

The strength of the man with self-affirmation is the strength of manhood. Being rooted in the spiritual integrity of his manhood frees him from the selfish materialism that destroys the moral fabric and the brotherly love in our society today. While the soul hungers for love and spiritual fulfillment, the ego hungers for power, glory and more and more material consumption for the body. In the history of the human race, too often might seems to destroy right. The ego becomes the master of the soul. The spiritual and loving ways of the soul-centered man is no match for the physical might and knowledge of the ego-centered man. The ego deals with the outer world of greed, power and fear, but the soul deals with the inner world of love. And in love there is no fear.

In the history of the human race, mankind has come to be convinced that **ego power,** not **soul power** is vital to his survival. Still religions teach that soul-power is vital to an individual's inner peace and happiness. But total self-affirmation is only for the people who strong ego-power coupled with strong soul-power. There has to be a delicate balance between spiritual fulfillment and material consumption. Man needs spiritual self-affirmation that works hard to get knowledge and material possessions.

All the great religions and all their great prophets teach about the destructiveness of selfish and materialistic ways of living. They all teach the denial of the ego-centered self and at the same time, they teach man to seek first the pathway of love and righteousness.

However, modern man has lost his soul and every wise man is forced to live in an ego-centered way. And in today's world self-affirmation is defined as affirmation of the ego-centered self. Living in a world of ego-centeredness, man is prone to all the evils of selfish materialism.

This is why our egocentric religions of today must teach self-denial, rather than self-affirmation as the path to salvation.

The danger is that in today's world, self-affirmation has become the victim of egotism, even among the most religious people. Mankind's only chance to have inner peace and at the same time have peace on earth goodwill to all men is to build his cultures rooted in the holiness of soul-centered living and to teach every man to seek first **self-affirmation of a soul-centered self**.

Total self-denial only brings self-distraction to mankind. Wars and rumors of wars and ego-centered religions only bring mankind into a world of *spiritual emptiness,* a world void of soul-centered self-affirmation.

Feed the ego and starve the soul, so that man can live, and find *all* the glory of the ten virtues of love and celebrate life in the absolute power and glory of a soulful self-affirmation.

Wisdom
Wisdom is the quality of being wise. In all the glory of the technological and the information age today, however, as knowledge increases it seems that wisdom of inner peace and happiness decrease. Machines teach people to think less.

Knowledge increases wisdom, but the root of happiness is wisdom.

The **wisdom of the soul** is to hunger for love. We are born with the gift of this wisdom of the soul from cradle to grave, but we must seek first the spiritual fulfillment of love as the pathway to spiritual maturity. Then and only then can we find true inner peace and peace on earth goodwill to all men.

The wisdom of all creation is in the soul of a newborn child. The child's soul holds the seeds of the spiritual wisdom of loving motherhood that needs to be nurtured so they will flourish. It also holds the seeds of the wisdom of loving fatherhood, the wisdom of loving brotherhood, the wisdom of the ten virtues of love, and the wisdom that religions and colleges fail to teach. Last but not least, in the psyche of the child lies all the instinctual wisdom of creation. Unfortunately, it is not long before this unholy world teaches the child to suppress the hunger for love and contaminates its soul with selfish materialism.

Many men go to college and earn a Ph.D. yet still cannot find love and happiness simply because they do not seek wisdom. They spend all their time seeking the glory of intellectual excellence and never read books about the philosophical virtues of wisdom.

Man needs wisdom and inspiration to follow his passion and hard labor, because they are the wellsprings of our lives. While going to college to get your Ph.D., make sure you seek all the things that are the wellsprings of your life. In addition to your degree, seek love, wisdom, knowledge and understanding.

Forgiveness
Forgiveness is the action that purifies the soul and brings peace and joy to a contrite heart. It opens the path to love and shows the path to faith, hope and redemption. Those who will not, or cannot, forgive will never find the light of redemption. They will always stumble in the darkness holding the sword of revenge. As adults most of us live in the consciousness of some hurtful feelings from the past. We feel terribly **unloved**, from the hurts of

childhood to the hurts of yesterday. We come to see a world with bad people who cause us grief. We have wounded souls. For some who try very hard to forget—to bury the hurts—the hurt just gets buried in the sub-consciousness, where the hurt manifests itself in self-destructive behavior.

Forgiveness is the only way to heal a wounded soul. Forgiveness is the only path to redemption.

Those of us who have been hurt badly in one way or another, especially if we were hurt in early childhood, face the emotional pain of living with wounded and tormented souls. Each day we must face a world that has wronged us, and we feel betrayed. We have the sword of revenge in our hands. Most of the time we try hard to love people, to love our children and family. But there is only one way for us to really experience true love, and it is the pathway of forgiveness. We must forgive those who have hurt us.

All the great religions teach **forgiveness** as the pathway to redemption and salvation. But once the hurt is seated in the belly of the soul, forgiveness does not come easily. For some people, it takes almost a lifetime to empty the soul of affliction and to fill it again with spiritual love. We must pray for the ability to forgive, for the gift of forgiveness. Religions teach the glory of forgiveness and teach people how to forgive, how to bring the power of the Holy Spirit unto the soul and how to love again.

A heart that will not forgive is open to anger and fear, and anger and fear lead to depression and self-doubt. Forgiveness is a one-way street—*my* forgiveness of someone is the only thing that matters. It doesn't matter what kind of evil someone has done to me, and it doesn't matter how he or she feels about me. The only thing that matters is how I feel when I think about the person. If I feel anger towards them, then I have not fully forgiven. I must pray to the Holy Spirit for more power of forgiveness.

Forgiveness is sometimes a long journey of praying and praising God.

194

Let me tell you I was very hurt by my very angry mother, and it has taken all my life looking for a spiritual filling station to find forgiveness. Even today I know I have not fully forgiven her.

How do I know I need more forgiveness? The day I think of my mother and feel a burst of love bubbling in my soul and filling my heart, I'll know I have been blessed with the virtue of total forgiveness.

On the other hand if I do or say something to hurt another person's feelings, it takes a lot of courage and humility to ask that person for forgiveness. Remember that forgiveness is a one-way street. It's up to the hurting person to forgive.

In the matter of parents and children, one person is hurting but stubborn and refuses to forgive. The other person, void of courage and humility, refuses to beg for forgiveness, and each winds up living with the pain of a tormented soul. There is nothing more likely to send a man to an early grave more than a tormented soul.

It takes a person with a loving heart to forgive. If you find it's very difficult to forgive, change the way you look at the world. Change the way you look at people and things will change for the better for you.

Forgiveness is a virtue that is twice blessed. It is a gift to the other person and also a gift to me.

Tranquility
Tranquility is that peaceful easy feeling inside. A tranquil state of being is more virtuous than for those who only seek glory and excitement. The quality of tranquility frees man from all the negative emotions that disrupt spiritual wholeness. Tranquility is a peaceful easy feeling, with tender loving feelings that flow from the fountain of the soul to quench the thirst of the heart. It's a state of spiritual bliss, a tranquil place that we go to find inner peace.

Anger and fear are the most common enemies of tranquility.

People who see the world as an unkind place and see people as bad are always quick to anger. But let me tell you, every time you get angry—it doesn't matter who's right or wrong—the anger disrupts your spiritual calm. When you lose your cool, you lose your tranquility.

Anger and fear are two sides of the same coin, wherever there's one there's the other. To every bout of anger there is some fear down below. Fear is much more painful than anger. Fear is terror, and fear steps in when a man ceases to love life. He moves from celebrating life to living in fear of life. The fear is buried in his subconscious and anger is there to see that he does not descend into the deeper pain of fear.

Man must be free from a state of anger and fear to live a tranquil life. He must be free from always blaming and complaining, and he must stop finding fault with the world.

If you do not have inner peace, self-examination is the only way to find tranquility.

Change yourself and your world will change. Pray that you see the world in a different light. See friends and family in a different light, and you will take yourself out of the darkness of anger and fear. Pray that you see love and put yourself into the spiritual wholeness of that peaceful easy feeling—the spiritual bliss of tranquility.

Kindness
In my book "Love, the Breath of Life," I define love as the ability to surrender without the fear of being conquered. Mankind is an ego-centered animal because of his high level of consciousness, his high self-awareness, the high anxiety about his future, and the consciousness of his mortality. Man is forever a tormented soul.

With his soul tormented and contaminated, the evolution of his ego takes man out of the bosom of love, the ego allies with the demons of selfish materialism that tries to conquer his soul. The soul hungers for heaven and is ready to surrender to love,

196

surrender for a soul salvation. Make yourself a fountain of human kindness—that's the pathway to a soul fulfilling life.

Kindness is the best way to show a person you care about them. The day we were born all we needed was tender loving care. We kicked, screamed and cried for TLC, calling for love and calling for more love, "**Love me or I'll die**." A loving mother pours kindness on the child's call for love, making the child feel loved. But a loveless mother pours contempt of the child's call for love, making the child feel unloved, angry and rejected.

From the cradle to the grave, everything we do we do for love. We either do things with love or we are **calling** for love. The spiritual integrity and strength of mankind is a world where we pour **kindness** on a brother's call for love. But a world where we pour contempt instead of kindness on another brother's call for love is a world of loneliness and sorrow.

Who will answer a brother's call for love? Who will pour some kindness on a brother's call for love? What does it take to answer a brother's call for love?

Listen, listen, love, love. Diligently **listening** to a brother makes him feel your kindness. You give him strength. Ignoring him or talking loud over him pours contempt on his call for love, and you weaken him.

Happiness is a community where people pour kindness on people's call for love and contempt is unheard of.

Mankind is weak and feeble. Man is a creature of suffering and is acquainted with grief. In his grief he calls for love. From the crib to the grave, mankind is on a long and dismal journey, calling for love.

Kindness is the only salvation in a world that's calling and bawling for love. Let every brother pour some kindness on another brother's call for love, and watch how your world becomes a better place.

197

If you feel lonely and unloved, try kindness. Go out and pour some kindness on some other person who is lonely and feels unloved, and watch what happens. Do something good for somebody. Call somebody just to say hello.

Selfishness is the opposite of kindness. Who can argue selfishness is not a virtue but a vice when it's been said that self-preservation is the first law of nature? Self-preservation is the first law of nature, but tell that to the infant child, the very sick, and even the very old. It is the source of human kindness that keeps the infant and the very sick alive. The only way to clear up this confusion is to put selfish and kind as allies and friends, but put selfishness the foe.

When the virtues of self-preservation are taken to the extreme, they then become a vice. In fact, any virtue taken to an extreme will become a vice. The big reality of human living is that man must live in fear of many dangers. We all live in fear of our lives, whether it's fear of earthquakes and hurricanes, fear of starvation or fear of harm from our fellowman.

With all this fear in his sub-consciousness man must live in the high consciousness of self-preservation in order to keep his sanity. Wisdom is the key to a happy life, the wisdom to differentiate between selfish and selfishness. People with selfishness must forever feel lonely and unloved, because every time someone comes close to them calling for love, the selfishness pours **contempt** on them.

Put ten selfish people in a room and have everybody call for love. No call will get answered, and the weak will get weaker. It's a room filled with contempt, so everybody feels lonely and unloved.

On the other hand put ten kind people in a room, and the weak will get strong, because kindness pours love and everybody's call for love is answered. It's about people praising, saying kind words to each other, and uplifting each other. Friendship and love abound, and trust, hope and faith prevail.

When I love my brothers, I feel loved. A world creed for kindness.

Gratitude

Give thanks and praise for the gift of life. The optimist, the positive thinker, and people with high hopes and strong faith all have one thing in common: they have an attitude of gratitude. They say, "Thank you," "Please," "I appreciate that," "You're welcome," and "You are a good person."

As the world becomes more selfish, all these kind words have become few and far between. But these words of kindness are virtues that serve to uplift the spiritual integrity of the self and also uplift people in your presence. Every man lives to hear the words, "Thank you."

Wake up in the morning the man with gratitude thinks of many things to be thankful for. He sees the glass half-full, while the man who is thankless sees a half-empty glass.
Gratitude frees a man from the sorrows of blaming and complaining. It frees him from the vices of greed and envy and gives him a better chance for inner peace and happiness. Gratitude also decreases material desires. The man filled with gratitude can have nothing in this world and still have everything. His gratitude cultivates satisfaction, and it is satisfaction that cultivates inner peace and happiness.

Ingratitude is a cancer that eats away at the moral fabric of our society today. It has created a culture where people put things before people. They seek to find better relationships with machines than with people. We do not have to say, "Thank you," to a machine. Ingratitude is the enemy of loving relationships with people, but it's easy for them to fall in love with machines. Children who are not taught to give thanks grow up believing this world owes them something, and they have a very hard time in life.

There is something in the psyche of every man that makes him wonder about all the goodness and mysteries of nature. It fills his life with meaning to give thanks and praise to a higher power for all the goodness of nature. It can be said that religions grow out of man's need to give thanks and praise to a higher power for tender mercies and for health and strength and daily food. **Gratitude fills life with meaning**.

In America today we have an abundance of material riches but sadly, we also have an abundance of selfishness. Selfishness dries up the source of human love. There is an abundance of people thanking God for everything, but it is the source of human love that keeps humans alive in the crib, in sickness, and in very old and feeble age.

If we want a better world of love for our children, we must promote more gratitude for human love.

Truth/Reality
Truth is the light that takes man out from the darkness of ignorance. "The truth shall set you free." Truth is reality—the only reality.

In this age of technology we hold on to the illusion that information is the source of happiness. But misguided, misleading and even useless information today only causes confusion because wisdom and truth are no longer the golden rules.

"Man, know thyself." Only the truth is real, and only love is real, **so truth is love**. I am my true self only when I feel love. Anger, fear and self-doubt are only ego perception and are the illusions of the truth.

"Come Holy Spirit, let me see love. Let me see truth and take away my illusions of fear, anger and self-doubt.

A lie is an illusion. "Oh, what a tangled web we weave when we practice to deceive." Fools hold on to the illusion that if you don't get caught, there can be virtue in a lie. But every time we cheat or tell a lie, it diminishes the integrity of the self. When we don't get caught, we face a bigger danger of leaving the world of

200

reality and holding fast to an illusion that eats away at the moral integrity of our self.

Truth is the golden rule that promotes self-love and self-affirmation. "It's okay to cheat on my school test or tell a lie as long as I don't get caught" is the wisdom of a fool who has lost his grip on reality.

Since the beginning of time, man has been in a struggle searching for truth. The truth that is not only vital to his survival but it is also vital to his soul salvation. The great men of the ages are those who have uncovered the truth to show the way and the light. Science seeks the truth about the biological wisdoms of the body. Religions seek the truth and enlightenment about the spiritual wisdom of the soul, and psychology seeks the truth about the mental and emotional wisdom of the mind.

Who am I? How little of the truth do we know about ourselves? Man is born more animal than human. The baby that kicks, cries and screams, calling for love in the crib, behaves more like an animal than a human.

But let me tell all you super humans the bad news. The baby's nature is closer to God's creation than any adult human. The baby's nature is true to human nature—true wisdom, true instincts, true to all the virtues of nature than any adult.

To find the absolute truth about human nature, we must look in the crib.

In the crib we see man whole and holy, living centered in his soul. But in his egotistic way of living, **man pours contempt on his true soulful nature.** The adult human has lost the truth and reality of himself. He needs a spiritual rebirth to find himself.

Every adult in this ego-centered, materialistic society has to face contempt of his created soulful self, and so the truth of the inner self is lost. The big ego takes on the task to gain a world of vanity and illusion, trying to save a soul that is lost.

201

Who am I?

Only with truth, honesty and the wisdom of the soul can man find the answer to the question in a way that will take him out of the darkness of ignorance. Out of the illusions of fear and self-doubt and into the enlightened path of truth.

Truth is the path of inner peace and happiness.

ELEVEN

THE TEN BARRIERS TO LOVE

The "Course in Miracles" says love is the only reality in life, and the opposite of love is fear. But since love is all encompassing, love has no opposite. It's okay to say everything in life is love or if not, it's a call for love.

As we describe the ten virtues of love, we have defined the reality of love. We also describe each one as a **call** for love. The call is when we escape the reality of love and move into the illusion of fear. Because life is the celebration of love, when we move away from love, we move into the illusion of fear. We either love life or we live in the fear of life.

It's safe to say that in life's journey we experience either an open pathway to love as reality and truth or we experience barriers to love as fear and illusion. All the ten barriers to love are experiences of fear.

Imagine going down a highway in the light of love—cool, calm and collected. All of a sudden your headlights go out, and you must continue in darkness. You feel fear of fear itself and fear of the dark. You call out for love and call out for light. The darkness is real, but only because the light of love is gone.

Each one of these **ten barriers to love**, as you will see, puts us in the darkness and we are afraid of the dark. Love is faith, and with faith there is no darkness. Creation is light, and God said, "Let there be light." As light is full of love, darkness and fear are empty of love. That's why they call out for love.

The human soul knows only one reality—the reality of spiritual love. When we live in a soul-centered consciousness, we are in the **reality and faith** of "what is." But when we escape reality and move into an ego-centered living of fear and illusion, the ego lives in the **fear** of "what if." **What if something goes wrong, even when everything is right?**

In this chapter we will outline the ten vices as barriers to love that bring us into experiences of a loveless life of spiritual emptiness. All the joys and fulfillment in life are experiences of love, high self-esteem, high self-affirmation, gratitude, humility, and kindness. These and more are all manifestations of love—the virtues of love and the light that brightens our pathway. We see clearly a world that is real and true. We see only love, and we walk in the reality of faith and truth.

We do not walk in the **illusion and in the darkness of things only the eyes can see**. Our eyes will always deceive us because they must have the light from this world, a world where darkness abounds. But with faith, hope, kindness and humility, we walk with an inner light, the eternal light that burns from the source of the holy creation. It is the inner light of peace on earth goodwill to all men that is the strength of love. Love for God, love for self and love for thy brothers.

As one faces all these many barriers to love, we walk in the domain of the ego. The ego deals with fear and darkness and in the darkness, the ego must fight to open pathways to love. Sad to say, the ego's ways of love are with the sword of anger, fear and self-doubt, fighting and struggling with the outside world that calls for love, begging, "Love me, love me."

Some would say hate is the opposite of love. We say not so. We believe love is life's only reality and love has no opposite. Hate is

204

not the opposite of love but the absence of love. There are many who hate, and they can hate only if their hearts are empty of love.

A heart empty of love is wide open to hate because it is a heart in the terror of sorrow and a heart in fear of life. A heart empty of love is in more terror than a belly empty of food. An empty belly struggles to live, but an empty heart does not want to live.

Darkness and light. Every time we show loving kindness and forgiveness to others, we move into the infinite light of creation. Life is love, and we are in the celebration of life. But every time we show anger, arrogance and selfishness to someone, we move into the darkness of destruction, and we move into the fear of life. A selfish person will not find true happiness.

GOD IS LOVE
The loving grace of God is in every living soul. God's grace abounds in the souls of little children. But every adult has suffered some measure of spiritual separation from the grace of God. Unlike the innocent child, most adults live in the **consciousness of God—worship, prayer and praise—**to draw them closer, back into the grace of God. **Without the grace of God in the soul, life is empty and meaningless**.

Religions: Good And Evil
All the great religions practice God or god's consciousness, a supernatural higher power that keeps man in the light of spiritual love. All the great religions also are students and teachers of the ten virtues of love. They seek to unblock man's path to love, as well as to block his pathway to sin and self-destruction. They seek to open man's path to faith, hope and eternal salvation nesting in the light of creation. All religions seek spiritual consciousness.

I believe the Holy Bible is the best book ever written. It gives strength to *individuals* who go to it, and some have used that strength to show goodness and mercy to mankind. But too many use the strength to put a **holy label on evil actions against**

mankind. The evil man uses the Bible just a well as the righteous man.

The infant child, innocent and holy, has no consciousness of God but is filled with the grace of God. But the adult who knows good and evil and whose soul is contaminated with evil needs a religion. He needs to have a consciousness of an infinite holiness that will take him from the darkness of evil back into the truth and the light.

Man is born righteous, whole and holy. He is born in the bosom of God, innocent and whole. In his infant days of innocence, he has no religion, and he has no consciousness of God. In these days of innocence, he also is soul-centered and egoless—which is very important.

But the baby is a physical cripple and a mental midget and to stay alive, he needs constant tender loving care from humans. The baby is in a state of spiritual infancy and physical immobility. His path to love is not open until adult caregivers open it. Every adult is alive today because someone opened his path to love with some kind of care while he was a child.

The source of human love that opens the path to love in children is the savior of mankind. And at the same time the barriers to the source of human love has been and will forever be the destruction of mankind.

As the path to heaven, mankind must seek first the ten virtues of love as explained in this book. If he doesn't he will find himself in the darkness stumbling against the barriers of love on his way to hell.In the issue of human development, tender loving care to infants is the only way to take the infant in excellent development from spiritual infancy to spiritual maturity. Tender loving care opens the infant's path to love, the light is shining bright, and the candle is aglow.

At about three years old the ego comes into its own, and when it comes into the light, it surrenders to love in harmony and in oneness with the soul. The roots of spiritual maturity begin to

206

take root in the glory of light and love in the life of a person with tender loving feelings and tender loving ways. If the infant gets a lot of tender loving care, he or she feels loved and at about three years old, feels ready for the ego to enter. When the soul and the ego are aligned, the child will live all through life with inner peace and happiness.

On the other hand, a lack of tender loving care or neglect and abuse of the infant will put **barriers** on the infant's path to love. The light in the soul grows dim and dimmer, and soon, the soul is in distress. That's when the ego comes to the rescue of the body and the soul. However, in this case the ego comes not to surrender but with the sword **fighting to open the path to love.** The ego is the mental and mind capacity that takes about three years to develop.

The ten **virtues** of love are the ten **candles** that light the path to love. But the ten **barriers** of love are **swords** fighting to open the path to love. Love is everything in life. We either live in the light of love or we live in the darkness, fighting for love.

The Candle And The Sword
Life is a journey from cradle to grave. If we walk that journey in the light of love, we are like a candle. Darkness disappears wherever we are. In our glow of love—rooted in the source of the eternal light of love—we become the light of the world. On the other hand, if our journey is void of love, we walk in darkness with a sword in hand, fighting and struggling to remove the barriers of love that has robbed us of the light.

The soul-centered innocent child in spiritual infancy is transformed by this world of sin into an ego-centered adult of selfish materialism. And so it came to pass that the people journey from cradle to grave in a state of spiritual infancy.
Imagine an adult that still lives in a state of spiritual infancy. If he is unable to love, he is like a spoiled child. He still is programmed to receive but cannot give. He is selfish, possessed with anger and fear, unable to control his emotions. He wants everybody to show him love and attention, but he cannot show love to anyone.

It is said, "**Ye must be born again**." In this second birth we are capable of prayers, praise and worship. In this second birth we cry out *not* to human weakness and selfishness as we did before but to **God. "Save Me!"**

We can say the strength and virtue of all the great religions is rooted in man's hunger for love and spiritual maturity, from the strength of that infinite higher spiritual power. All we need is faith to take us out of the darkness of sin and spiritual emptiness into the light of spiritual righteousness and spiritual maturity.

The Ten barriers (1B to 10B) to love, we call the swords fighting for love.

The Candles

1A—Spiritual Maturity
2A—Faith
3A—Humility
4A—Self-Affirmation
5A—Wisdom
6A—Forgiveness
7A—Tranquility
8A—Kindness
9A—Gratitude
10A—Truth/Reality

The Swords

1B—Spiritual Infancy
2B—Fear
3B—Arrogance
4B—Self-Negation
5B—Ignorance
6B—Resentment
7B—Anger
8B—Selfishness
9B—Entitlement
10B—Illusion

Spiritual Infancy
Imagine a child, kicking and crying, blaming and complaining. It's crying for love, and it always wants to receive but is never able to give. It's unable to control its emotions. This is spiritual infancy, and it is rooted in anger and fear. If the child is given tender loving care soon, and very soon, all this spiritual infancy will grow into spiritual maturity.

The trouble is, too many adults grew up without feeling loved in childhood, and they're still in that state of spiritual infancy. They're starving for love and calling for love. "Please, please, please," they call to the outside world. "Give me some love and attention."

208

Spiritual infancy is okay for a helpless child because a child must be taken care of and receive love. **But life's journey of holiness must start in spiritual infancy with tender loving care to little children that comes from the source of human love and transcends into spiritual maturity with tender loving kindness in adults, in actions of human love.** We must be like a candle, each man a little light in the world.

The path to love is blocked for any adult who, like a child, is unable to give love. He must live in the darkness, always looking for love. He must fight the outside world with a sword in his battle for love. Or he can take to a religion that teaches him or her to find spiritual enlightenment and raise spiritual consciousness.

A baby that is left alone to cry helplessly for long hours feels the greatest terror on earth. "Love me or I'll die," he cries. "Pick me up or I'll die."

This is terror and hell. It's the reason for spiritual separation and it keeps people in spiritual infancy all through life's journey. It puts the adult in the darkness of ego-centered living. The ego takes up the sword to fight the outside world in a spiritual battle. It fights to escape inner darkness and for the light from an outside world of selfish materialism.

Loving parenting is the only road from spiritual infancy into spiritual maturity. Tender loving care from parents keeps the soul of the child in the light of spiritual bliss, which is spiritual maturity. When the ego comes into maturity, at about three years old, in the light of love, it surrenders to the soul without the fear of being conquered by the outside world.

Love, oh love. Thou be so tender and so sweet.

In the state of spiritual infancy, we seek **survival** in the dim light from the outside world. But in a state of spiritual maturity, we seek **salvation** from that bright inner eternal light in the soul. The biggest human dilemma is that we must seek survival before salvation and revenge before redemption. In times of dreadful human destructiveness, salvation is a luxury that the strong must ignore and the weak are denied.

I am the light of the world.

Fear
God bless America. We live in the land of the free and the home of the brave, and we have nothing to **fear but fear itself**.

Faith is the opposite of fear, and a faithless man lives in constant fear. While faith opens the path to love, fear blocks the path to love. Some say that faith in God is the savior of mankind. Faith in the goodness of mankind removes the fear of rejection, which is the barrier of friendship and trust.

If the path to love is blocked, fear enters the human soul. Life is love, and love is life. If love is blocked, life itself is blocked, and we live in fear of life. The fear of life is caused by an inner spiritual emptiness, an inner place where fear, anger and self-doubts lurk in the darkness.

But fear can be good. Since it's an inborn instinct seated in the psyche, it's the reason we run from danger and avoid pain. The fear of life is from an inner spiritual emptiness, while the fear of death is different. The fear of death is a consciousness of danger in a material world. The fear of life is an inner spiritual emptiness—man's deepest terror of walking half alive and half dead.

Today we say. "God bless America," and we are relatively free from the physical dangers of the outside world. American's greatest danger today is a fear that comes from the inner world. Our increasing selfish materialism is blocking our path to spiritual love, and as the light of love grows dim and dimmer, the darkness of fear grows darker as well.

People in America, let's love one another.
It's the only way to remove the inner darkness of fear.

The fear of being alone is one of the most terrifying feelings in human experience. This terrifying fear becomes rooted in our personality in our days of helplessness, before we can walk and talk. It begins in the days when our life depends on the source of human love. Left alone for too long in infant days, the fear of life haunts almost every human in this world of sin and selfishness. God said, "It is not good for man to be alone," so he gave man someone to love. As the story goes, however, Cane killed his brother and the darkness of fear covered all of creation.

My life can be described as a man of sorrow acquainted with grief against the world. I'm a man with a bubbling fear in my soul that causes me pain and robs me of the freedom to love. I've always felt lonely, because I felt nobody loved me. I feared that I was going to get sick and die, even though I was in perfect health. I was filled with anxiety and panic attacks. I was afraid of my shadow.

I feared if I moved toward any intimate relationship with any woman, she would reject me. My **fear** of **rejection** made me find fault with every woman who came close to me. I rejected them before they rejected me. Feeling rejected is one of the most painful feelings, even more painful than a broken arm.

Fear and anger

In every bout of anger there's some fear undertow, because fear and anger are two sides of the same coin. The source of this fear and anger, however, does not come from the outside world. It's an inner state of a broken spirit.

While fear is a flight mechanism, anger is a defense mechanism. A person with a broken spirit is in a constant state of flight from the issues of life. Fear puts a man in hell on earth, while anger is there to make sure he never gets to feel the hellfire of the fear. That's why some of the most fearful people never really feel the fear. Their anger protects them from feeling the fear.

Any experience of anger is painful and spiritually distressful, but anger is our weapon to fight against a deeper terror—**fear**. Fear is a potent energy bubbling in the bottom of the soul and it takes a lot of courage to even admit we have fear. It also takes a lot of

211

mental energy to suppress it. Fear even puts a lot of stress in the body, but let me say:

To every burst of anger, some fear is an undertow.

Mankind is born in a perfect state of being. The source of our living is a wellspring of emotion. We call it love and it flows from the soul into the heart and into the ocean of life, the outside world.

But this selfish materialistic world of sin and shame is very unkind to the flow of an infant's emotions of love, joy and infantile wildness. This world pours scorn on infantile behaviors, such as crying for love and attention. Every time the baby cries it gets a dirty look. Every time it's hungry, the world says wait, and when it jumps on the furniture it gets hollered at, "Go to school or sit still." The baby's spiritual emotional aliveness comes into conflict with this unkind world. The child must learn very quickly to dam-up its feelings.

The damming of feelings causes fear. The entire physical body gets uptight and ready to take flight from life. The neck is uptight, the belly aches, joints get stiff, and fear brings on every kind of psychosomatic sickness in the damming of feelings. Then the ego— uptight and angry at the outside world—comes into play with a sword to stop the flight and start fighting for survival.

A trembling soul a dam of fears, love is dammed, dammed up emotions, fear is everywhere.

Arrogance
Humility is like the bulldozer that opens the path to love, but arrogance is like the big oak tree that blocks the path of the bulldozer. This world of technology and super information gives us so much material prosperity, but as knowledge and intellectual power increases, arrogance also increases.

The arrogance of power, intellectual arrogance, has been the downfall of all the great nations in history. It seems today America is going down the path of the arrogance of power.

Love must grow in the soil of humility, which is for the humble and the meek. But the arrogance of power is the sword, so it is much mightier than humility. Love is only mighty when it is able to surrender without the feeling of being conquered by the sword. Power can be holy and it can be a friend to love, but only when it is mixed with humility.

Power mixed with boasting, false pride, egoism and arrogance is the enemy of love. An arrogant man pours contempt on every weakness he sees in his brother, and he cuts himself off from brotherly love. A humble man pours kindness on his brother's weakness and becomes his brother's keeper. Humility is the way to friendship and trust, and the way to promote the brotherhood of man.

Self Negation

Self-affirmation is the manifestation of self-awareness, self-expression and self-control. Self-love is at the root of self-affirmation, which is a very good way to build self-esteem. But man must first build self-love before true self-affirmation can be experienced. He must have the integrity of self-love—must **know** himself through self-examination—before he can truly affirm himself.

Self-negation gets in the way of self-love by weakening integrity and bringing low self-esteem. It can even destroy the integrity of the self. Too many people can experience self-affirmation only when another person affirms them. This way of living also stands in the way of self-love and lowers self-esteem. For every time man feels affirmed, he often feels negated ten times. Somebody comes and bursts his bubble.

The best way to lower self-esteem is to experience negation. This occurs when a man cannot stand firm in honor, trust, truth, forgiveness, faith and last but the least, love. If he cannot stand firm and steadfast in these things, he is on the path of self-negation and the path of diminishing self-esteem. He must be very careful and wise in how he seeks self-affirmation.

213

The **ego** has many ways to deceive. A man on an ego trip may feel confident about himself and confident about making himself feel good. But in the ego's ways of doing things, self-affirmation is just an illusion. The ego's ways of giving is to give to control, not to fulfill but to glorify the self. This way of giving diminishes the integrity of the self.

The ego says, "If giving to others is without joy, then I can only feel good about myself when I give to myself." This is a false ego assumption.

Giving from the heart is the gift of love, and love is self-affirming. But to the man on an ego trip, giving to others becomes a vice and giving to himself seems a virtue. He goes on ego-tripping and seeks self-affirmation in selfishness, as he plunges himself deeper and deeper into self-negation. In the ego's way of self-affirmation, self-love is only an illusion because giving brings sorrow and receiving brings joy. There will be a quick burst of self-affirmation but in the long run, the ego only brings self-negation.

Seek self-affirmation as the path to love.

Ignorance
Wisdom is the virtue that lights the path to true love, which is an instinctive emotional experience. Wisdom and truth are the sources of happiness. This is the age of information and technology, but machines can only be a conduit for wisdom and truth, not the source of them. Machines cannot be the source of happiness.

I'd rather be the wise man with little information than the foolish man with all the information in the world. Little children have more wisdom to love than some men with Ph.D.s. It's said, "He who knows not and knows not that he knows not is a fool." He has a double dose of ignorance and has lost his chance to be wise.

The most self-defeating aspect of ignorance is the man who thinks he knows it all. He doesn't listen to anyone and he cannot learn anything. Most damaging of all he cannot love anyone but the ego-image of himself.

Knowledge increases wisdom and information increases knowledge. Wisdom, knowledge and understanding are the foundation of love. These three will remove the darkness of ignorance and light the path to love. There's a saying, "If you think education is expensive, try ignorance." But it's the quality of the education that counts, not just the quantity.

Some of the wisest people in the world have no higher education, but they are not ignorant because they learned the knowledge of love. They are smart in many ways, such as how to make money, how to spend it wisely, how to invest some wisely, and how to save some. Some of the wisest people in the world are self-educated.

The quality information grants the wisdom of kindness. Quality information enlightens my self-examination to make me a better person. But most of all, quality information gives me the wisdom to build loving relationships with family and friends.

Resentment
Forgiveness is a gift unto one's self—the act itself is self-fulfilling. On the other hand, any kind of resentment is self-negating.

Every human who lives long enough to be an adult has sometime in the past had their feelings hurt by someone they expected to show them love. Whenever we are hurt or wounded, anger is the natural response. Resentment puts it mildly. For the wounded, forgiveness is the only way to salvation and redemption.

The deepest kind of resentment is caused by not feeling loved in childhood. If we did not feel loved, it could take a lifetime of blaming and complaining about the world and not being aware of the early hurts that are the source of our grief. People who have been hurt in early childhood live a life of contempt for people who are close to them.

Wounds that were open in childhood are the most painful and the most difficult to forgive. Most of the time the owner of this contempt blames present conflicts for the source of his grief. He lives an unfulfilled life of resentment and sees no need to forgive.

It makes no difference who happens to be right or wrong. Anger and resentment still eat away at man's ability to love and become a barrier to love. For people with resentment against anything, any person or any place, forgiveness is the only path to inner peace. Often we see people who run away from themselves and can never settle down emotionally. This is a sign of inner hurts buried alive in the bottom of the soul. The only salvation is to run into the arms of forgiveness.

Dark clouds of sorrow from days of my youth plunged my soul into the valley of resentment. These sorrows of my resentment were against a world that failed to open my path to love. To the world out there, I kept crying, "Give me a light, give me a light," and my resentment kept falling on anyone who failed to light my candle. My ego became an ally of my resentment, wrestling with the outside world and seeking a light from a world that I happened to resent.

In my loneliness fear of the darkness gripped my soul. My resentments against the outside world made my darkness darker and darker. I needed love and attention from a world that I resented. I became a man of sorrow, with fear and grief against my world. I was in a dreadful dilemma.

But forgiveness was like bleach—it washed away the stains of resentment that put dark spots on my soul. Forgiveness lit the candle on my path to love.

Every child born in this world of selfish materialism, who receives an inadequate amount of tender loving care, holds some kind of resentment against this selfish world. But this resentment, or even anger, must be buried because the child depends on people for living. As a result, many people have bad feelings against a world they cannot live without. Resentment and anger

216

seek revenge at the same time that our souls are starving for love. We need redemption.

What is the answer to this dilemma? It's simple. He who needs redemption must first give up all resentments.

Forgiveness of others is my only escape from the darkness of anger and resentment, my only escape from the darkness of blaming and complaining. Forgiveness lights my path to love. Forgiveness is my salvation.

Anger

Tranquility is that inner peace that puts man in the arms of love and happiness. On the other hand, any kind of anger disrupts spiritual calm and is a barrier to love.

Let it be understood that anger is a positive emotion. It's one of the three primary emotions, and the other two emotions are love and fear. If someone or something is coming to hurt you, your anger gives you extra physical strength and courage to fight back. If the path to love is blocked, it is your anger that takes up the sword to fight to open the path to love.

We start our journey in life with the emotional instinct of anger, but this anger is only to be expressed when something is life threatening. Look what happens to the helpless infant, a life without tender loving care *is* threatened. Any child that is denied loving care is angry at the world.

The baby's cry is instinctive anger fighting for life itself. It is a soulful expression of sorrow and anger. Because a baby is in a state of helplessness and spiritual infancy, it must cry for love. If the cry for love is answered every time, then the darkness of sorrow and anger is removed. The baby will grow up with a tranquil soul and spiritual materiality.

This world of selfish materialism diminishes our ability to love. As a result, most adults are angry at the world. Their inner anger sees a world that's ready to attack, so it's only wise to attack first. And because anger sees the world as a place with bad people, it travels with fear. It drives out inner peace and tranquility.

Ours is a world of good and evil, anger and tranquility. We must accept our anger, while we remember that it is grief. We also must realize that wrong thinking precedes every burst of anger.

We must change our way of looking at the world before we can stop being angry. There is always a better way, a different way to look at whatever is causing us to be angry.

After the initial burst of anger I say to myself, "I don't want this grief. I want to see this differently." I also pray to the Holy Spirit, "Let me see this in some way that will bring me tranquility."

Most the time our anger is caused by an ego illusion, seeing something that is not there. The brother who makes me angry is not a bad person. He is just calling for love, but I pour my anger on his call for love.

Call the Holy Spirit into your life to take away the anger from your soul and give you inner peace and tranquility. If there is tranquility in your soul, there is no place for anger. When your inner world changes, all the bad people in the outside world suddenly become good people.

Selfishness
It is said that self-preservation is the first law of nature. Too many people use this to glorify selfishness. **Selfishness does not work**. He who is too selfish is lonely and unable to love. He is cut off from any spiritual connectedness with his fellowman.

Selfishness may be the first law for *survival* but *kindness* is the first law of *salvation*. To those who merely want to survive, I say, "Go ahead, be selfish. But be ready to accept an empty and lonely life without love."

If your life is lonely and you wonder why the world is so selfish and uncaring, there is something you can do about it. Instead of always wanting people to help you, try the habit of always helping somebody else. Ask not what someone can do for you but each day, ask what you can do for someone.

I am my brother's keeper. When I love my brother I feel loved.

All the great religions teach the virtue of kindness. Acts of kindness fill the soul with the joy of spiritual love. Think about the Supreme Being who has unconditional kindness for even the most selfish people who worship him. There is no more comforting feeling than to know there is one who never fails to be kind to us.

The trouble with the world today is the abundance of human selfishness and the short supply of human kindness. A world without kindness is a world where people, even little children, are programmed to receive. It's a world of selfish people, people who pour contempt on acts of kindness. In a world where selfishness pours contempt on others weaknesses, the weak get weaker and only the strong survive.

Selfishness breeds a culture of contempt and materialism, where the ethical and spiritual fabric of the culture are in a state of corrosion because it's every man for himself.

In a culture of selfishness, sometimes our most selfish acts are words that hurt other's feelings. Words of "blaming and condemning" are evidence of the sorrow in man's soul. It makes him hurt the feelings of other people every time he speaks.

Burdened with our own selfish attitude, we are unable to consider other people's feelings. Instead, we always have an irresistible need to vent our own wounded feelings. A selfish man is a lonely man. Even his wife and children cannot get close to him, because every word he says glorifies his ego image of himself and nullifies the image of others

Self-righteousness promotes selfishness. It's all about the ego— all the kind words must be about us, and we feel put down by people who fail to see our glory.

America is the richest country in the world. We have an oversupply of material wealth, and we have a good supply of generous people who give away some of their oversupply of material things. But we also have is an **undersupply** of spiritual wealth, an undersupply of kind words. As a result, we have spiritual emptiness.

If we are to walk the path of brotherly love, we must leave footprints of **kind words** in the soul of every brother we talk with.

It is very strange how selfish people find it hard even to say kind words. They feel as if they are losing something with every act of kindness. The fail to understand that there is nothing better to lift and fill the spirit than **words of kindness**. Words like, "I love you," are sometimes the greatest acts of kindness. Others include "Thanks," "You're a good person," and "You look good today."

Praising someone can be the greatest act of kindness. Praising your child can be the greatest self-esteem builder. Words of praise are great acts of spiritual kindness, and even listening to someone can be very kind.

To every parent who says a college education is the best thing they can give their child, I tell them, "A good education starts with high self-esteem, and high self-esteem starts with kind and loving words."

On the other hand, unkind and selfish words wound the very soul of the child. Unfortunately, these wounds can last a lifetime and can lower self-esteem. In this selfish world a man can grow old and never hear a kind word.

Selfishness promotes greed, envy, loneliness and materialism, all the barriers to love. But kindness promotes compassion, friendship, humility and spiritual connectedness among people. Selfishness is a dark cloud on the path to love, but kindness is the light shining bright on the path to love.

Entitlement

There is none more ungrateful and so disgusting than he who thinks he is entitled to everyone's generosity.

The attitude of gratitude is, "I am thankful for everything I receive." But the attitude of ingratitude is, "I am entitled to more than I receive." Gratitude promotes joy and satisfaction. Entitlement promotes greed and disappointment.

A person with the attitude of entitlement feels no need to show love to his fellowman, because he believes he is entitled to love from them. He is an adult but living like a helpless little child.

Entitlement is a self-defeating vice and it's a big barrier to love. It promotes a kind of selfishness that destroys loving relationships with family and even relationships with strangers. The attitude of ingratitude is, "Why do I need to thank someone for giving me something that is my God-given right?"

Entitlement is a trap. It gives you an unquenchable desire to use and abuse others. It builds you up every time someone is nice to you and lets you down every time someone refuses to show you kindness. You live in misery because for every time you get lifted up, you get let down ten times. Entitlement promotes ungratefulness and as my mother use to say, "Ungratefulness is worse than witchcraft."

This world of materialism and selfishness promotes spiritual emptiness. Any kind of inner emptiness promotes an obsessive attitude of wants and desires. Because we live more in a material than a spiritual consciousness, we are programmed to look to the material world to fill our spiritual emptiness. Every obese person is trying to fill a spiritual emptiness. Every action of greed is trying to fill a spiritual emptiness.

As infants we were not spiritually empty but all our wants and desires had to be filled by the outside world or we would not have lived to become adults. Every adult alive today owes much *gratitude* to the source of human love.

221

But the source of human gratitude to other humans is in dangerously short supply. There are too many people who can give praise only to God and cannot love their fellowman. This world needs more people praising people.

When I awake in the morning, is my glass half full or is it half empty? It depends on my attitude of gratitude or ingratitude. It depends on whether I give thanks for some of the good things in my life, or if I'm going to "blame and complain" about all the things I am entitled to.

I am entitled to life, liberty and the pursuit of happiness. In reality, in order for me to have and hold these things, I must be grateful to every person who helps open my pathway to all my entitlements.

Illusion

The "Course in Miracles" says, "Love is the only reality in life, anything that is not love is just an illusion. What is truth? Truth is reality, truth is life, truth is love and love is life."

An illusion is to believe or to see something that is not there. If something is true it means it is factual. But the truth is subjective, and a lie is the intent to deceive. Many times ignorance or a lack of knowledge stand in the way of truth. At the same time, they are the mothers of illusion.

The truth is God created me with value and virtue equal to every other man. What happens if I don't know this simple truth? Then my truth is covered in darkness and in my darkness, the illusion grows and grows that I am worth the exact amount of attention people pay me. But every long lasting illusion only lives because the illusion is planted in the garden of truth, which in turn is covered in darkness.

Fear also feeds an illusion, when we are afraid to face the truth. If love is the only reality, everything that is not love is an illusion. In our selfish society today, it's safe to conclude that the illusion of love is more abundant than the reality of love.

222

The truth is, man cannot live without love. Love is the truth, love is the light and love is the way of life. Even when the truth is covered with darkness, in the darkness there is still love. Someone calling for love is the illusion of love.

Truth in the darkness is the mother that nurtures every illusion.

How do we get rid of an illusion? Shall a mother kill her child? No! The child must find the light and escape into a new birth of truth and light. There are many ways to destroy an illusion but only light can reveal the truth.

Suppose you try to destroy someone's illusion just by telling him all the wrong things he is doing. He'll get angry with you. Now, suppose you give him the truth and the light. He will quickly escape the illusion. People will hold on to an illusion with their life and will only let go after the truth is revealed.

Truth and illusion are the best of friends. We use the subjective truth to defend our illusions. Never ask a man to give up his illusions, just give him the light. The illusion is like a termite, it cannot live in the light.

Enlightenment is the best antidote for any illusion. In our selfish world of spiritual emptiness, illusions often blossom and flourish in the garden of truth. Enlightenment is the only thing that can set us free to embrace the truth.

All the great religions seek the path of enlightenment as the way to salvation. All the great religious books and writings are documents of spiritual enlightenment. We pray for wisdom, knowledge and understanding. Man cannot find joy in life without truth and love, so enlightenment is the only way to destroy illusions. It reveals the truths that give us the freedom to love.

My experience with love, truth and illusion is a long story. Let me give one example. All of my life I felt unloved, alone, and in sorrow with feelings of rejection. I built my hope of happiness on getting rich, thinking money would make me happy. The truth is

223

we can't live without money and material things. But my truth about material things was wrapped up in the illusion that material things would let me escape all my sorrows and fulfill my deep hunger for love.

I had built for myself a very strong and high wall in my darkness. I held fast to my wall of illusion of material desire because I held it as the **truth.** I got very angry with anyone who stood in the way of my material progression.

My illusion brought me into the valley of the shadow of death. It was after my second divorce, when I was fifty years old. I had plenty of money in the bank and I was in good health. But there was a day when I did not want to live. **My empty life without love was not worth living**.

How did I go from illusion to reality? Just getting rid of my material possessions only left me in the darkness, hungry and broke. *I needed enlightenment*. That is why for the past thirty years, I have been reading books, saying prayers, meditating, consulting psychotherapists, and reading the Bible. I even took the "Course in Miracles."

I do this in an effort to know myself and the world around me and in an effort to seek truth, wisdom and understanding. (My mother used to pray for all her children to get wisdom, knowledge and understanding.)

Truth is the light but without wisdom and enlightenment, the light is buried under a bushel of dark clouds. Illusions conquer the truth. My perception of truth about materialism was wrapped up in an illusion that put me in fear of life and caused loneliness, emotional pain and sorrow. It left me in spiritual emptiness.

In my pursuit of happiness, I write about these "Ten Virtues of Love." Every one of these virtues is the truth, the light and the way to love. Then I write about the "Ten Barriers to Love." Every one of these ten barriers feed the weeds of illusion growing in the garden of truth.

Enlightenment is the only way from darkness to light. We must know the truth about kindness before we can destroy the illusion of selfishness. We must first know the truth—kindness brings fulfillment and selfishness brings inner emptiness—before we can let go of the illusion of selfishness.

We also must know the truth about faith before we can destroy the illusion of fear, and we must know the truth about spiritual fulfillment before we can destroy the illusion of material desires.

Last but not least, I must learn the truth and reality about Asher before I can escape the darkness of my illusions about happiness. First, last and always I must seek enlightenment. I will continue to read the Bible and all the other holy books of religions. There are many spiritual books out there. Every one of my illusions is like a termite, afraid of the darkness. And so I will seek the enlightenment that reveals the truth and lights my path to love and happiness.

Light: Truth. Illusion: Darkness
Every illusion is like a termite, afraid of the light. But illusions feed on the fabric of truth and flourish only when the truth is covered in darkness. Bringing the truth into the light is the way to destroy any illusion. Faith is one of the ten virtues that removes the darkness and brings truth into the light.

Truth and light destroy all fears and illusion.

If the man who has a crippling fear of snakes sees a stick lying in the dark, he will start to panic. Telling him the truth may not diminish his fear as long as the stick still lies in the dark. But turn the light on the stick and the truth is revealed. His fear and illusion will be destroyed.

Born True And Holy
Mankind is born perfectly rooted in the wholeness of life, born in the consciousness of pure spiritual love as the only reality in life. Mankind is born knowing the truth and the light and on the way to salvation.

At birth the infant has no illusions about love and life. It's pure truth, pure light and pure love totally immersed in a unified self. But look at the baby just after birth, lying of its back. It cannot move, can't even put hand to mouth to feed itself. The survival of every infant is up its adult caregivers—often ego-centered, materialistic, sinful and shameful caregivers.

In today's modern world, caregivers who do not provide an adequate amount of loving care contaminate a child's soul. The creator created every baby, but until the creator comes down and feeds and comforts the baby, this world of sin is going to lead every child into the path of unrighteousness.

Every time the child cries to an adult for love and attention, some small amount of inner spirit is lost. The baby cries and cries with fear until ego steps in to stop the flight of fear. The ego uses anger and resentment to fight for survival and calm down the child. When the child stops crying, ego triumphs. Faith in mankind is lost. The truth about self, love and happiness is lost.

As a result, when the child cooks his first pot of food, he becomes selfish and materialistic, and he pours scorn on love. But God loves him and God will save him. However, if he does not believe in a God, he will say, "I must save myself." The atheist has lost faith in everything.

By the time the infant learns to walk and talk, some of this wholeness is lost. Some truth is lost, some light is lost, and the child is plunged into the darkness of an illusion. The illusion is about what it takes for love and happiness. As the child grows, so does the illusion, the illusion that selfishness and materialism leads to love and happiness. The child does need selfish materialism to survive, so the illusion is rooted in some truth. But truth covered with darkness makes illusions grow.

The illusion is like a flashlight in the dark showing the way to survival. That's why mankind will cling to an illusion with dear life. But mankind needs more than just to survive. He needs salvation, and the only safe way to rid himself of his illusions is to love.

We must learn to love again. We must experience a spiritual rebirth that lets us walk in the light and salvation of love. And in the light of love we will throw away the flashlight.

"I am the light of the world, forgiveness is my salvation, and gratitude is my attitude."

TWELVE

SPIRITUALITY AND RELIGIONS

Creation: Soul Of An Infant

A baby is born with pure love and pure spirit with plenty of faith in the bosom of creation and celebrating life. It is a place of pure love, filled with the grace of God.

Religion has no place where the baby lies. All the Holy Books are written for adults and all have conflicts with love and the nature of the child. Many children of deeply religious families grow up feeling unloved. I believe a child can be taken to religious school to learn about a higher spiritual power and moral and ethical ways of living, but the way of religions is obedience, while the way of the child is love.

A baby is not born in sin. It is born in a sinful world shaped in iniquity, but the soul of a baby is pure and holy. The source of spiritual love that bubbles in the baby is more plentiful than that in any adult. The baby's breathing is deep, its body grows fast, and it learns quickly. Every baby is like a brand new Rolls Royce in perfect shape.

God never makes a mistake, so everything is created in perfect shape. Look at the vast expanse of creation. Everything is

229

wonderfully perfect and holy, and mankind cannot be the only exception.

The difference is mankind has choices. He has high ego-consciousness, and the ego makes choices of good or evil. The ego is an earthly creation. It sins and makes holy wars. At the end of life man is separated, soul from ego. His soul goes to heaven and his ego goes to hell. God repossess the soul and the devil takes the ego. Heaven must be an egoless place.

The fate of mankind is to break the string from the puppet master. He ceases to *BE*, and he becomes a co-creator. He becomes all he can BE and lives up to all the glory of his human potential.

Let's look at mankind in the good old days after birth but before the ego comes to dominate his personality. As shown in the hand illustration, on the back cover, we are imbued with the grace of God. We have no concept or consciousness of God but make no mistake about it, these egoless days are the Godliest days of our lives.

Any adult who loves the baby will be drawn close to God. Look at the smile on the baby's face—its worth more than anything money can buy. The baby has no sin, no shame, no evil thoughts, and no evil actions. It's just pure love, faith, and spirit.

In a baby's personality, faith is strong. It's a faith rooted in a deep lust for life, an open active lust that moves the baby to kick and cry if the mother—the support of life—moves out of sight. Ego-centered adults see this kicking and crying as disobedience and even sin. It takes strong faith to learn to walk and talk. It is said that by the time a child is six years old, it has learned half the lessons it will learn for the rest of its life.

All babies need is love, some milk and a warm, soft loving body to lie on. Babies do not get depressed and worry about life. They live in the moment, and they live in celebration of life. Jesus said, "Suffer little children to come unto me for such is the kingdom of heaven."

Grace Of God

Babies are born filled with the grace of God and filled with a spiritual grace that flows from the infinite source of creation. Their spirit-fullness is manifested in emotional feelings that flow from the soul to fill the heart with love, the mind with inspiration, and the flesh with life.

This spirit-emotional grace is the source of life for every man, from the first day of life to the last. Even when a man who is totally empty of spirit and love takes his own life, as many men have done. Mankind is a spiritual being that lives in a material body. The spirit is life, and the body is just the consumption of life for the short time each man lives.

The soul of an infant is pure and holy, like a freshly minted coin without a scratch or a blemish. It is not like the adult soul, which is contaminated, battered and bruised. To prove it, hold a baby in your arms, look into its eyes, and ask yourself one question. "Is this sin and shame or just pure love?" If this is your child ask yourself, "Did God make a mistake by creating something that is sinful or is this pure love?"

The book of Genesis contains a lot of violence, but when I look at a baby in my arms, I see pure love. I ask myself, "Should my religion teach me about creation or is this creation in my arms?"

If they believe babies are sinful and unholy, it's easy for self-righteous adults to neglect or even abuse little children. My mother was deeply rooted in her Christian beliefs—more than any other person I know. But her Christian beliefs came onto conflict with raising her children. Throughout my life, I've noticed that some of the most deeply rooted religious people are the worst fathers and mothers.

Self-righteous people who force or even punish a child to bring it to God do not understand the virtues of human loving kindness. The child grows up rebelling against them and their patents' Gods.

In fact, some preachers' children are the most rebellious of all.

231

They rebel with every kind of chemical addiction, they wind up in prison, and they can't find happiness in life. They have every kind of emotional problems, but if they're lucky, they may end up in church praising God for his saving grace.

All the religions of today fail to adequately promote the tender loving care of children. There is a conspiracy of silence among all religions about loving children. While religions try to save man from spiritual emptiness, their jobs would be much easier if they spent more time nurturing the soulfulness of spiritual birth and nurturing the innocence and gracefulness of little children.

Religions And The Soul
All the great religions believe there is a soul in man. They believe in the spiritual essence of mankind and believe spiritual significance is a greater virtue than material significance. Religions never promote any virtues in the flesh. Instead, they promote spiritual virtues, morals and ethical principles.

The soul that is the spiritual essence of mankind is mentioned many, many times in all the scriptures and religious writings. But it is hardly ever explained. It's just assumed that the soul is the innermost spiritual part of us. Religions fail to promote the spiritual purity and absolute truth and light of the infant's soul as shown in the hand graphics.

The soul is the seat of man's emotional life. He who suppresses his feelings suppresses the expression of his soul and feels a spiritual emptiness inside. Soulful expressions are spiritual, and emotional expressions are soulful. They are the innermost expressions of the self.

Love is the soul-filled expression of a spirit-filled life. But anger and fear are soul-filled expressions of a broken spirit. Love is the normal expression of life, while anger is the emotional force to defend life, and fear is a desire for flight from life. A person who is empty of love has plenty of fear inside and is always running away from himself. He runs so he will never have to feel the terror and fury of the fear.

I believe only the things that unite souls can unite the human race. Until religions become more soul-centered and less ego-centered, there will be no peace on earth goodwill to *all* men.

If babies could walk and talk, they would unite the world. This would happen because babies do not have an ego, which is the agent of fear. Babies live a soul-centered life, a life of love and unity.

If we want peace on earth goodwill to all men, we must be as humble and have as strong a faith in humanity as a little child. We must live centered in the expression of the soul, not of the ego.

Some will say babies are narcissistic and selfish, not loving and kind. Indeed, it may seem that way when babies cry for everything. Also, they have no material things to give and in this world, everybody sees love only in a material light. But I believe babies are loving and kind. Their souls are filled with love, and they have a loving smile and hugging ways. Babies' emotional and intimate connections with their mothers are stronger than any two adults could have for each other. Babies' expressions of love are spiritual expressions flowing from the soul into the heart and into the outside world. Babies love the whole world with pure love. They cannot have any hate, greed or envy, but only those who live in a spiritual light can understand this kind of love.

The higher self, the self that is pure and holy, is created from the spiritual fountain of life. The soul is the core of this innermost self and at the root of the significance of the self. The man who has lost his soul has lost the significance of his higher self and lives with a self that is alienated from the source of creation. He has moved from the light of the celebration of life into the darkness and the fear of life.

All religious dogma and doctrines written in books are ego-centered documents. They cannot compare to the divine virtue flowing in the soul of a little child who cannot read or write a book. Babies don't have to read about love. They *feel* it, and they *express* it.

233

Child abuse is very widespread in this selfish materialistic world, because we have failed to fully comprehend the holiness of children. We've failed to understand that to love a child is the most spiritual act on earth. People who love God will not neglect or abuse something that is holy. They will understand that the most holy place on earth is the place where babies lie.

People of God must realize the most holy thing they can do is love little children. People "talk the talk" of holiness, but to "walk the walk" in the path of righteousness they must nurture with love the grace of God in the souls of little children. The way to unite the world is for every adult to pour love into the soul of every child in every part of the world.

If we could love little children with holy and absolute spiritual love, every prison would close, every drug dealer would be out of business, and most the sins of the world would cease to be.

Because religions have so shamefully neglected to promote the soulfulness and holiness of babies, most religious people are unable to understand the need for tenderness and love in little children. Deeply religious people fail to understand babies' emotional aliveness and how it needs to be nurtured if the child is to grow up with a satisfied soul and a life filled with meaning and high self-esteem.

Babies do not need the golden rules—they need unconditional love. When the child cries for love and misbehaves to get attention, do not tell the child what the Bible says. Man wrote the Bible, but the soul of the child is rooted in the spirit of God. When a child cries out for some of your love, please give it unconditionally.

Every baby's cry is a soulful expression of the lust for life. The cry is a deep emotional expression of the soul. It unites body, mind and soul in yearning for life. Every baby's cry is a defeat for the celebration of life and a triumph for fear.

In fear, the baby calls to the mother, "Come feed me, come lift me up, and come give me life." If the mother gets angry, or gives

234

the child an angry look or the "evil eye," it frightens the child. From that the child learns to suppress its emotional expressions and the spiritual aliveness of its soul. The child suppresses soulful expressions, cries no more, grows up and gets tough. But he is left with a broken heart. He is spiritually separated, his soul is lost, and he must go on an ego trip to gain the world.

Too many people who grew up in religious homes do not believe in God. Or they rebel against God because of the terrible way they have been treated by people of God in their childhood. Too many people who grew up in religious homes have lost their soulful emotional expressions.

Most of these people do not even understand the loss of soulful expressions. They see them without any significant self-expression. They see them mired in self-doubt and insecurity, and they rebel against themselves and the outside world. They rebel with anger, fear, low self-esteem, selfishness, and every kind of chemical addiction.

I believe discipline is a vital part of raising children, but good discipline is a component of love. The parent who loves the child will discipline the child in a loving way, knowing that good discipline is what strengthens the integrity of the self. Love without good discipline can be said to be a lack of love.

Plenty of love mixed with good disciplined is the formula for a happy life filled with meaning. The formula is to love first, listen to the child's thoughts and feelings second, and discipline last. If you want your children to grow up to be happy, this is the formula. It's not about how much money you spend on the child. Too many rich people's children are not happy.

All religions teach about the virtues and the light of spiritual consciousness. They teach about spiritual enlightenment and aim to light the path back into the kingdom of the soul to find God. But religions must start teaching more aggressively about the glory of **spiritual birth,** and all the religions of today must unite under one philosophy of holy spiritual birth. Until they do that, peace on earth goodwill to all men will be only an illusion, and wars and rumors of wars will be our reality.

One religion of Spiritual Birth will unite the world. Every man will be his brother's keeper, and brotherly love will be the revolution to unite the world.

The philosophy of holy spiritual birth would change the world. Every religion would find common ground in spiritual wholeness and would unite all of humanity with one spirit of holiness. Religious leaders would all look to little children for lessons of holiness and we could have one big book of holiness that is used by all religions. Then it would be easy to love children.

What a wonderful world this would be, a world with one Brotherhood of Man, one God, one spirit, one creation, one religion of love.

Self-Possession And The Soul

Babies have full self-possession. They have full unity of self—body, mind and soul—and total inner peace. Babies have the ability to deeply express every part of the self with full emotional integrity. Babies are emotionally and soulfully vibrant and free, and their passionate love for life and the joy and fulfillment of the soul is strong.

If all this self-possession in little children is true, then why do some religions teach self-denial so the spirit of God may be strong within? Instead some religions teach, "I should decrease so that God will increase in me." This kind of religious teaching fails to understand the inner quality of the self. There is the soulful self and the ego self. Spiritual separation is *dis*-unity between soul and mind/ego.

The soulful self is rooted into the grace of God from the day we are born. Man is born soulful, innocent, holy and pure. If one loses this soulfulness, he loses the inner grace of God, no matter what his belief. Some atheists are very loving people. They're good fathers and good brothers, and they have the grace of God in them, even though they deny it.

236

Before anyone teaches denial of self, they should differentiate between the soulful self and the ego-full self. The soulful self is created in the spiritual image of God, and man became a living soul. If we lose our soulfulness we lose God, and we are alienated from God because we have lost our soul.

Religions spend all their time studying the nature of God and too little time studying human nature. Human nature in the way we are born is filled with soulful spiritual essence and significance.

At birth the baby is egoless, and the ego takes about three to six years to fully develop. The ego develops into each person's mind to disobey God and please the outside world. The ego's role is to move mankind from the consciousness, the truth and the light of pure spirit and pure love. It moves into the darkness and illusion of material consciousness.

Many religious activities are just a journey into the spiritualization of the ego in order to dim material consciousness. If religions would teach nurturing and sheltering of the soulful self, then every child would be given plenty of unconditional love. Then as the child grows older and into ego domination, religions should teach denial of the ego self. Decrease of the ego self means increases of the soulful self.

Next time you hold a little baby in your arms, look deeply into its eyes and say, "This is the spiritual image of God. I must nurture it and water it with unconditional love so that the grace of God may increase."

If You Can Read This…

If you can read this chapter, you are old enough to understand about who are you, and I have good news and bad news for you.

I'll give you the good news first because there's plenty of it. You were born pure, innocent, whole and holy. You came out from the pod of creation seeking only to be loved. You were emotionally and spiritually alive, and your soul was filled with the grace of God. You were a child of God.

When your mother first picked you up, put you on her chest and gave you the breast, you were in paradise. You were totally united within the self, totally in love with self and totally in love with your world and all the people around you. Love was your only reality. If she fed you with milk every few hours and kept you in her arms or at her side twenty-four-seven, you stayed in your paradise for a little while longer.

In the months after birth the whole universe was your playground. You saw everything you looked at through the eyes of love. Your breathing was deep and strong, joy abounded, and you were in a place of spiritual bliss. Your were born free—free from hate, free from envy, free from greed, and free to give and forgive. Even though you have nothing to give but a loving smile. You were free from materialism.

When you were born you had no sin and no shame. You were not even conscious of your nakedness, just like Adam and Eve before they ate the apple. Tender loving care was all you desired and as long as you got it, you were satisfied. Your soul was satisfied, and your heart was satisfied. Your paradise was a warm and tender lap, a warm and tender chest and a breast to lie on. If they had offered you all the world's riches, you would have ignored it for just one drop of milk from the breast and a warm and tender body to hold you.

When you were born you had full spiritual and emotional self-possession. You could cry deep, deep tears one minute laugh the next and get angry the next. You had total emotional and spiritual freedom.

Free to be everything God created you to be, free to grow and reach the fullness of all human potential. Free from the fear and fury of an empty life. Free to love life, free to live in the celebration of life. "Unless ye be like a little child, ye cannot enter the kingdom of heaven," Jesus said. When you were a little child the kingdom of heaven was within you. You came into this world in a Spiritual Birth, and the kingdom of heaven was in you. You had no religion—you did not need one. It's only after you have been with ego and

238

been spiritually separated that you come to know sin and shame. Today you need redemption. Every adult needs a Spiritual Rebirth.

Self-righteous parents who say they must take a child to God make a big mistake. The child is Godlier than any adult can be, and loving a child will bring the adult closer to God.

Now For The Bad News
If you can read this you have suffered some spiritual separation. Ego separates you from your soulful self. In the time you have lived, you've traveled from being a soul-centered infant of pure spirit, pure love and pure light into the darkness of an ego-centered consciousness. The ego takes sides with the flesh, abandoning the soul to seek favor and survive in this material world. This selfish materialistic world has contaminated you. It has you thinking more about material consumption than the spiritual fulfillment of your soul.

If you have been given love, love, love and plenty of tender loving care, mixed with tender discipline, you're lucky. It's safe to say you have inner peace, high self-esteem, and plenty of self-love. You love the whole world, you see love in everything, and you love everyone.

If all this is true of you, you are the exception. The rule is today parents have to work too hard, shop too hard, and consume too much. People don't have enough time for pure love and to spend adequate time loving children.

If you were born in a home that was deeply religious, they probably believed obedience is of more virtue than love. Parents will quote the scriptures to you, a set of rules you should obey. Too many times these rules are in conflict with loving you and in conflict with the tender loving ways of your true self. Too many times these rules help separate you from your true soulful self. As you grew older and your ego comes into play, your parents will do everything to support the egos way of materialism while your soul starves.

239

Even when they took you to church, mosque or temple, everything is materialized. Everything is so much symbol and images, filled with myths. Your poor soul cries out for spiritual love and food.

If you grew up in the home of an atheist, they told you there is no God. Rest assured, the grace of God was in you where you were born. Today you need something to believe in, a spiritual power higher than yourself. You can call that higher power anything you want, but you must have faith in something spiritual, because the man who believes only in his material self is faithless. At the core of yourself, you are a spiritual being and your soul needs spiritual food. Spiritual emptiness brings anger, fear, loneliness and feelings of rejection.

If you were woefully neglected or abused as a child, chances are you are living in hell, not just spiritually empty but spiritually broken and living with emotional pain. You may have plenty of anger and fear inside of you, while you may try to be a good person. To be polite, you cover the resentment, anger and fear you have against the outside world that erodes your self-love. But too often, these feelings burst out, ruin your day or even ruin your life.

You need a **spiritual rebirth**. All the religions work towards more spirituality, seeking truth, light, inner peace and love. Prayer, praise, worship, meditation, psychotherapy, and self-examination, all can help. You must learn to love again, to be like a little child. You must reconnect with the little child inside of you, still crying out for expression. If you do this, you can leave the fury of hell and inherit a little heaven on earth.

Also if you can read this, you will soon have children of your own or you already have children or grandchildren. If you grew up neglected or abused and didn't feel loved, the record shows you most likely will pass your anger and fear down to contaminate your children from generation to generation. Please remember this and be consciousness of it so you can break the chain of sorrows.

240

Love is the most important thing for children to grow up with high self-esteem. However, if you did not get love as a child, it's hard to show love to children or spouses. Please try your best to love your children, and try your best to break the chain of sorrow. Try your best to rebuild your own tower of self-esteem.

In all things spiritual, we are as one with the palm.

If you look at the hand graphics, you will see that the palm is like the soul of an infant. This place of infant *spiritual birth* is a place of unity and oneness with all of humanity. There is no separation whatsoever because pure love has no separation.

Spirit has no separation, faith and human spiritual consciousness have no separation, and soulfulness has no separation. In all things spiritual, we are as one with the palm. The Holy Spirit sees only one humanity. Separation comes from the ego.

All the religions that teach and preach separate God or gods. They separate dogmas and doctrines and they do it with ego-centeredness. The ego believes in "divide and conquer"—divide the world within and conquer the outside world. The ego sees unity as a threat to its power.

Rooted in the essence of our spiritual birth, we live in a pure spiritual consciousness. All we need is love, love, love and more love. But as we grow old we grow away from the bright spiritual consciousness and into a brighter material consciousness. This happens because the material flesh puts such a big demand on us. It demands more and more material consumption, material comfort, and convenience as we get less and less spiritual fulfillment.

Holy Birth In A World Of Sin And Iniquity
The baby exits its mother's womb pure, innocent and holy, but it's born into this world of sin and iniquity. Sometimes the pregnant mother is under stress and the baby is born with anxiety, causing some psychological problems. DNA also can cause some biological issues.

241

But spiritually speaking, the baby is pure love and pure spirit. Throughout history mankind has failed to understand or failed to fully investigate the spiritual aliveness of human birth. We have not been able to understand the emotional aliveness, purity and strength of the human soul at birth.

Science has done wonderful studies on the neurological and biological makeup of babies, but who will study the spiritual make up of human nature at birth? If we say children are sinful and we must take them to meet God, we say God made a mistake in his creation. That's implies that if man begs for mercy, he can correct God's mistake. The mistake was made by man's ego. If mankind is born sinful, then there is no hope for mankind in this world.

EGO means "*Ease God Out*."

When a child is between three and six years old, the ego comes in and captures its spiritual consciousness. The ego takes sides with the flesh, using weapons of fear. Like a flashlight in the darkness, it searches for material power and glory and a brighter material consciousness. People say children don't need to be treated like the holy child of God, because they're not pure until ego-centered adults bring them to God to cleanse them from their sins.

This is a big mistake. This is why it's so easy for so many self-righteous religious people to neglect and abuse children. If we believe the only righteous people on earth are those with egos who praise and worship God, there never will be peace on earth goodwill to all men.

Everything in creation is created whole and holy. There are no mistakes in creation. How can mankind nurture and shelter all of creation when we look and see ungodliness all over it? The ego was not created because at birth, we are egoless. The ego is an outgrowth of mankind's super bright self-consciousness and self-awareness. It's also our consciousness of death and a life after death.

242

The ego is the mental consciousness of the mind that is cultivated and shaped by adults.

The soulful emotional expressions of little children must be nurtured with unconditional love and later, discipline. When was the last time you heard a sermon about loving children and loving families? Most adults do not remember or they block out the memories of crying in childhood.

Sigmund Freud and many of his fellow psychologists studied the development of the ego, the id and the super ego. They found all kinds of conflicts in development that cause emotional neurotic problems for adults all through life. I would like to ask these psychologists, "What about the human soul? What about the souls of little children in the days of ego development?"

What do science, theology, philosophy, and sociology have to say about the tender loving souls of children? Shamefully, they say very little. And what do they have to say about the mountain of faith, hope, forgiveness and gratitude in babes? Next time you take a baby in your arms, look at him or her and say, "This is God's little holiness. This is the love of God. This is me, the way I was born."

Separation

In this world where selfish materialism keeps pushing technology to the outer limits, there is not enough love and tender care to keep the soul of babies rooted in the spirit. By the time the child learns to walk, talk and read a book, he or she suffers a spiritual separation. It moves from the core, the roots of the self of soul-centeredness into the trunk of the self of ego-centeredness. This is called *spiritual separation*. Just like Adam and Eve suffered in the Garden of Eden and suffered the consequences of the ego—sin and shame.

In the process of spiritual separation, emotions of spiritual love flow from the innermost parts of the soul into the heart. "Feelings are suppressed" and a split in the personality happens. Man becomes alienated from himself. He is separated from his spiritual roots of the grace of God, and his ego takes over his

243

personality. Faith in his fellowman to love him is lost, and he feels alone and empty. He longs to go back, to find the grace of God.

This spiritual separation happens so early in life that it causes some people to believe mankind was born with it, born sinful. Man becomes estranged from his inner world, as his ego/mind and all his mental capacity grows. He takes on the task of fighting and negotiating with the outside world for his survival. But mankind needs more than survival. He needs the salvation of love to feel filled with meaning and life.

Separated from his inner world of love, truth and light, man finds himself wandering in a no-man's-land of sweat and seeking knowledge. Feelings of insignificance keep him searching for God.

In his world of spiritual separation, man drifts—faithless and empty—in self-alienation. He builds castles, wonderful worlds outside himself, but the inner emptiness haunts his dreams by night and darkens his consciousness by day. He is unable to find inner peace and happiness outside himself. The words of all the great prophets and all the scriptures and holy literature written by all the great religions is the only pathway to salvation for mankind. So it's safe to say religions are the prescription for spiritual separation. They are the only path to inner pace and spiritual rebirth.

In any ego-centered world, a religion of self-destruction will find you. But the ego glorifies separation because it knows not the glory of God. The ego is isolated from man's spiritual birth. It knows only power and excitement. It tells you, "You can rule the world even though your world inside is crumbling."

But peace will come only when mankind is reunited with those emotions of love that are seated in his soul. The ego is a voice in the head that separates thinking from feelings. It separates them, leaving the soul behind while the mind and body seek to gain the material world. The soulful little child trapped inside every man and every woman is left behind, crying for expression and salvation while the ego seeks to gain the material world.

Ego-Centeredness

Most adults from all over the world grew up in homes with some kind of religious teachings that promoted love, inner peace and spiritual fullness. The great spiritual men who were the fathers of every religion conquered ego, got spiritual enlightenment and became filled in the light of spiritual consciousness.

Ever since the dawn of mankind, man has been the only creature with an ego, which separates him from his creator. Ego-centered living has been the way of life for the survival of every culture. Cultures that live only in a soul-centered way are wiped out by the ego-centered cultured of military might. The strongest cultures in history are those who use the inner source of spiritual holiness, combined with the glory of a super ego, a combination of candle and sword to fight all enemies.

Spiritualization Of The Ego

The ego's code is "divide and conquer." Even in the ego's most spiritual moments, it sees no virtue in unity. As long as we live centered in egotism and religions are ego-centered, there will be separations in every aspect of human living. Wars, greed, selfishness, materialism, and every kind of human destruction will reign. The ego sees no virtue in love and when love is gone, fear is king. The ego's ways of fear will forever keep us in wars and separation.

In the hand graphic it seems I give all religions **equality**, but fundamentally, religions have more in common than they have differences. They all seek to bring spiritual enlightenment, for inner peace puts its devotees in a dim material consciousness and a bright spiritual consciousness.

I am a Christian, and I do believe in the gospels of Jesus Christ, Matthew, Mark, Luke and John are the greatest documents ever written. They teach unconditional love, love for children, love for God and Brotherly Love.

245

THIRTEEN

THE ESSENCE OF BEING, THE ART OF HAVING

"What is a man, what has he got, if not himself then he has not?" These words of a song by Frank Sinatra are very true. A man can have the world but if he doesn't have true self-possession and true self-expression, he has nothing.

Everything in nature, all creatures great and small, are just as they were created to BE. All animals follow exactly the spiritual laws of nature laid out for each species. They are born, eat, have sex, have babies, and die. They have no need to possess anything but themselves, and they do not have to work for a living or build big buildings. Animals live their whole lives in the essence of their BE-ing.

Mankind is the only creature that lives outside the spiritual laws of creation. We cannot just BE—we must HAVE and BECOME. For mankind the meaning of life is to stay rooted in his BE-ing and grow with wisdom and knowledge into becoming everything possible in his human potential.

In the story of Adam and Eve, God cursed Adam, saying, "By the sweat of your brow you must eat bread." After he been separated from his glory of innocence and love, man must

247

struggle between the knowledge of good and evil and work hard for his living.

Labor is one of the first and most profound experiences that take man from the essence of his BE-ing and put him in a struggle to HAVE and BECOME. His hands become his tool for survival while his soul is imprisoned. As mankind works with his hands and thinks with his mind for survival, his soul hungers and thirsts for salvation.

I must go back once again to the infant child. Its soul is free, full and in the total expression in the essence of BE-ing. But the essence of this infant BE-ing is a place where an adult's love and tender care keeps the infant alive. God's creations leave the life of the infant in the care of sinful adults in this world of shame and iniquity.

Born to be in the essence of his BE-ing, mankind must be spiritually separated from his soulful self and become short of the glory of God while he seeks the ego's glory of wealth and power. Creation births a human creature as a unified whole, sinless and shameless, and in harmony of body, mind and soul.

The baby, in the embrace of spiritual birth, could not care less about the things and the sins of the world. The baby just wants food and pure love. He needs only spiritual self-expression and a warm body to rest on.

Physical or emotional pain diminishes the essence of BE-ing, and the baby will kick, cry and scream with any pain or physical discomfort. More important, a deep pain and terror engulfs the infant if he is left alone for a long time. The feeling of aloneness bleeds away life support in the consciousness of the infant. Kicking and crying are the expression of the infant's lust for life that comes from the soul, crying out, "Come and get me, come and get me, or I'll die."

Back in the tender arms of his smiling mother, the baby is once again in paradise, free from sin and shame, free in the expression of the essence of BE-ing, and free to love and be

248

loved. On mother's breast sucking up milk and love, the baby is free like every other creature in creation. All babies are born to BE, free as the wind, and living in the essence of BE-ing.

The nature of all living things is to BE and to follow all the spiritual laws in the essence of BE-ing. The rosebush that grows from seed to shrub produces a rose to brighten and sweeten the air. Just as human nature is to be as God created us—to BE.

Meaning and happiness will come only when we live within the boundaries of our God created BE-ing, not just when we make money or win the Olympics. True meaning and happiness will be ours only when we experience the things that contribute to the growth and development of our inner BE-ing. We must have a high consciousness of self— what we call self-awareness—and a deep amount of self-possession to be fully seated in the essence of our self.

I'm fully aware and confident in who I am. I have full self-awareness and full self-possession, and I can feel strong emotional rivers flowing inside me. I'm free from spiritual emptiness, my actions are motivated more by my feelings than by my thinking, and I can feel the pleasure of emotions running through my body. But when sorrow abounds, I also can feel it and I cry to liquidate it.

The essence of BE-ing is a full and vibrant inner emotional aliveness. In other words, I am free inside, free to feel joy and free to feel sorrow. I am in possession of my soul, my mind is aligned with my soul, and my bodily feelings are united in harmony. I am fully rooted in the essence of my being. I am in the place of my spiritual birth or spiritual rebirth.

This place of spiritual bliss and essence of being is the place of little children. Adults who want to be in this place must be born again. They must have a spiritual rebirth to find the love, faith, hope and forgiveness that are found in little children. On the physical plane, it may seem that little children have nothing going for them. All they do is cry and want, want, and want some more.

They only want to play and run without discipline and act out of control.

But this is just a physical appearance. Children are very centered in self, and they have plenty of love, faith and goodwill to all men. Children are happy with themselves only if they are getting tender loving care. They have no ego-tripping, no false conceited uptight ways about them.

Children are for real—what you see is what you get. All they need is love and without it, they develop all kinds of illusions about themselves. This causes them to put on a mask of deceit, with a total denial of self.

Little children who feel loved may have many moments of jumping for joy, moments to just BE. They have no great plans to go anyplace or to do anything, or to possess anything. They are just happy in the moment. Very few adults can live in the moment. Instead they live with hurts of the past or in the anticipation of happiness in the future.

Man's two deepest desires are his hunger for spiritual love and his hunger for biological food. These are the two things that keep him alive. The food is for material survival and without it, he cannot live. The love is for spiritual significance and without it, he does not want to live. The essence of being is the satisfaction of these two yearnings. One yearning keeps the physical body alive and the other keeps the eternal soul from the torment of spiritual emptiness.

Self-Possession
If man is emotionally vibrant and spiritually filled and if his thinking is aligned with his soul, he is intimately in touch with the innermost core of himself. He has self-possession.

Most people do not remember when all they had was mother's milk to drink and mother's chest and lap to lay on. They had everything, because they had total self-possession.

In those good old days of total self-possession, you also had total self-expression. Every emotion—joy, love, happiness, sadness, anger and fear —were fully free to be expressed, yet you cried. You had no self-control, because self-control comes when you learn the art of living. So you cried.

As you now know, crying does not sit well with ego-centered adults. In fact, they pour scorn on it. But when you were a baby, you didn't know that. If you were left alone, lonely, hungry or wet, you cried and cried until you grew weak and couldn't cry anymore. Finally, you stopped crying and emotions of love, joy and sadness welled up.

You do not remember when you stopped crying or how you had to hold back the anger and fear when nobody came to see about you. You do not member the fear of being left alone, nor do you remember how adults were pleased because you were not a crybaby anymore. They were proud that you were growing up. You do not remember when you started to suppress your inner emotional aliveness just to please this material world of sin and iniquity.

You lost your soul and you lost your intimacy with God. You lost faith, you lost your spiritual significance, and you lost your self-possession. You also lost your self-expression and your true self. You gained self-control and learned to suppress your inner emotional aliveness.

Then you began to walk and talk and think big and bigger. Your ego took on a false image of the self, and you and your ego faced the outside world, seeking the inner truth and light that was lost.

This is the story of most adults. This is the reason religions are the most powerful forces on earth because devotees seek and find spiritual enlightenment. They find a lamp to light the path back into to a spiritual rebirth.

"Ye must be born again," said Jesus. The power of religions comes from telling of a paradise call heaven and a fire fury call hell. They say they will save you from the fear of the fiery fury.

251

Could it be that heaven is a **spiritual rebirth**, back to be born again? And could it be that hell is an ego trip in the spiritual abyss of a Godless bottomless pit?

The Essence Of BE-ing
All of creation lives in the essence of BE-ing. Creatures live within the boundaries of the spiritual laws of creation. Creation is a mass and movement of physical energy, living flesh and blood, but one universal spiritual law of creation rules it. Animals live by these universal laws of creation, but in all the Holy Scriptures the sheep is seen as the best example of holiness. It is seen as the animal closest to God. It shows no anger, no aggression, and it is humble and peaceful.

The lamb is the best example of a creature that lives in the consciousness and tranquility of the inner self.

A little child is like a lamb to the slaughter—they are innocent, helpless, defenseless but holy. If you neglect or brutalize a little child, all they have to face it with are their tears. And some self-righteous, ego-centered adults will punish the child for crying, adding insult to injury and putting fear and the demons of hell into the soul of the child.

If ever you want to see what the essence of BE-ing looks like, just look at the lamb. The lamb does not have to struggle against a super ego to stay in the presence of God as humans do. Lambs travel in flocks, but they do not need the obsessive love and attention to lift self-esteem as humans do. The sheep's instincts for motherhood and fatherhood are in line perfectly with the spiritual laws of their nature. They will not neglect or abuse their young as humans do.

In the essence of God's creation, the baby sheep (the lamb) and the baby human (the child) are alike. They are sinless, egoless, spotless and living in the essence of BE-ing. The human child can be called the Lamb of God. It lives in a holy place, heaven on earth. Adults are commanded as a matter of instinct and duty of love to nurture and shelter the celebration of life in the kingdom of heaven. We do that every time we love a little child.

In the essence of BE-ing, thinking is aligned with feelings. Ego and soul are aligned and in perfect harmony. This inner unity gives the whole personality a consciousness of living in the moment. Each moment is experienced in the "I am where I want to be, seated in the joy of spiritual bliss. I have no need to run away from who I am or where I am."

In the essence of BE-ing, the mind's thinking ways are aligned with the fulfillment of the soul and the good health of the body. The flesh will consume just enough for good health and the fulfillment of soul, because in the essence of BE-ing, there is harmony between body, mind and soul.

In the essence of BE-ing, the mind thinks of soul satisfaction. Man pays attention and hungers for more spiritual fulfillment. There is no need to try to fill an empty soul by eating too much. There is no need to try to fill an empty soul and low self-esteem with worldly material possessions. There is no need for glorifying ego trips and an obsession with image and material possessions.

Ego Aligns With Soul
A man who lives in the essence of BE-ing stands strong and steadfast with self-confidence. He or she lives with a high spiritual consciousness and high self-esteem. When the ego is aligned with the soul, the mind pays attention to spiritual things that fill the soul, rather than paying attention to material things to be consumed by the flesh. The ego is free from fear, self-centeredness and materialism, because its yearnings are rooted in the desires of the soul.

That inner unity is the truth and the light shining at the core of the self, and unity of body, mind and soul gives you a feeling of inner peace and tranquility. When the ego is aligned with the soul, it gives a feeling of a high spiritual power and a feeling of being close to God.

God is love, you feel loved, and you love the world—all because of the soul-centeredness of the personality.

But man cannot live only by BE-ing himself, because that stifles his human potential. Rooted in the essence of BE-ing, we slowly but easily move into learning the art of having and becoming. I'm sure you remember a moment of spiritual bliss at some time in the past when you loved everything about the moment you were in. You felt exactly as you wanted to feel and you hoped that moment would last forever. Your heart and soul was filled with joy and laughter. Those moments for me were as a young boy, on a Saturday night dancing rock and roll with a pretty girl.

In moments like those, you were filled with the inner light, truth and spiritual essence of yourself. Those blissful moments, unfortunately, are too far apart and too few between in this busy world of obsessive material consumption. This world of materialism is not built on the essence of being. Rather, it is built of the art of becoming.

The Art Of Becoming
If you are rooted in the essence of BE-ing and have a strong integrity of self, you can find the ultimate joy and fulfillment in life. You do it by learning the art of living and by learning the art of becoming.

The fate of mankind seems to be learning the art of living. Evidently, he was not meant to BE, totally. He must cultivate a personality and become something more outside himself. Scientists will tell you because of man's super large brain he lives in a super high consciousness of self-awareness and super mental capacity to think and reason.

Seated In My Being
Seated in the essence of by BE-ing, I am reunited with the throne of my spiritual birth. I ascend from the smoking mirrors of the ego images of myself into the substance at the spiritual core of myself. I feel whole, united and complete with the awakening of self-awareness, and I have emotions moving through my body. This bright self-awareness gives me total self-possession of who I am. I have the possession of a unified inner self, the inner peace of unity in body, mind and soul.

254

Seated in the essence of my being, I am the Lamb of God, like a little child, with the light and love of God shining into my soul. I am in the glory of a spiritual rebirth and I stand firm and steadfast in the arms of faith, seated in the essence of my BE-ing. The outside world falls from my shoulders and into my lap.

My innermost being embraces the outside world. Not with the image of my material self, stumbling in darkness and fear, but seated in the innermost part of myself. I embrace the world in the consciousness of a spiritual inner light, a light that frees me from envy, selfishness, greed and materialism.

I am seated in the source of life and seated in self-love. I am who I am, because I am everything I'm created to be. The material side of me, the body, is stress free, confident, certain and secure. Spiritual love is my salvation, and I am feasting at the table in the kingdom of spiritual holiness.

Just as I am, I fear not. I am as meek as a lamb, not as self-confident as a lion. I am all I've got.

But the winds of my material desire keep knocking at my door and tormenting my soul. Ego also keeps knocking at my door with its weapons of anger, fear, greed and envy. "You cannot come in," says the voice from my soul. "You want to become the master of fame and, fortune, but I am grounded in the essence of my BE-ing. I am everything God created me to be. I am seeking first self-examination, and I hunger for the meaning of spiritual. Love fills my soul, and I am free from the loneliness and afflictions of spiritual emptiness."

My emotions flow from the depths of my soul. They flow into life and everything I do, I do with passion. It fills my life with meaning. I have an inner stillness, consistency, courage and perseverance. My sorrows are short and my joys last longer. My faith in myself, in God, and in my fellowman is strong. I stand in each moment filled with joy and laughter.

The Lion And The Lamb
The lamb is seen in most religious scriptures to be meek and

holy. Man is a spiritual being and at its core, the essence of that being is a spiritual significance—meek and humble like a lamb or a baby.

But the lamb is no match for the sheer self-confidence, swiftness and strength of the lion. The lion uses its swiftness and strength for survival, but man cannot live by survival alone. He will feel powerless and insignificant. Man must live by the power of love. He must be meek and humble and filled with faith, for that is what makes his life worth living.

Some men will have everything that need for material survival, yet spiritual emptiness will push them to the edge of sanity. They will tremble with fear and tell themselves not to jump.

The art of living means mankind must be like the lamb and the baby, seated in the kingdom of salvation where he was born. He also must learn to be like the lion because he must roam in the forest of survival.

The nature of the lamb abounds in babies—they are soulful, meek and humble. But babies do not run the world. People that are filled with egoism and with a lion nature run this world. These people have plenty of ego self-affirmation. The world needs men who at the innermost part of themselves have the soulful nature of a lamb while on the outer ego level, he has the strength and self-confidence of the lion. There would be peace on earth and goodwill to all people.

To have the power of survival and the glory of salvation is to have the formula for the art of living.

The Art Of Living
The art of living is to be seated in the essence of your being, seated in the essence of faith, love and soulfulness. It means to be transcended, but not uprooted, into the art of
BE-coming.

The art of becoming is the art of living. It's being on a constant search for knowledge, getting a college education, and learning how to make and invest money. It's also learning how to have intimate and friendly relationships with people, and working hard and smart to build a better and brighter future.

Wisdom, rational thought and sound reason are the components of the art of living. Strong spiritual self-affirmation, good judgment, rational and intellectual thinking, strong willpower, courage, and perseverance—these are the virtues that give man the art of living.

The art of living is to find the path to happiness. In today's world of total material consumption, happy people are the exception. Instead, bored, stressed and unhappy people are the rule. The art of living is not easy to find in a material world, because people are searching for more material things that leave them spiritually empty.

As we move from the spiritual consciousness of our spiritual birth into the material consciousness of egoism, everything we touch and the material monster that leaves our lives meaningless and unfulfilled contaminates all our experiences. The material monster is a bottomless pit. Its unquenchable thirst of material desires put us in the chains of envy, greed and selfishness, all the chains that shackle our happiness.

If we want to find happiness we must have diminishing material desires and an increasing hunger for the spiritual fulfillment of love, faith, hope, forgiveness, wisdom and gratitude. These are the ingredients for the art of living.

I often wonder why church people are no less materialistic than people who don't go to church. They shop all week to buy the best clothes, cars and jewelry to wear to church.

"What is a man and what has he got, if not himself then he has not?" are the words in a song by Frank Sinatra. Many people cannot stand being un-busy and alone with themselves and their thinking. Their minds always run with things of the world and can never focus on the inner workings of self. People who cannot be still experience inner feelings of pain, fear, anger, and no inner peace. That's why they must run to the outside world to find refuge. Someone who cannot stay in one place for long and cannot finish anything is running away from self. They try to be still, but the inner storm won't let them.

There are other people who cannot think for themselves, who are afraid to be an independent thinker. They have lost the virtue of self-affirmation and so only want to be what they think the outside world wants them to be. They care more about the image of the self and have no consciousness of the substance of the inner self. These people have lost a chance to find the art of living and so they live a meaningless and unfilled life.

There is an attitude of gratitude and forgiveness that promotes the joy of living, to give thanks for what we have and cultivate satisfaction rather than desire. But too much desire is just for the pleasures of the flesh.

We should instead seek things for the joy of the soul. Happiness is a soul, meek and humble as the lamb, but with a full ego, brave and self-confident as the lion. To be meek, to be kind, to be forgiving, and to be humble—these are the virtues in the art of living. These are the virtues of self-love, without which there can be no happiness.

Rational Thinking
Rational thinking is a key ingredient in the art of living, the way man thinks about himself, and the way he thinks about the outside world. Negative thinking is thinking people cannot be trusted and the world is a bad place.

If a man thinks he is not worthy, he always feels he is being attacked and is always ready to attack the world. Inner anger and fear rob him of rational thinking and give the illusion of danger lurking in the dark. His mind is filled with irrational thinking. In the darkness a pebble sounds like a thunder roar, so he must attack or be attacked.

In truth, this world can be a loving place with kind people. If a man feels loved and is filled with plenty of faith and hope, he thinks positive. Happy is the optimist—he lives in the truth and the light of love.

Rational Self-Examination
Negative emotions are the most common reason people are unhappy. Negative thinking triggers these emotions and for the most part, negative thinking is in conflict with truth. It's an illusion of the real situation.

Man may get very angry because he thinks someone is verbally abusing him, but the truth is words cannot abuse. Words are just the mind's way of imposing false ideas on the self. A system of rational, positive thinking and self-examination is the prescription for freedom from the hurtfulness of the anger of any possible verbal abuse.

In the human psyche, perception too often is stronger than fact. Most of the time it's our perception of things that cause emotional grief and unhappiness. We need to use self-examination to rid the mind of negative thinking and negative feelings. Self-examination is the first rule in learning the art of living.

For example, it's negative thinking if I say to myself, "I am stupid for making that mistake." It's in conflict with truth and reality, because the truth is even the smartest people in the world make mistakes. It also gives rise to negative emotions and conflict with myself, and I get angry with myself. Notice that negative thinking precedes the negative emotion of anger. My anger gives me grief and causes me to lose the art of living.

If an issue causes anger, it is because you see the issue in a negative way. Stop, examine your thinking, and start thinking in a positive way. Next time, you will not be angry, and you'll save yourself some grief.

I may say to a friend, "You hurt my feelings with negative words." It's not true. The truth is I *think* your negative words hurt me, but I know words cannot hurt. That's the truth.

259

There is a set of five rules to follow in rational self-examination. They obey the laws of rational thinking.

1. It is based on objective reality
2. It protects my wellbeing
3. It achieves my goal
4. It keeps me out of trouble with others
5. It keeps me out of trouble with myself

My thinking affects my emotions. Positive thinking gives me positive emotions, and I feel good. Negative thinking, on the other hand, gives me negative emotions and I feel bad.

If I can make myself think only positively, will I never be angry again? No, it's not true, because sometimes my bottled-up emotions are triggered before I have time to think. When they rise, they can stay and hurt long after I've started thinking positively.

The art of living is not just positive thinking. It also includes using self-exanimation to rid yourself of any fear and anger bottled up inside your system. The art of living is to have a positive attitude of gratitude when you wake up in the morning. It's saying, "Today is a good day. Something bad might happen, but it's still a good day. I will keep a delightful attitude."

The art of living, the art of giving, and the art of loving are very important. People who give with love seek to find fulfillment in giving, not just in receiving. People who seek fulfillment and joy will show love and don't just look for someone to love them. They are learning the art of living. The art of love is central to the art of living, but the art of love is rooted in the art of BE-ing. If you are untrue to your heart and soul, the innermost part of the self, you will be unable to love. You will be unable to find the art of living.

Self-Righteousness
Self-righteousness is a big barrier to learning the art of living. The self-righteous man suffers from ego inflation. He has lost humility and meekness, and he has lost the virtues of listening, He has lost the art of living.

People who stand firm and deep in their religion find it easy to fall into the grips of self-righteousness. They think they're better than other people because God gives them special favors with wisdom, knowledge and understanding. They lose their ability to listen and learn, and they fall in conflict with even their own children, who rebel against them and even rebel against their God.

Self-righteous people are slow to understand and forgive but quick to judge and condemn others. They live in constant self-doubt, which can put them in conflict with children, family and the world. They're disconnected from their inner feelings, and they live by a set of self-made ideals or some Holy Book. They think it's hell for those who disagree with them or those who come into conflict with their righteousness.

The art of living is to find a loving heart and kind ways. That's what allows man to have compassion on his fellowman and why he pours kindness and empathy on others with personality defects. The art of living, the essence of BE-ing is happiness with self and happiness with the outside world.

Self-righteousness comes in conflict with the ways of love. That's why it's so difficult for deeply religious people to love children. Kids rebel against self-righteousness in a conflict between ego-centered self-righteousness and soul-centered love.

Love is meek and patient. Love listens to the child. Love is forgiveness and humility, and love is what's right for the wellbeing of children.

Man cannot BE-come more righteous than when he was born. The self-righteous person lives in an illusion, and the unrighteous person needs a spiritual rebirth to be reunited with the righteousness of birth.

Conflicts Of Desires
A big component in the art of living is to learn to diminish desire. To possess everything, man should desire to possess nothing. In order to arrive at being everything, he should desire to be

nothing. Happiness is cultivating satisfaction, not the satisfaction of desire.

To want less is a virtue, and less satisfies you more. To seek happiness only in the satisfaction of material desires is holding to an illusion. The more you get, the more you want, and you never find full satisfaction.

Become the seeker of wisdom and truth, rational thinking, and sound reasoning. Seek to align your thinking with things to fulfill the soul, not the desires of the flesh. Happiness comes only when consciousness is in line with fulfilling the soul and not only the desires of consumption of the body.

Differences Between Being And Having
In the BE-ing mode, man has an in-the-moment three-dimensional experience. Body, mind and soul are united in three-part harmony. Any experience of BE-ing is an inner-soul-fulfilling, mind-stimulating, body-consuming experience. It's the totality of being, the totality of an integrated self, and a oneness of BE-ing. Body, mind and soul are attached to the experience and all desires are fulfilled. "I'm where and what I want to BE."

But in the having mode, each experience is met with detachment. The inner core of self is detached from the experience. There's an inner void of fulfillment that fuels desire for having more and more as the whole personality seeks satisfaction.

In the BE-ing mode satisfaction and joy are found with a oneness in time and space. Satisfaction is found in a oneness with self, a oneness in the satisfaction of BE-ing a oneness with nature, and a oneness with subject and object. It's also a oneness with passion and affection, and a oneness with the Holy Spirit. This oneness subject and object fills each life experience with meaning because of a full soul embracing, mind embracing and body embracing. Each experience is all the three dimensions of man's existence.

In the BE-ing mode, satisfaction comes alive and all desires in life are sent to the grave. Man becomes all in everything because he desires nothing from nothing.

In the having mode, however, desire comes alive and satisfaction is sent to the grave. Life's experiences are incomplete with detachments, while the ego and the mind have a good time seeking more and more to gain from the world and looking for power and glory in material objects. The inner spiritual self just goes along for the boring ride.

In the having mode, the detachment of inner self from the objects of superficial excitements leaves man in a half-empty mode of satisfaction and a growing amount of desire. In the having mode, this growing desire lets man eat too much in an effort to fill an inner spiritual void.

In the BE-ing mode, walking brings an experience of being in step with the earth and the air. It's a journey of joy. But in the having mode, walking is detached. "I walk to a destination and my journey is joyless."

In the having mode, material consciousness grows brighter and seeks to fill the inner emptiness with material possessions or having things. Everyone knows material things cannot fill spiritual emptiness, but man is not conscious of the spiritual emptiness so he lives for the glory and excitement of one more material possession as the object of desire.

In the BE-ing mode, man feels spiritually fulfilled because he uses human kindness, loving and giving to fulfill the yearnings of his soul. In the having mode man feels spiritually unfulfilled because he is programmed to receive and possess. Hoarding is the name of the game, and greed and envy are the weapons the ego uses to build an empire of material desire.

In the BE-ing mode, man has an inner stillness and tranquility. Gratitude is the attitude and it cultivates satisfaction. "I find happiness just by BE-ing who I am. I know who I am. I find confidence and self-love in who I am. My soul if filled, and my

263

ego is aligned with my soul. I am in this world and share myself with this world. I do not lose myself to the world."

In the BE-ing mode, I stand firm in my individuality but at the same time, fully integrated in this world. In the having mode, I lose myself in desire to the objects of this world.

In the having mode, man runs away from the inner empty feeling of self. If he tries to be still and to BE, negative feelings begin to rise, making him feel tormented. He must constantly have something to do and places to go. He must always be on the move. His ego/mind runs fast and he thinks of changing the outside world. At the same time, his inside world —his inner feelings from the soul—cry out like thunder wanting to be expressed.

Having And BE-Ing Modes
On the issue of having and BE-ing modes, it's not an either-or situation. In fact, man must have (possess) things to live in comfort and convenience. He must have a place to sleep, food to eat and money to live a good life. So the Having Mode is necessary to live a good life.

To find happiness and fulfillment in living, however, man must find a delicate balance between the having and the Be-ing mode. He can own material things without investing his self-esteem in them. The main ingredients for the art of living are plenty of money, a good education, and a good job.

But spiritual love is the essence of life. Love, reason and productive activities are the source of the inner aliveness that gives meaning to life and grows only to the extent they are practiced and experienced. They cannot be bought, consumed or possessed as things in the having mode can be.

Unfortunately in today's world of high technology and materialism, the orientation is towards the art of having. People build self-esteem on more and more material possessions. In fact, a person who is rooted in the essence of BE-ing and neglects to follow society's orientation toward **having** can be seen as foolish.

Journey Of Self-Discovery

Let's say you wake up in the morning feeling low down. You think another boring and meaningless day is ahead. What do you do?

You have three choices. One, get out of bed, turn on the TV and shuffle from the couch to the refrigerator as you wallow in despair. Two, let your mind take off in many directions, planning all the different great things you can do today and thinking about all the different places you can go and keep busy all day. But all this planning and great thinking about staying busy is just a way of running from yourself, running away from inner feelings of worthlessness.

The third choice is the best. You can seek inside yourself to uncover the feelings of worthlessness that are casting a dark cloud over your soul and making you feel low. Then, you can reconnect with the essence of your BE-ing and seek the strength of your significance from the inner source of life inside of you. You'll be lifted up from the spiritual source within you as you travel on a journey of self-discovery through self-analysis, prayer and meditation, or psychotherapy. You won't run to the outside world in the having mode, looking for the next thrill and excitement in the illusion of material egoism.

How do you travel the inner journey?

People who are seekers of inner spiritual fulfillment and spiritual significance use prayer, meditation, and reading the Bible, the Koran, the Torah, the Bhagavad-Gita or other Holy Books. They think these practices will grant them spiritual enlightenment and a lamp to build faith and hope to light their path back into the kingdom of the soul.

People who take a psychological and philosophical view of life dig down into the depths of their feelings and get in touch with their emotions. There are many secular spiritual books available

265

on this subject. They tell you how to unite mind/ego and soul to find the inner harmony that will uplift the spirit so you begin to feel joy in life.

 Acceptance is a very good place to start on your journey back into the essence of your BE-ing.

The Serenity Prayer
"Lord give me the serenity to accept the things I cannot change, the courage to change the things I can and the wisdom to know the difference."

GLOSSARY

1. ANGER
Anger is an emotional experience. It's the emotion that kicks in to defend love and life. The mechanism of anger is rapid but very deep breathing to get enough energy to fight any obstacle to the wellness of life.

The common sentiment about anger is that it's always bad for you. But when used in its right place to defend and not to offend, anger is a positive emotion. People with self-hate and low self-esteem will be angry at the world and too often, they will use anger mixed with rage and violence to seek revenge on the outside world. This gives anger a bad name.

Self-expression is the key to happiness. Freedom to feel the emotions of anger and love are vital to self-expression.

2. ATTENTION SPAN
The attention span of humans is alive from cradle to grave. Every day of living we crave attention. Every great action of man is done with some motive to get love and attention. Some of the most destructive acts of man are motivated by feelings of rejection. Children too often use destructive behavior just to get attention. In the psyche of man, love and attention keep us alive.

As babies we would actually die without love and attention. As adults, memories are made of those infantile days when the fear of death would grip us if we were left alone for too long. Getting attention seems to be mankind's most important need. We live for it or we will die for it. Let me say to all adults; please remember to give what you seek. The easiest and best way to get attention is to give it.

267

3. CREATION AND EVOLUTION

There is and always will be a big debate over creation versus evolution. Was the earth created by some supernatural force? Or did a chemical Big Bang form the universe?

I believe all life on earth is created but at the same time, I believe the evidence for evolution is so strong that it cannot, within reason, be ignored. So I believe creation and evolution are compatible.

The story of Adam and Eve in the Garden of Eden is the story of every human. Born innocent and holy but suffering spiritual separation, sin and shame in later years with the development of the ego.

My hope is that some day in our future, scientists, religious leaders, psychologists and philosophers will sit down in a room and agree that there's virtue in everyone's theory. Then I hope they combine forces to make a better world.

Science deals with facts while religion deals with faith. Man must have the facts to understand and develop his material self, but he also must have faith to understand and develop the spiritual core of himself. Man cannot live without the facts, but he also cannot live without faith.

4. FAITH

Faith is belief without evidence. In the reality of life, faith is stronger than facts. We can have all the facts of life and still walk in darkness. With faith there's no darkness. To be fully embraced in love, we first must have faith. Faith holds the key to happiness.

Can we live without faith? An infant must have faith in its mother's breast and faith in the first step to rise when it falls. We must have faith in a spiritual higher power or we will despair in the facts of this material world. We must have faith in order to love those and ourselves we need to love. Surely we must have faith, because without it we become sterile, hopeless and afraid to the core of our beings.

268

5. FAMILY

In building cultures, the most important virtue is to build one rooted in strong family units, a culture where people put motherhood, fatherhood and brotherhood first. A loving family where every member feels loved is the source of a wholesome and strong society. People who were not raised in a loving family have to struggle all through life looking for happiness and peace of mind, with the winds of despair forever haunting their dreams. It's sad to say many of these people struggle all their lives but still never find any peace of mind.

The first six years of life are the most important in determining whether a person will go through life with high self-esteem and a firm inner peace. There's an important paradox in human living. People who, for lack of tender loving parent, grow up insecure with little or no self-worth always see fit to work very hard. They burn the midnight oil, seeking fame and fortune, but even when they find it, inner emptiness remains. Then they self-destruct.

6. FEAR

Fear is the most emotionally crippling experience man can have. It's easy to feel frightened when we stand on the edge of a cliff or in front of a speeding train. It's terror. But man's deepest fear and terror does not come from the outside world. That fear comes from the spiritual emptiness and the spiritual volcanoes that are felt deep inside the human soul.

Fear is the opposite of faith. Man loses faith in life when he loses his capacity to love. Love is the essence of life, so when love is lost faith in life is lost. Fear of life becomes man's constant companion.

The mechanism of fear is short, shallow breathing. Babies have the best quality of breathing, they breathe easy and deep with the spiritual calm of love. But as babies become adults, they begin to breathe in fear, suppressing their feelings in order to cope with the burdens of the outside world. Fear is like the very breath of life being taken away. Fear is the urge to flight, whether it's flight from an oncoming outside danger or flight from inner emotional torments. Fear becomes man's greatest enemy.

269

Fear is a sleeping lion that lurks in the soul of man. Too many times troubling life experiences come to awake the sleeping lion. Sexual aggression, anger, rage and violence are the weapons we used to fight back at the outside world to avoid waking the sleeping lion within.

7. FEELINGS AND THINKING

In addition to the three primary emotions, we also feel a range of dozens of emotions. These include rage, hate, envy, sadness, joy, tranquility and more. These emotions are called feelings. Feelings are spiritual sensations that flow from the soul into the ego consciousness of the flesh/body.

Feelings must be clearly distinguished from thinking. Thinking is in the head. It's the consciousness of words and thoughts, our intellectual and mental power of wisdom, folly and reason. Feelings are emotional, while thinking is mental.

The human personality is an integration of body, mind and soul. With harmonious integration, we feel good. Disharmony causes us to feel all kinds of inner conflicts and afflictions.

In this world of sin and shame, human suffering is more the norm. We have become too ego/mind-centered, and we live with inner disharmony and suppression of feelings. We suffer because we have lost the freedom of inner self-expression.

8. FORGIVENESS

Forgiveness is a gift to ourselves. It's a one-way street. Forgiveness removes all the pain, anguish and hate from our inner self and sets us free to feel the freedom of joy and love. Forgiveness brings redemption but un-forgiveness seeks revenge. Those who will not forgive will never be happy because revenge activates negative thinking and sorrow. On the other hand, redemption gives positive feelings of joy.

If you have one drop of grief or anger toward any person, place or thing, search your soul to find some love. Only when you feel love toward that person, place or thing will you know you have truly forgiven.

270

9. GRATITUDE

The person with gratitude wakes up in the morning and sees his world as a glass half-full. He's thankful for a half-full glass. His attitude of gratitude opens him to show love and kindness. He lives a satisfied life.

On the other hand the man with ingratitude wakes up in the morning and sees his glass as half-empty. He sees a world where he must blame and complain about a half-empty glass. He must struggle each day to grab what's coming to him.

Ingratitude gives man a life of increasing desires and little or no satisfaction.

10. HATE

Love is the water of life, flowing like a river into the sea. Anger is the soldier fighting to remove any obstacle to the flow of love. If the river of love—free flowing emotion—becomes frozen, fear becomes the riverbed and anger keeps chipping away at the ice.

Hate is the fearful riverbed, with anger chipping away at the frozen emotions of love. Bottled up anger and fear are the foundations of hate. Low self-esteem, loneliness, and isolation happen when the river is frozen. Then fear and anger turn to hate. Hate is fighting a battle against a loveless, empty life.

11. HUMILITY OR ARROGANCE?

Here's an example of the difference between humility and arrogance. If a man has humility, when his neighbor's dog comes and messes on his lawn, he cleans up the dog's mess, keeps his cool, and keeps a friend. His humility makes his life easy and fills it with meaning.

When a man with no humility sees the dog's mess on his lawn, he gets angry, goes to his neighbor, demands his rights and privileges, and makes an enemy. This arrogant man has a very hard time in life, and his self-righteousness and false pride disconnect him from his family and friends. He has constant feelings of isolation and unhappiness.

271

12. INNER PEACE

The history of the human race is defined by man's search for inner peace. Since the beginning of time, mankind has struggled to understand his inner world. Religions, voodoo, myths and magic have all come about from the inner wonderland of mystery in the human mind and the soul.

The biggest mystery about inner peace is that mankind was born with it. Babies came into this world with inner harmony, with body, mind and soul in a tranquil state of being, egoless, innocent and holy. But sure enough every adult human has lost the intimacy of inner connectedness and is alienated from his inner self—the abode of God, peace and love.

A loss of inner connectedness splits man into a civil war, man against himself. The inner soul hungers for love and salvation, but the outer ego seeks to grab power and admiration. This split robs man of any inner peace and is the source of all the acts of human destructiveness.

Jesus Christ said, "Ye must be born again" to inherit the kingdom of heaven. He also said that the kingdom of heaven is within. The greatest mystery of human living is the adult human who spends his life seeking something he was born with but lost.

Mankind seeking inner peace is like looking for gold in a silver mine. We seek inner peace by looking toward the outside world for love, power, fame and fortune when all we need to do is turn the searchlight inward to reconnect with the little bundle of peace, love and inner harmony we were born with.

13. INTELLECTUAL SPIRITUALISM

A wise man once said, "When man discovered the mirror, he lost his soul." I take this further to say, "Each move to advance the industrial and technological revolutions is a setback for the soul-centered spiritualism of humanity." As intellectual power grows, thinking becomes more sophisticated and mankind loses faith in his inner spiritual self. At the same time, he increases his faith in the intellectual power of his mind.

Evolution has given humans a bigger brain with more mental and intellectual power. As mankind gains more and more mental power, he uses that power of the mind to suppress his feelings and the spiritual vibrancy of his soul. I can see why all the evolution intellectuals have little faith in the spiritual power of the inner soul.

Modern man has become too smart for his own good. He fills his head with so much intellectual power that the arrogance of that power has cost him the loss of his soul. It has cost him the loss of inner peace. Spiritual aliveness is expressed in emotional feelings that rise up into our consciousness—emotions of love, fear and anger. But if held up to rational and intellectual scrutiny, these emotions will fail the test.

There are times when the deepest and sweetest moments of love seem like folly. Many times our rational mind says we should not be angry, but anger keeps building higher and higher. If you are a highly intellectual and rational person, do not let your inability to love with forgiveness and humility let you fall victim of your own success.

14. IN THE MOMENT
Happiness, joy, and peace of mind are all in-the-moment experiences. It's a shame, in this world of so much fear and self-doubt, that people equate happiness with being busy. People get overworked and travel all over the world looking for joy and happiness. They don't know that the foundation for happiness must be built from an inner harmony of body, mind and soul.

When man has unresolved inner conflicts, running away from self seems to be very exciting. It lets him avoid the dread of in-the-moment inner disturbances.

The experience of love also is an in-the-moment experience. A man in love lives each moment in the presence of joy and self-assurance. He is where he wants to be and he wants to stay there.

But inner conflicts, fear, anger and self-doubt motivate too many people to keep running away from themselves. If ever they try to be still and silent, negative feelings begin to rise in their consciousness. All of a sudden they find a million important things to do, and they go from one exciting moment to the next.

Many religions practice pray and meditation to find peace in the moment.

15. LOVE
Love is life's only absolute reality. Everything we do, we do for love or else we do as a call for love. Life has only two modes— one answering the call for love and the other calling for love.

Love is any emotional experience of spiritual fulfillment. Love is the ability to surrender without the fear of being conquered. When love is present, we surrender and live in celebration of life. But when love is gone, we struggle and live in fear of life. Love is life, love is God and creation, and God is love.

Parental love nurtures the essence of spiritual birth in little children, giving them the foundation for a life of happiness and a life of inner peace. It also gives them high self-esteem and high spiritual self-affirmation.

Brotherly love promotes peace on earth and goodwill to all men. Brotherly love means every man is his brothers' keeper, uniting every man's soul in harmony with one humanity.

Romantic love is driven towards sex, the agent of procreation. It is driven towards family and nurturing children, which is the strength and foundation of any society.

16. MORAL LAWS
The moral laws of life are written by nature. In other words, nature and the universe are run by a set of moral, ethical and spiritual laws. Everything in creation follows these laws. This includes the ebb and flow of ocean tides, birds as they build nests and fly to get food to feed their young and trees as they take food from the air and the soil and give back to nature the same goodness to the earth and the air. The sunshine and the

rain, and the thunder and the lightening all follow exactly the laws of nature.

Humankind is the only subject on earth that's able to break the moral and spiritual laws of nature. We selfishly want to take more and more from nature and give back nothing—making it easy for us to break the spiritual laws of nature. Mankind is the only subject in nature that needs to write books with a set of Golden Rules to follow. Then we turn around and break those rules and cause destruction on nature and on our fellowman.

Mankind is created just like all other creatures, wired with the ability to differentiate between what is moral and right and what is immoral and wrong. But on the way to ego maturity, we become spiritual outlaws. We become disconnected from the true moral laws of Mother Nature. As a result we write millions of book about man-made moral laws all because we have lost touch with our inner spiritual self and the universal spiritual laws of the universe.

17. PARENTING
For adults who are struggling to find a little meaning in life, struggling to find one drop of self-affirmation, each day is a

struggle against depression and despair. It's most likely these people started life in childhood on a dark journey of loveless parenting. Nurturing children is nurturing the source of life. There's nothing more spiritual than to nurture life.

People need to understand that nurturing an infant child brings them closer to God than anything else man can do. The angels rejoice and celebrate the glory of life every time a child is loved. All the great religions make a tragic mistake when they fail to promote tender loving parenting as the source of spiritual fulfillment.

I am a volunteer chaplain at a prison in Florida. Almost without exception, every inmate I counsel never felt loved as a child. They all come from homes with bad parenting. Some even come from Christian homes where parents ruled by the Golden Rule but with little or no tender loving care.

There's not enough tender loving care for children in families today in this selfish world obsessed with material consumption. So every adult must seek the path of self-discovery and self-examination and the grace of the Holy Spirit to reverse the effects of being raised in a family with inadequate love.

18. PASSION
Passion is the juice of life. A passionless life is like a juiceless orange. The passion of life is the lust for life. It makes you rejoice in life. With passion the flesh is filled with spiritual emotions, and the mind is free to think and reason. Body, mind and soul are in harmony, dancing to the rhythm of life.

In today's world of technology and information, we have lost the passion for life. Our lust for life is a romance with machines, while children suffer from feelings of loneliness and isolation. It's all because we give them a world without passion.

19. SELF-CONTROL, POSSESSION, EXPRESSION
We are born rooted in self-expression and self-possession. Self-possession means to have and to hold a unified and harmonious inner self. Babies have this strong possession of self—with body, mind and soul united in spiritual holiness and harmony. Babies feel a strong expression of love. They breathe easy, they breathe deep, and they have soft skin because of quality breathing. They have high self-worth and high spiritual self-expression. Hope and joy abound.

But by the time babies become adults, this material world of sin and shame imposes on them inner conflicts, spiritual oppression and suppression of feelings. They suffer loss of true self and loss of self-possession.

Self-expression defines the way of babies. When my granddaughter was about eighteen months old, I watched her express the full range of emotions—anger, rage, fear, then joy and laughter—in just a few minutes. For most adults, however,

276

thinking has become so dominant in the personality that it undermines every attempt at true inner emotional self-expression.

Self-control is one virtue babies do not have. Babies are defined by being out of control. Ego control does not come to infants until they're about three years old. Tender loving parenting and discipline are the keys to a healthy life of self-control for adults. But on the other hand, neglect and punishment of an infant (even with discipline) gives the child self-denial, not self-control. The danger is it's hard to differentiate between self-control and self-denial.

"What is a man, what has he got, if not himself, then he has not." These are the words of a song by Frank Sinatra. "What good would it do if a man gained the world and lost his soul?" These are words from the Bible. The person who has lost his or her soul has lost the integrity of the inner self. He is split and divided within himself. It's very sad to see some of the most polite and the most successful people on earth who have lost the integrity to express inner feelings and gut thinking just so they can gain power and glory from the outside world.

20. SELF-EXAMINATION
A wise man once said, "The unexamined life is not worth living." That may be true but sometimes, self-examination is like pulling teeth. It drives fear into most people. This is the reason so many people live lives that are not worth living.

Every adult needs to practice self-discovery by way of self-examination. However, in this world of selfish materialism, we grow up with inner emotional and spiritual brokenness. If we do not examine our self, we see no fault in our self but see all blame in our outside world. We wind up fighting the outside world to seek change, when we can only be happy with change from within.

21. SPIRIT-FULLNESS
The most important thing to say about spirit-fullness is that we are born with it. The creator giving the gift of life imparts on

mankind all the glory of love, innocence and grace. But in this world of sin, shame, selfishness, and materialism, we suffer spiritual separation before we learn to walk, talk and read a book. This is due to inadequate loving and not enough tender parenting.

Spiritual emptiness and spiritual brokenness are the root causes of most of human suffering. This is why all the great religions have such power and glory in all of humanity. They offer doctrines to combat spiritual conflicts.

22. SPIRITUAL BIRTH
The creator did not make a mistake when he created man. Every man is created and born in spiritual holiness. While the parents may be in sin and iniquity, the child still is born innocent and holy. The whole human race has failed to fully nurture with love the spiritual essence of human birth.

The failure to fully comprehend and fully nurture the essence of spiritual birth is the greatest tragedy in the history of the human race. As a result we have built cultures of selfish materialistic warriors, cultures void of true love and tenderness.

In centuries past before swords, guns and machines, mankind used to put tender loving parenting first, and spiritual holiness covered the land. In modern times spiritual holiness is no match for weapons of war. In the name of survival, man must deny himself the glory of love for the glory of war.

23. SPIRTUAL SELF-AFFIRMATION
At the core of our humanity we are spiritual beings. The spirit in us is eternal, a universal energy of life. The flesh is weak and mortal. It's just a consuming sponge in life. If we must be true to self, at the core of self, we need to feel and live in the consciousness of spiritual expression. Life itself is rooted in self-expression.

Spiritual self-expression is the essence of life.

24. THREE PRIMARY EMOTIONS

In nature there are three primary colors. Red, yellow and blue mix together to make all the colors of the world. The same happens with human emotions.

Love, anger and fear are our three primary emotions. All the many, many different emotions we can feel are a mixture of the primary three.

Love is the emotion of life and it gives spiritual life to the flesh. Anger sets up the body to fight for life and fear sets up the body and psyche to take flight from the dangers and conflicts of life.

ABOUT ASHER
10-10-07

I was born in Jamaica West Indies, in 1941. My childhood was a lonely journey filled with suppressed anger, fear and deep feelings of rejection. You see, I am the last of six children. With an angry mother, and a distant father, working too hard planting food and they had no concept of showing tenderness and love to children. I suffered the human sorrows like too many little children, neglect and punishment. I Left school after the sixth grade went to youth camp which was a little Self-assuring.

After youth camp I went to Kingston to learn a trade, Electrician. In 1964 I went to New York City the big Apple looking for love. At the church I sang in the choir, made good money as an Electrician, and got married in 1970 for the first time but my dreams of finding love was still crumbling. Looking for love I tried everything, psychotherapy, studied religions, and studied everything about spiritual fulfillment. I did plenty of self-examination and self-discovery, trying to ease my emotional pain.

At about fifty years old I discovered inside me, *the little boy inside the man,* starving for love, filled with fear and trembling because of living a loveless life. One day I separated the Spiritual Essence of the little boy inside crying for love form all the Religious teachings. That was the day I started the journey to writing this book.

Spirituality Without Religions.

Music sweet music, the sweet passion of my youth, from
Manchoniel to Long Road, Hectors River, Dance Halls and Juke
Boxes in Kingston town, to Night Clubs in New York City. I was
the King of song and dance, I can see me dancing
with pretty girls.   Each day a song in
my Heart, sweet lyrics of love on my Lips and dancing in
my Feet. In all my dark nights of mourning,
music broke the dawn as refuge.
Music, sweet music was the joy that freed my soul.